I, DRAGONFLY

I, DRAGONFLY

A Memoir of Recovery and Flight

KERRIE BALDWIN

Foreword by Gwyneth Olwyn

ISBN 978-0-692-04636-4 (trade paperback edition)
ISBN 978-0-692-04635-7 (e-book edition)

This is a work of memoir. Some names have been changed to preserve privacy; a few incidents have been condensed or reordered for the sake of narrative; dialogue has been recreated to the best of the author's recollection. The events described herein are included and portrayed solely to illuminate the author's physical and psychological transformation.

The information provided in this book is designed to provide helpful information on the subjects discussed. This book is not meant to be used, nor should it be used, to diagnose or treat any medical condition. For diagnosis or treatment of any medical problem, consult your own physician. The publisher and author are not responsible for any specific health or allergy needs that may require medical supervision and are not liable for any damages or negative consequences from any treatment, action, application, or preparation to any person reading or following the information in this book. References are provided for informational purposes only and do not constitute endorsement of any websites or other sources. Readers should be aware that the websites listed in this book might change.

Catskill Mountains photograph by Michael Hunt
Dragonfly wing photograph obtained through CC0 Creative Commons
Author photograph by Leyla Cadabal

Front cover design by Michael Hunt

For my father, Geoffrey D. Baldwin (1950–2016),
who would have been proud of his daughter, the writer

FOREWORD
Gwyneth Olwyn

Almost six years ago, as an average-sized woman with no personal or family history of an eating disorder, I found myself wanting to get healthy. I had just emerged from several years of suffering with undiagnosed celiac disease and I was one of those patients who gained weight with it.

In adult-onset celiac disease, weight loss or weight gain can occur while the patient remains undiagnosed and consuming gluten.[1] However, gluten does not cause celiac disease and the activation of celiac disease is not generated by the presence of gluten in one's diet, either. The genetic predisposition is inherited and the most common activators are gastrointestinal illness (the culprit in my case), significant life stressors, and/or hormonal changes.

While my various symptoms had drastically improved within two weeks of shifting to a full gluten-replacement diet, I believed I could improve lingering symptoms and "tone up" by focusing on "healthy eating" and exercising. Everything in quotation marks denotes what I thought to be true then.

I was using an online site for tallying calories and exercise and found myself scrolling through one of their forums dedicated to health-related issues. As a patient advocate, I had spent many years researching information for newly diagnosed patients. Most of my work centered on chronic conditions—anything from cancer to multiple sclerosis to rare congenital conditions. At that point I had no more than a passing understanding of eating disorders, but my instinct was telling me that I was looking at the blind leading the blind on that forum. Fully one-third of the

---

[1] R. D. Zipser, S. Patel, Y. Z. Yahya, D. W. Baisch, and E. Monarch, "Presentations of adult celiac disease in a nationwide patient support group," *Digestive Diseases and Sciences*, 48, no. 4 (2003): 761–764.

active participants appeared to be attempting recovery from severe restriction of food intake and the advice they received seemed as steeped in anxiety as what drove their concerns in the first place.

So I did what I do in my job—I began combing the research to understand the condition: its etiology, diagnostic frameworks, prognoses, and treatment modalities.

An eating disorder (a spectrum that includes anorexia, bulimia, orthorexia, anorexia athletica, and binge eating disorder) is a chronic, incurable, and sadly often fatal neurobiological condition. It is the deadliest of all mental illnesses. Standardized mortality ratios (SMRs) for eating disorders range from 1.92 to 10.5.[2,3,4] A SMR is a scientific way of identifying the increased risk of death associated with a particular condition when compared to a random healthy group of human beings. The SMR for a random healthy group is set at 1.00. To reframe the SMR ranges into something more tangible, eating disorders have approximately a one-in-four to one-in-five fatality rate over a twenty-year period. SMRs vary from one trial to the next because causes of death for those with eating disorders can range from heart failure to suicide, and extracting accurate data is not always possible if a patient's underlying contributing condition (namely the eating disorder) is not identified on a death certificate.

But an eating disorder can be nudged into full remission and that remission can often be permanent. Full remission is the complete disappearance of all clinical and subjective characteristics of a chronic or malignant disease.

And at its onset, just as eating wheat does not cause celiac disease, restricting food intake (dieting) does not cause an eating disorder. However, dieting can activate an eating disorder if the person has the genetic predisposition to develop the condition. Voluntary or involuntary (surgery, trauma, illness) restriction of food intake will activate a series of neural anomalies for these genetically predisposed individuals that spirals them into a space of eating less and moving more.[5] We have only some tentative candidate genes that are implicated in the onset of an eating disorder and

[2] G. Paulson-Karlsson, I. Engström, and L. Nevonen, "A pilot study of a family-based treatment for adolescent anorexia nervosa: 18 and 36 months follow-ups," *Eating Disorders: The Journal of Treatment and Prevention* 17, no. 1 (December 2008): 72–88.

[3] F. C. Papdopoulos, A. Ekbom, L. Brandt, and L. Ekselius, "Excess mortality, causes of death and prognostic factors in anorexia nervosa," *British Journal of Psychiatry* 194, no. 1 (2009): 10–17.

[4] C. L. Birmingham, J. Su, J. A. Hlynsky, E. M. Goldner, and M. Gao, "The mortality rate from anorexia nervosa," *International Journal of Eating Disorders* 38, no. 2 (September 2005): 143–146.

[5] R. A. H. Adan, J. J. G. Hillebrand, U. N. Danner, S. C. Cano, M. J. H. Kas, and L. A. W. Verhagen, "Neurobiology Driving Hyperactivity in Activity-Based Anorexia," *Current Topics in Behavioral Neurosciences* 6 (2011): 229–250.

we are likely a long way off from identifying the entire genotype.[6] And having the genotype, or genotypes, will still not confirm that you will ever develop an active state of the condition. Restrictive eating behaviors are driven by a threat identification system in the brain that has mistaken food as a threat. Now of course the patient is not consciously experiencing her condition as a threat response to food. Food cannot possibly be a threat in any logical way. Nonetheless, every time she approaches food, the threat system is fired up. The conscious mind scans the environment for a likely cause of the internal disturbance, and then the conscious mind does what it does best—it makes an educated guess. The reinforcement and practice of restrictive behaviors is dependent on innumerable sociocultural, physical, and psychological inputs, and for each patient those influences will be unique. In our modern cultures the common educated guess is that the food will make her fat. Several hundred years ago, the common educated guess was that the food would render her less spiritually connected to God.

Even today, fear of fatness will not always be how someone with an eating disorder frames her anxiety, behaviors, and torment. Many will talk about ingredients, "frankenfoods," macronutrients, and wanting to live a long and healthy life (orthorexia). Others will talk about how a level of restriction knocks down emotional distress, or that bingeing and purging offers a release of emotional distress upon which they depend (bulimia). Some will indicate they don't fear any food at all, but after an injury suddenly their food consumption plummets because they depend upon the calorie burning of exercise to allow for food consumption (anorexia athletica). There are a growing number of those with eating disorders who will have long lists of forbidden foods on the grounds that such restrictions resolve a host of idiopathic physical symptoms. And most will careen through all of these conscious educated guesses for why they feel what they feel and do what they do. An eating disorder sits under the broad umbrella of anxiety disorders.

After two solid years immersed in the topic, I created the website Your Eatopia [now The Eating Disorder Institute] in 2011. Originally I used my name as the site name but quickly discovered that I didn't want the focus on me, but rather on the science I was synthesizing and analyzing on the blog. And through the forums I supported on the site, I soon met Kerrie in February 2012, when she asked about hormone replacement therapy that had been prescribed because she had amenorrhea after weaning her twins. Of course meeting in an online sense is unique. I couldn't even put a face to her name until she wrote a guest blog post in 2013, and not until 2015 did I hear her voice for the first time on the phone.

---

[6] T. K. Clarke, A. R. D. Weiss, and W. H. Berrettini, "The Genetics of Anorexia Nervosa," *CliniCal pharmaCology & TherapeuTiCs* 91, no. 2 (2012): 181.

I have actually been waiting for this book since long before Kerrie began her journey. While the statistically significant scientific data on my website is compelling, at the end of the day, if you are thinking about getting out from under your own eating disorder, you want to hear from someone who's been there. I have a suggested reading section on the site, but it has listed only one firsthand experience book on recovery, *Brave Girl Eating* by Harriet Brown, which is about a mother navigating her young teenage daughter's recovery process. But very few on the website forums are mothers seeking firsthand experience as a way to help their eating-disordered children. Those who stumble onto the website are almost all adults who have likely spent more years alive with an active eating disorder than not.

The prevalence of eating disorders in the general population is a matter of contention, as meeting diagnostic criteria may not be the most suitable way of measuring who might benefit from treatment. But even when we use those somewhat arbitrary and narrow diagnostic criteria, approximately 25 million Americans will have an eating disorder in their lifetime.[7]

Type in "memoir + eating disorders" into your trusty Google search engine, and you'll receive 469,000 results. And whether you want to classify those memoirs as "wannarexia" or "pro-ana" (essentially how-to books for maintaining restrictive behaviors), or de-glamorizing efforts to try to warn others ("Thar be monsters!"), I've read a few, and you won't find much in the way of what the process of recovery is all about and what full remission looks like.

Most of these memoirs speak of the inexorable frog-in-beaker progression into ever-increasing levels of restriction, terror, and compulsion. Some include the moment at which the author reaches out for help and an epilogue describes the present recovered space of fulfillment and peace. Except that no one recovers, and the vast majority of these epilogues describe a life of harm reduction and not remission. This harm reduction, which may involve returning to a more average weight yet continuing to restrict, albeit not to such an extreme extent, still means progressive disability, pain, suffering, and early death.

Certainly harm reduction is preferable to an unmanaged active eating disorder, and full remission may not be the best course for some of the most severe and enduring cases. Also, remission rates are severely impacted by the number of months a patient is actively restricting before she seeks help. After two years, the remission rate plummets from 75% to 35%. And by year five, only 25% will reach full remission.[8] But the option of complete

---

[7] F. R. Smink, D. van Hoeken, and H. W. Hoek, "Epidemiology of eating disorders: incidence, prevalence and mortality rates," *Current Psychiatry Reports* 14, no. 4 (2012), 406–414.

[8] James D. Lock, University of California San Diego Eating Disorder Conference, October 2014.

remission is not nearly as against the odds as the above statistics would suggest.

But if complete remission from an eating disorder is possible at any age and with any number of years actively restricting, why are there such abysmal outcomes for adults?

One critical contributing factor is that we have created a culture that fears fat. We don't realize that fat is not a storage unit, but a hormone-producing organ.[9] We don't realize that dieting destroys cells throughout all our organs equally. While resistance training during starvation can slow the rate of lean body mass destruction, it is not sustainable beyond three months.[10] We refuse to accept that our weight should never be manipulated, as it has an inherited set point.[11] We doggedly believe, against all scientific evidence to the contrary, that food and activity levels correlate to the size of that fat organ.[12]

And all of these misconceptions relegate those with eating disorders to recovery efforts that rest on this tenet: recover, but not too much.

A recovery effort that usually involves significant bloating, water retention, and a temporary overshoot of one's optimal weight set point will seem a pointless undertaking with a self-sabotaging loss of social status and identity in our fattist culture. Still, with the knowledge of what recovery may bring, after more than a decade of starving, Kerrie decided to recover from an eating disorder. And I cannot tell you how thankful I am that she has written about what that recovery process actually entailed and what full remission really looks like.

I am immersed in very dry, very arcane scientific literature on the topic of eating disorders when I prepare to write blog posts. But when I navigate the website's forums I connect with the human beings for whom all that science matters. There I cry for their losses, I cheer for their successes, and I marvel at their spirit. But all of that are still just post-by-post moments or

---

[9] E. E. Kershaw and J. S. Flier, "Adipose tissue as an endocrine organ," *The Journal of Clinical Endocrinology & Metabolism* 89, no. 6 (2004): 2548–2556.

[10] R. W. Bryner, I. H. Ullrich, J. Sauers, D. Donley, G. Hornsby, M. Kolar, and R. Yeater, "Effects of Resistance vs. Aerobic Training Combined With an 800 Calorie Liquid Diet on Lean Body Mass and Resting Metabolic Rate," *Journal of the American College of Nutrition*, 18, no. 1 (1999): 115–121.

[11] L. M. Redman, L. K. Heilbronn, C. K. Martin, L. De Jonge, D. A. Williamson, J. P. Delany, and Pennington CALERIE Team. (2009), "Metabolic and behavioral compensations in response to caloric restriction: implications for the maintenance of weight loss," *PloS one* 4, no. 2 (2009): e4377.

[12] "Part I and Part II: Systematic Review of Weight Gain Correlates in Literature," *The Eating Disorder Institute*, accessed October 11, 2017, https://www.edinstitute.org/paper/2015/1/21/part-i-systematic-review-of-weight-gain-correlates-in-literature?rq=systematic%20review and https://www.edinstitute.org/paper/2015/2/26/part-ii-systematic-review-of-weight-gain-correlates-in-literature?rq=systematic%20review.

vignettes of any one individual's entire arc of recovery. To read Kerrie's book, which I struggled to put down, was phenomenally intense. To witness the realization of transformation unfold page after page was profoundly moving.

Kerrie begins with snapshots of what it is really like to live inside that space of telescoping anxiety, but, as she has written a memoir of recovery and not of restriction, you will be brought to her moment of choosing recovery within the very first chapter.

The straightforward, science-based approach to recovery that she next describes is called the Homeodynamic Recovery Method, which reflects the clinical data gleaned from the Minnesota Starvation Experiment[13] and the Maudsley Family-Based Treatment[14] approach used for children and adolescents with eating disorders, along with countless peer-reviewed published results. The minimum calorie intake guidelines are set using doubly labeled water trial method data for non–eating disordered age-, height-, and sex-based equivalents.[15] The doubly labeled water trial method is the only way to dependably identify actual energy requirements in humans.[16] In the Homeodynamic Recovery Method, the three pillars of getting to full remission are re-feeding unrestrictedly, resting fully, and involving appropriate psychotherapeutic support to retrain that threat identification system. Additionally, psychotherapeutic support is also needed to uncover and address the personal circumstances and pressures for which continuing to practice restrictive behaviors had been beneficial.

Quickly Kerrie leaps and falls straight down the rabbit hole that is the recovery process. Like the white rabbit in Lewis Carroll's *Alice's Adventures In Wonderland*, Kerrie discovers that everything she believed to be real and true about body size and fitness is simply a mirage. Remission is not feasible when you cannot identify and then release the cultural fallacies that drive the desirability of thinness, the moral superiority of healthiness, and the hatred of fatness.

As Kerrie manages the rigors of re-feeding and resting while contemplating her past, present, and future, she faces the inconvenient truth that the body's timetable is never what your mind wants it to be. And

---

[13] A. Keys, J. Brožek, A. Henschel, O. Mickelsen, and H. L. Taylor. *The Biology of Human Starvation*, 2 vols (University of Minnesota Press, 1950).

[14] J. Lock and D. Le Grange, *Treatment manual for anorexia nervosa: A family-based approach* (Guilford Publications, 2015).

[15] "Homeodynamic Recovery Method, Doubly-Labeled Water Method Trials and Temperament-Based Treatment," *The Eating Disorder Institute*, accessed October 11, 2017, https://www.edinstitute.org/paper/2015/1/12/homeodynamic-recovery-method-doubly-labeled-water-method-trials-and-temperament-based-treatment?rq=temperament%20based.

[16] D. A. Schoeller, "Recent advances from application of doubly labeled water to measurement of human energy expenditure," *The Journal of Nutrition* 129, no. 10 (1999): 1765–1768.

as she struggles to juggle work, kids, and a marriage alongside a punishing recovery effort, she has to face the fact that restrictive behaviors are often practiced year in and year out precisely because they are a coping mechanism, even though they are self-destructive. Lying face-first in the dirt at the bottom of that hole can have anyone yearning to go back to the illusions that were once accepted as fact. In the realm of an eating disorder, that usually means relapse.

Instead, Kerrie gets up, dusts herself off, and begins the real exploration of her new world. Except, of course, this world isn't actually new. It's the world that has been underneath all along—the underworld from which the demands of an eating disorder systematically dissociate you. While rest and re-feeding most certainly allow you to think beyond restriction, achieving full remission requires more than thinking; it requires excavation, which Kerrie does with the assistance of a therapist. She carries the reader through this journey deep into her real world, which includes the grotesque, the bizarre, the tragic, and the miraculous.

Kerrie ultimately achieves remission, which is a daily practice for those with an eating disorder. This memoir shows you how it is done, and I know it will be both inspiring and reassuring to anyone about to embark on a recovery process. You don't need to be told where you've been; you want to know where you are going.

While each recovery effort is as unique as the patient undertaking it, there are markers and challenges along the way that are universal and reflected in Kerrie's journey, which spanned longer than two years. And despite the current odds suggesting that her success is the exception,[17] I believe that her experience can become the rule. No more "recover, but not too much."

December 2017

Gwyneth Olwyn
Patient Advocate
www.edinstitute.org
Author, *Recover from Eating Disorders: Homeodynamic Recovery Method*

Please do not ever begin a recovery effort from an eating disorder without first seeking medical assessment, input, and advice.

---

[17] James D. Lock, University of California San Diego Eating Disorder Conference, October 2014.

And the time came when the risk to remain tight in a bud was more painful than the risk it took to blossom.

—Anaïs Nin

1

Her weathered finger stabbed my stapled production schedule. "Did you change the price of this book?!"

Oh, God, I screwed up. I changed the price on the wrong book, or the right book to the wrong price. Somehow grinding my focus into the black print of the page summoned the answer. "Y-yes, I did . . . after you told me to."

My boss's eyes retreated to her computer monitor, e-mails flickering open and closed. She spat at the screen, "I don't remember that at all. I can't find anything here that says that should have been done." I studied the four burgundy upholstered chairs in Valeria's office, recalling on which one I had sat the day I scribbled price changes on scrap paper. *I wonder if I still have that paper. That will fix everything.* As her mouse continued to click away, I held my breath and noted how she resembled an owl, with her short salt-and-pepper hair petrified by gel into a swooping wave on each side of her squarish head. "So help me God, if I find out you went ahead and changed a price, I will RAKE YOU OVER THE COALS." Valeria opened more e-mails. Right then I wasn't worth even her most disdainful glare.

Stunned, I backed out of her office and hustled to my cubicle. I overturned every sheet of paper at my desk, but the evidence was long gone. Numb, I searched the keys on my computer keyboard as if it were an oracle. *I might be fired—a failure. But . . . maybe it's really for the best.* My phone rang and displayed her extension, and I braced myself for the end.

"Oh, ha-ha-ha-ha-ha! Kerrie? I found it. Yeah, it was after the big meeting. I sat you and the other production editors down for price changes. But after any meeting like that you should *really* e-mail me a list of everything that was said. Okay, bye!"

The hairpin turn in her tone rattled me. But I was disconcerted more that I was right, but somehow I was still wrong. Through my whole short life I had worked hard and done a good job, but under her scrutiny I always wrong. And at twenty-two years old I lacked the confidence and experience with that kind of authority to brush off her daily censures as a symptom of her own failings rather than of mine.

A month after I began that job, a handsomely suited Alex, whom I had been dating for just longer than a year, had strewn rose petals on the floor of my bedroom and got down on one knee to propose. Whittling off a few pounds before shopping for a wedding dress seemed the normal and expected thing to do, and eating a little less and redirecting grocery money toward wedding expenses seemed the perfect way to achieve my short-term goals. Then Valeria's relentless insults and threats and my growing terror of her unpredictable moods tipped what seemed like casual dieting down the slippery slope of what I much later realized was anorexia—a mechanism to control the outside of my body as a counterbalance to my trashed self-esteem and sense of professional accomplishment. Starving myself lent a sense of success, a way for me to be "right" on a daily basis. It was a death spiral; I was consumed by the overwhelming self-doubt that my boss generated in me and the command of the scale with which I was attempting to medicate myself. By my wedding day I had lost more than twenty pounds. My pelvic bones crunched together as I walked down the aisle.

One morning on our Parisian honeymoon, Alex and I sat at a thumbtack of a table in a frenetic café on the Left Bank, and I was trembling. Alex pressed one of my hands between his, and my other hand clenched the wobbly tabletop to keep myself upright as I screeched in my head for the garçon to get over here and take our order. I steadied my eyes on the gilt Belle Époque mirrors on the walls, noting the thrum of the crowd receding under the sound of my own heartbeat, quickening, thumping, threatening to cease. I envisioned a particularly refined interior for the French hospital where I would end up, since I would likely pass out soon or perhaps plain die.

Alex knew I wasn't eating enough; on another morning earlier on our trip I hadn't the energy to move from our hotel bed. I had made some noise about simply disliking the ubiquitous, small, eggy *petit dejeuners* I'd been passing over, and he had hunted the Ile St-Louis for a baguette and banana to present to me, a breakfast I scarfed with desperation and shame, a victory for my life force but a blow for the self-starvation that had become my sense of control and serenity.

Our table seemed forgotten. Alex hoisted me onto my jittering legs, then he grasped my shoulders in case I collapsed as he ferried us to an emptier café, where we sat in the breeze along the Seine and I ordered a huge bowl of relief—something with noodles; I consumed the whole thing before investigating the ingredients. As the nutrition traveled from my stomach to my veins and brain, the chestnut trees yellowing in late October fell into sharper focus. I felt like the energetic twenty-four-year-old I should have been. As we next walked three hours to tour Napoleon's tomb and through various Parisian neighborhoods, I was not only content and happy but reset for something new, better. And then, like a rock thrown upward, I eventually could go no higher. At our lunch stop I plummeted with the thrill of deficit, the willpower to turn away the second half of my sandwich *avec des légumes* after I'd barely cut my deep hunger, the beastly insistence on walking for additional hours in order to burn whatever I did consume, and the terror that my jeans could become snug if I ate one more bite.

For months afterward I continued to shrink, and I became paralyzed by depression because I couldn't just quit that job—Alex and I couldn't survive in New York City without my income. After two years I had lost a total of thirty pounds, but Alex didn't seem to attribute the loss to anything more than my hopelessness wrecking my appetite. Then, by some grace of the universe, my desperate job hunting finally paid off: I was offered an editorial position at another children's publisher, which I believed would be my salvation. But when my satisfying new work environment did not in fact dissipate my fixations on eating, not eating, and exercising, I eventually conceded to myself that I had developed an eating disorder. The number of calories I would allow myself to eat on a particular day was my first, deflating thought upon waking, and it bullied every hour of every day until I slipped into sleep, my only release. Although at my core I understood that this was no way to live, that this was wrecking my body, that normal people did not need to do this to maintain their weight, I could not find a button to mute the squalling tyrant.

I remained emaciated and tortured. Rather than seeking help, I pursued pregnancy, expecting that a soft, loving thing of my own might bring me some untainted happiness, that the required level of selflessness of motherhood would smack me out of the self-absorption of starvation. I ceased my birth-control pill, but my periods did not continue because they couldn't on their own. Until then I hadn't considered the damage incurred in my body. After scouring the Internet, I suspected that I had developed hypothalamic amenorrhea, when menstrual cycles stop because of a disruption of hormones secreted by the hypothalamus, the part of the brain that had determined that my ultra-low calorie intake and fat stores made me a poor candidate for growing another human being inside me. I reluctantly accepted that, if I was ever to have a baby, I needed to gain.

I finally divulged my darkest of secrets to Alex, in a cracked voice uttering the word *anorexia* for the first time. With the shock of the news, he kneaded his fingertips into his overgrown, coffee-colored hair, his nervous tic. Alex awaited the solution, remaining quiet as I explained my plan to slowly gain until my periods returned. He seemed a little detached, but I couldn't find reason to fault him for that, since only I could do the work to pull myself out.

I immediately doubled my average intake, but the scale did not budge. I was amazed that I could have been eating so much and feeling energetic while maintaining my severely underweight body. But I couldn't just stop there, and I stuck to my decision: *I'd rather have a baby than wear tiny pants. I need to gain weight to get my period again.* At my in-laws' Christmas Eve family party I felt so stuffed after spending the day and evening consuming a total of 2,500 calories—a normal daily intake for an average person—that I had to escape and lie for an hour on Alex's childhood bed. There he comforted me, assuring me he was proud of what I was doing and I would be beautiful no matter what. I burst into tears. I was trying so hard, but I still wasn't gaining anything.

I had to keep eating, and more. With persistently increased intake, the scale finally crept up just a few pounds, and a few pounds more. When my clothes started fitting a bit differently, anxiety crept up, too. To quell it I reduced my eating just enough for my weight to stabilize for a week or two, allowing me to become comfortable enough with that size before forging ahead. Soon I noticed that some flesh had developed between my upper arm and torso, that I was starting to look like everyone else. I was losing my identity as the thinnest person in the room. My smallest clothes were banished to the bottom of the drawer and the back of the closet with both pride and horror.

The gain was always deliberate; I carefully calculated calories so that my body would do exactly as I wished that week, whether staying at a precise weight or pushing ahead precisely one pound—maybe two if I was feeling extra brave. One day I would really go for it, eating 1,750 or 3,500 calories over a maintenance level, so gorged and reeling with sugar that I needed two Benadryl to pass out, and then the next day I would feel so ashamed at what I allowed myself to consume that, despite a deep hole in my gut, I would not feed it more than absolutely necessary to stumble through the hours until the embrace of sleep. I wouldn't allow my body to take the lead; I was terrified that if I kept eating like that I would expand indefinitely. Eventually I put on twenty-five pounds, but my eating remained no less disordered.

From across his glossy mahogany desk, the reproductive endocrinologist smirked at me and Alex as he tossed aside my printouts of Internet articles on the function of leptin in the resumption of menses, which I had presented to him with hope that he could prescribe some form of it. Instead he drew diagrams of follicles, demonstrated syringes, and explained that I would report to his office in the very early mornings, several times a week, for blood draws to monitor my ovaries and uterine lining as the drugs nudged my body toward that elusive ovulation. I tearfully begged for a strategy for fixing my body; he curtly countered with a glance at my flat torso and trim thighs in a tawny plaid pencil skirt and suggested that I "could gain five or ten pounds." That felt like a slap in the face, for I was convinced that I had already done the work to restore my weight to the point where pregnancy should be possible. But ultimately he was the only doctor to suggest that a medically minimum healthy weight might not be enough, that I might be self-sabotaging.

Alex and I silently rode the subway from Manhattan to our Brooklyn apartment that slate-gray winter afternoon, stunned that we were now navigating the waters of injectable hormones and intrauterine inseminations, that first I would have an MRI to check for a pituitary tumor, a hysterosalpingogram to ensure that my fallopian tubes were clear, and blood work to establish my hormone levels, and that Alex would have a sperm analysis. Just those upcoming months of preliminary testing were overwhelming, and I was devastated that I wouldn't be able to conceive our first child in our bed, in a tender or lustful act of sex or, given my very low libido since the onset of anorexia, at least a loving if tepid attempt at conception. No, instead I would gaze up at a fluorescent light, my socked feet in medical stirrups, as this doctor threaded a thin tube through my cervix and plunged Alex's purified sperm into me.

With bitterness, I capitulated to the brokenness of my body. I was angry that I could never escape this nightmare, that I would be punished for the rest of my life for stumbling into a job that whipped me into a submission from which I could never recover. There seemed no longer a point in maintaining the twenty-five pounds I fought to gain and then endured with angst for many months. *If I can't get pregnant naturally, then I should at least have a body I'm comfortable with.* Plus, we had a beach vacation coming up. So the number on the scale went down.

It took three tense cycles of injections and appointments, but I was pregnant and elated. I believed this would deliver me from my disordered behaviors, at least by the time of birth. I expected I would become utterly immersed in motherhood, the attention that a tiny, shiny-headed being would require of me. Because how could I calculate the calories in a five-ounce piece of salmon when a small child needed to hear a little "Twinkle, Twinkle"? I read that some eating-disordered women's behaviors flared during the increased hunger, weight gain, and body shape changes involved in pregnancy, but I found that time an oasis, a place where my body had a purpose other than being thin and looking great in any clothing item I pulled off a rack. With another life inside me, I finally had a bargaining chip against anorexia. I had fought hard to conceive this baby, and I was determined to provide the fuel to grow it properly. I rigorously researched the different caloric requirements and ideal weight gain patterns and totals for normal and underweight women, and I aimed at a point in between. I knew that growth spurts and increasing water retention could throw off my intended gain curve, but I was determined to use math and self-discipline to encourage fetal development while minimizing maternal weight gain. And I loved my newly increased daily totals, which no longer included a glass of wine or a vodka tonic on the weekend or at a restaurant. I was now free to consume those calories in the form of food, and I was relieved not to feel so starved. My body cooperated quite well with my efforts, gaining on the established arc until our last-hurrah trip to Mexico, where I stupidly ate some local water-washed salad on an outing to Maya ruins and I came down with the infamous diarrhea. I continued to eat my daily amounts through the rest of the trip and then back home, but a week after my intestines calmed, the scale showed that I had not gained anything in three weeks.

My beloved midwife, who knew about my history of severe anorexia but not the subsequent years of continued food control, encouraged me to increase my calories and scheduled an ultrasound to check on the baby's growth when I was almost eight months along. I was mortified that I may have miscalculated or, worse, that I had erred on the side of the eating disorder. I feared that I may not have been consuming enough, and that meeting only absolutely minimal nutritional requirements may have been putting my baby in jeopardy. I increased by a few hundred calories and went for the ultrasound, which showed a cyst on the placenta but overall normal growth. However, a follow-up ultrasound a couple of weeks later revealed that the baby's abdomen growth had slowed, a sign that insufficient nutrition was traveling through the placenta. Right then, at thirty-six weeks' gestation, my midwife strongly advised me to let my publishing group know that I would be commencing a "home rest," where I watched TV, read, and took short walks—as far as I could, with my pelvic bones and muscles aching easily—in the late summer sun. My lessened activity level tempted me to commensurately lower my food intake, but I couldn't allow myself to eat anything less than heartily; at that point my baby's health was a priority that could muffle the shriek of anorexia. A week later, some routine blood work showed a very low platelet count, which led to a diagnosis of HELLP syndrome (Hemolysis, Elevated Liver enzymes, Low Platelet count), a rare and potentially fatal form of preeclampsia. HELLP usually presents with high blood pressure, but throughout the pregnancy mine had always been low, perhaps due to my food restriction. Thank goodness my midwife had ordered that platelet count, because to save two lives the baby had to be delivered immediately.

❖

Freshly home with our newborn son, in those endless delicious hours of simply holding that sleeping creature against my chest, I marveled not only at his tiny body but also at how the tendons in my feet resurfaced, which Alex jokingly dubbed "anorexic feet" without realizing how very true that still was. Even with much heavy, swollen breast tissue, each morning the scale showed another drop until at eight days postpartum the needle settled just a couple of pounds above my pre-pregnancy weight. I fit right back into my skinniest jeans. One day during those first weeks, while wearing a tight camisole, I was boosting my less-than-seven-pound son in his stylish black-and-red stroller up a long Flatbush Avenue hill when an approaching older man regarded me and stopped in his tracks.

He picked up his jaw and asked, "You're not that baby's mother, are you?"

Straightening up and beaming, I replied, "Yes. Yes, I am."

He literally tipped his tan bowler hat to me and I felt on top of the world. I felt amazing for kicking those pregnancy pounds to the curb with my superior willpower, and I was still enamored by and engrossed in my son. I was supermom.

That is, until a checkup showed that Charlie had not gained any weight in a handful of days, and my self-worth immediately crashed. The terms *lactation consultant* and *supplementation* thunked like boulders in the pediatrician's exam room. I spent the rest of the day in tears, trying to nurse him every two hours and calling down the list of consultants. I was gripped with the terror that this was my fault, that I wasn't eating enough and this was the repercussion, that my selfish drive to be a certain size was putting at risk not only any future in breastfeeding but also my son's life. The next day we visited a lactation consultant who confirmed that he was gleaning very little at feedings likely because, as she explained, babies born before thirty-eight weeks' gestation are often very weak suckers. She showed me how to use a supplementation tube system that allowed him to obtain extra breast milk (which I would first extract with a rented medical-grade breast pump) while learning how to feed off me. And thus began a messy, complicated feeding regimen that was barely doable with Alex's assistance and plain crazy-making when I was alone during the workweek. But I could acquit my restrictive behaviors of their implication in the temporary situation. They could remain my trusty, friendly coping mechanism.

After Charlie grew into a strong enough nurser that we no longer needed the feeding apparatus, I felt I had room on my plate for motherhood, a low-gear freelance editing and writing career, and obsessive calorie counting. The eating disorder seemed manageable; breaking up with it seemed more trouble than it was worth. On outings I wore Charlie in a carrier—first on my front and then on my back—which not only made navigating New York City sidewalks, subway stations, and narrow bodega doorways much easier than with a stroller but also provided extra resistance on our lengthy walks through gentrified Brooklyn neighborhoods. These marches served partly to trade hours in our three-room brownstone apartment for some fresh air but also as exercise calculated to rectify food indulgences or "save up" for them. Despite occasional playdates with my new mom friends, I was lonely, so our escapes became more frequent, sometimes in the sticky city heat for a full hour just so that I could guiltlessly eat a 200-calorie snack at the end. And then I would be one hour closer to Alex's evening return, when I could escape into the other room to exercise even more, which I justified as "me" time.

On a summer night almost three years later, writhing on a lumpy bed in ER triage, I progressed to full dilation. On the way were two more babies whom I believed would make our family and my life complete, and perhaps provide enough leverage to heave the self-starvation over the edge forever. When the attending doctor noted that I was ready to deliver, I begged her, but she would not simply pull out breech twin A, even with his or her tiny foot apparently dangling through my cervix. I was wheeled immediately into the operating room with no time for an epidural, and right before I fell unconscious under general anesthesia I begged her, "Please cut really low." At that moment my most pressing fear was not the welfare of my babies, which perhaps I took for granted as the given top medical priority, but that I'd never wear a bikini again, that I'd never show off what I had worked so hard for. When anxiety was running the show, the eating disorder held the microphone.

Upon waking, a masked nurse told me with the ceremony of a weather announcement that I had birthed two girls, who were now in the NICU. It was far from the ecstatic "it's a . . ." moment, but I didn't care much, as I was too hazy with morphine for pain and magnesium to prevent any seizures associated with HELLP syndrome, which had recurred. Tethered to the hospital bed by a catheter and IVs, I pumped colostrum whenever I was awake, and my first glimpse of my fraternal twin daughters' tiny bodies was on Alex's cell phone. The following day, when the medications were stopped and I needed only the occasional ibuprofen, my consciousness fully surfaced and my world crashed down. I learned that my in-laws had already visited my babies in the NICU, before I had a chance to. No doctor had told me how they were doing and when they would be let out of those plastic prisons. No one had told me when I would be able to get out of bed and see them. I just wanted to hold them in my hospital bed as I had with my son. *Why was that asking so much?* Still too nauseated from the drugs to eat, I couldn't funnel my distress into food control; I had to feel every emotion. I felt ignored when I was most vulnerable, and I spent hours crying like a shattered little girl.

Later that day, after apologies from doctors for the miscommunications, my catheter was removed, and with my husband, son, and mother behind me I was wheeled to the NICU. Alex could have already held the larger, stronger baby if he wanted, but with immense sensitivity he had reserved the honor for me, the heartbeat that the girls would recognize, the woman who fought to conceive them and then carry them as properly as she could, and the person who would spend the majority of her time feeding and caring for them for months and years to come. I deserved that moment, and when Josie grasped my finger with her tiny hand with impossible strength, I knew we would be okay, even though her sister, even tinier, was covered with respiratory apparatuses and I couldn't do more than stroke her loose-skinned limbs through portholes in her isolette.

For days following, as Alex somehow managed our home in upstate New York and arranged childcare for Charlie so that he could visit me and the babies daily, I lived in the eye of the storm, quiet in my hospital room, alternately pumping and resting to heal my incision as my liver enzymes, elevated because of HELLP, slowly normalized. I left the room only to plod to the NICU and the floor cafeteria. No one seemed to know for sure when I could go home, and my daughters' discharge was even more uncertain. One day I was told that Josie would likely go home with me, leaving Eliza and her lung development issues behind at the hospital, but on that cloudless August Saturday when I was discharged and Alex drove us the forty-five minutes home, there were no infants in the back seat. And back at our house, with my son and sunshine and privacy, my hospital world persisted: round-the-clock pumping, soreness in my stapled abdomen, worry and sadness at not having my babies home, and anger that I was deprived of not only a birth in which I actively participated but the tender aftermath, too. The finish line of bringing them home and feeding them directly from my body was a moving target, as stretches of hopeful twice-daily reports from NICU nurses were demolished with news of another breathing episode. I was powerless to do anything but pump and shuttle a milk cooler to and from the NICU, where I held them and sang Bob Dylan's "Don't Think Twice, It's Alright." As an infant, Charlie had chosen that as his lullaby, perhaps soothed by a singing voice as endearingly off-tone as his father's.

The girls came home one at a time: Josie at a week and a half old, and Eliza a week and a half after that. The next morning—my thirty-first birthday, no less—I could have drowned in the delight of the sun-speckled sheets in which all five of us lounged in the big bed, finally a whole family. But soon my attention turned to my pooching abdomen, as the post-surgery swelling was slowing its deflation. I was larger postpartum after this second pregnancy, and I felt that the fat absolutely had to go, and immediately. I reasoned that if I had to weather my babies being such poor nursers—weighing all of five pounds each and having gotten too used to being fed by tube and bottle in the hospital—then I could treat myself to being enviably small again, finding solace, control, and victory there. And it wasn't a difficult task: since my body prioritized the use of calories for milk production rather than maintaining fat stores, I pumped eighty to ninety ounces a day while my body began thinning. About a week after both babies were home, I was at my pre-pregnancy weight, and I found that I had to eat more than ever just to stop losing weight, which quickly became more tiresome than exhilarating. Alex had returned to work down in Manhattan, so I alone faced the elaborate, lengthy breastfeeding ritual that involved individual attempts to breastfeed each baby, followed by bottles and pumping some more for the next feeding, eight or nine times per day. I barely had time to eat the five meals a day I needed to maintain my size. I never knew when one baby would wake up and cry, and I was still taking care of Charlie, who also needed to be shuttled to and from his new preschool. Even after hiring an occasional sitter for Charlie to lighten the load, I felt backed into a corner. In my eating-disordered brain the solution was to restrict, thus breaking the pact I had made with myself years prior never to fall below a certain weight that I had believed would always keep me afloat. But with such high daily caloric requirements, I felt that losing just five pounds would be so painless, and feeling just a little thinner would probably make me feel better. Those five pounds were gone by the end of October.

In November, I skidded into a world of powerlessness and worthlessness as acute as my first dive into anorexia many years earlier—hours, days, weeks, months lost to memory, to misery. I became a zombie of pain, a robot dedicated to infant feeding and diapers, a martyr to unpredictable and inconsolable wailing, both theirs and mine. I couldn't bring myself to joyfully engage in play with my son or do anything more than wave some jangly toys in front of my daughters. I wept until Alex came home—he stayed over in the city twice a week to avoid excessive commuting—after which point I could curl up on our bed until I had to open my shirt again for the babies. One day my friend Amanda arranged to come over with her son to play with Charlie and visit me and the girls for a time slot perfectly convenient to my schedule, and she even brought along bagels for everyone. But like a harpy I screeched for the boys not to play with more than a few toys at a time because I couldn't face another cleanup task, another moment of chaos I was supposed to resolve. I was reacting to my life rather than acting in it, and I felt terrible about who I had become.

Winter set in, as well as full-blown depression. I checked out of my family and into an extended bed-in with my eating disorder. My rules of engagement expanded beyond daily calorie allowances calibrated by exercise; now I was balancing minutes sitting and standing, my mind a perpetual hurricane of numbers squelching the mewling of infants and the maternal guilt accompanying my inability to remain on the floor to stack blocks after my self-allotted "sedentary time" had expired. I kept my weight perfectly stable, and the disorder had me in a stranglehold I hadn't experienced in years. The shock of my newly hectic and frustrating life had inflamed my behaviors, a seeming solution that lent only more fuel to the fire of anxiety, the futile reach for control, the fight for stillness. I became hollow and helpless, so weakened that friends convinced me to seek a therapist, the first one I had ever consulted.

She and I discussed easing the self-judgment, cultivating an inner mother, and reframing my existence as the primary caregiver of two infants and a toddler as a temporary role. Quickly I discovered that this therapist did not diagnose as much as act as an intelligent mirror so that I could delve more deeply into myself and find my own answers. I began regretting not having sought help when I was severely starving at the start of my disorder, but back then I had been convinced that the only solution was to leave the job that had pounded me down, that I didn't need someone telling me what I knew so well, that I was haggard and miserable.

When the therapist and I broached the transformation of my initial dive into starvation and emaciation into an ongoing exercise of control at any weight, I held such hope that she could name it for me, that I could go home, type that term into a search engine, and learn ways to overcome or at least manage this condition. I had already a dozen times searched the Internet for other people not quite starving yet imprisoned by a calorie-counting obsession, but no one else seemed destroyed by this; rather, online references to such intense food control seemed to be revered as the height of health, beauty, and triumph over the human form. But my therapist also had no solid answer, so I felt more isolated than ever in the preoccupation that I yearned to shake off. I couldn't stand that my consciousness had become no more than a pedometer, and I felt great regret that I had squandered years' worth of hours that could have been used productively and enjoyably. I reminded myself that in high school and college I had maintained my weight just fine without micromanaging my physical activity, that many years ago I didn't know the calorie content of anything and nonetheless my size didn't waver much.

As a baby step toward recovery, I took what was for me a leap of faith: I built familiar meals without the use of measuring cups and food scales. I experienced a rush of freedom, but after a few days, hunger crept up and I panicked. I realized I was subconsciously erring these meals and snacks on the small side; I had been eating by numbers so long that I feared I couldn't trust my body's appetite. I tried to capitulate to my hunger, but quickly I became too uneasy that I might start to gain. After not even a week's experimentation, I returned to counting calories, and I didn't see that therapist again.

As dark greenish-gray clouds gathered, and the predicted summer thunderstorm seemed just minutes away, I wrestled my three kids into their car seats and drove to the exit of the park, away from the public wading pool where they had been splashing around. I slowed to a stop, glanced in both directions, and nudged the car to cross the intersection at no more than five miles per hour when from my left I heard a frantic honking. Emerging through the seamless horizon of slate blue asphalt and sky was a car as muted a green as the surrounding pre-storm trees, without daytime running lights, barreling toward us. I braked to stop our roll and waited for the car to swerve around us, and my breath caught in the hope that it could do so without crashing into a telephone pole or rolling over. Instead, the car roughly scraped my front driver's side corner, rotating us forty-five degrees but crumpling and tearing off much of its own front. The kids and I were fine—the former virtually unfazed, in fact—but the other driver sustained minor injuries, likely from the steering wheel or airbag. Next was an hour of negotiating EMTs, police officers, firefighters, and tow truckers, while I panicked that my kids, now almost two and five years old, wouldn't understand what was happening and were probably absorbing every ounce of my anxiety. A mother I had just met at the pool let my kids sit in her minivan with hers, where they all contentedly munched on snacks while she sat with the injured driver and I made calls to Alex in the city. After an hour, the excitement settled, vehicles pulled away, and that kind fellow mom drove us home.

After settling all the kids into their afternoon nap, I ate a small lunch, drank a large vodka tonic, and cried out of trauma, out of gratitude that none of my children were hurt, and out of guilt that the accident could be considered my fault because the other driver had the right of way at that intersection. I felt terrible that the other driver was injured enough to need medical attention. The event was an unfortunate convergence of circumstance—the dark sky, the dark car speeding—but I feared that my failure to discern the car was the critical factor and my slowly deteriorating eyesight had been the culprit. I wondered if my persistent starvation had contributed to my recent need for glasses.

Still, I was not moved to recover. In the aftermath of car repairs, I chose to lose a few more pounds to allow my hips to narrow in proportion to my chest that had recently shrunken by weaning the girls, and also to ensure that I could fit in a dress I intended to wear to a friend's wedding in a couple of months. That goal was quickly achieved, but I was clenched by another apprehension: we were gearing up to launch six to eight weeks of renovations to expand bedrooms on the second floor of our house, during which we would all sleep in an RV in the driveway, next to a freight container holding half of our belongings. While packing the second-floor bathroom items, I nestled my cherished scale in one of the boxes, concluding that sustaining a very precise weight through the construction commotion would be too much of a burden. This would be an interesting experiment, I thought—to do it without a scorecard.

The daily disruptions of the renovations distracted me from the grind of incessant meal planning, but I could feel my mental hems unraveling, especially as we embarked on an exhausting preschool schedule in which my son attended five sessions a week and my daughters two sessions, all without overlap. My freelance work offers ramped up, and the roof and walls on the second floor were being demolished. To end those days by walking outside at night to sleep on a plastic bed in a poorly insulated RV in close quarters with three young children felt like resigning to a new circle of hell. One morning, the tarp over the exposed roof collapsed under heavy rain, which then streamed through the ceiling vents into the kitchen and dining room. The eating disorder became my life raft.

When I wasn't freelance editing or fulfilling my compulsory parent helping duties at the preschool, Alex and I were packing up the necessary items from the functional half of our house and moving ourselves to a rental house five minutes away in order for the crew to repair water damage from the tarp collapse. Here was much needed quiet, but also further displacement and restlessness. Not only was the renovation now requiring three months altogether instead of two—so was the quarantine of my scale in the freight container. I was alarmed when I noticed that my jeans were consistently snugger, which had long been another tool for measuring body change since new fat sprouted first on my thighs and hips. I rotated in front of the bathroom mirror in the rental house, scrutinizing my lower half from every angle, trying to gauge the extent of the damage. I decided to try not counting calories but eating only enough not to feel overwhelmingly dizzy or cranky.

Now starving even more, my body sought other sources of calories, such as the sugarless gum that for years I had been using to suppress my appetite and preoccupy my mouth when I wouldn't allow it food. I could easily process thirty pieces a day, cramming my mouth with piece after piece—one or two not enough, three or four too much at a time—forever trying to settle on the perfect mass to satiate me. Flavor ran out, hunger mounted, and the cycle repeated endlessly; by dinnertime I was often doubled over with excruciating gas from swallowing air all day. I knew it was a destructive habit, but I didn't know how to stop, just as I didn't know how to stop counting calories and worrying about maintaining a specific weight. And the less food I ate, the more gum I needed, until my body found those negligible calories far too little for the increased daily deficit I was creating. I then craved a mountain of peanut butter, which I tried to avoid with samplings of safer food before I found myself in an almost catatonic state at the counter, spoon in hand, shoveling half the jar into my mouth. I thought I was pathetically weak, capitulating to the stress of three chaotic months of house renovation and a bit steeper of a calorie cut. I was ashamed at my lack of willpower. However, I had read that an undeniable urge for a specific food was often a signal that my body required some nutrient in it, which in this case was likely the fat that I always skimmed from my meals due to its high caloric value and low bulk. So instead of restricting even further for the next couple of days to erase the mistake, I let those peanut butter calories stand. It felt odd to honor my body rather than fight it, but I let myself enjoy my full belly. The scale would hammer down the verdict soon enough.

We moved back into our repaired and renovated house. We slept like dogs in our old beds. I saw the scale in the bathroom and hopped on, expecting my weight to be higher than three months earlier—but it was lower by a few pounds. I was electrified by this surprise accomplishment. I theorized that the powerful clothes dryer in the rental house had been shrinking my jeans, and that the peanut butter binge was my body crying for calories. *I wasn't such a weakling after all!* But, as always, the high didn't last long. At 7:30 a.m. on the first weekday back in the house, I received a call that painters would be taking over the entire second floor to apply another coat to the hallway and girls' bedroom, and my babysitter called in sick. I caromed around the house to get the kids fed and dressed and to pull out diapers and everything else they would need for a whole day. I called Alex at work, wailing that I wanted those workers out of my house, out of my life, that I just couldn't take it anymore, hollering so threateningly that they all slunk out to their cars apparently to call the contractor, who soon appeared at my kitchen door, as gentle as a crisis specialist.

I knew that the very first step was to regain at least to where I was before the renovations, but the eating disorder was hissing at me that life is always easier a few pounds less. Plus I was already ahead of the game—a state I'd always relished—to lose a few before we took a family trip to Key West in less than two months. So I maintained the loss. But the urges to "binge," often at the end of a long, stressful day of restricting and child wrangling, became more frequent. I thought I was losing my edge, my self-discipline, but what I was really losing was my health: I came down with a terrible sinus infection that traveled to my ear. I was in throbbing pain, with my hearing potentially damaged, yet I spent hours researching online whether the tapering weeklong dose of prednisone would cause weight gain, as steroids can. This reaction was nothing new; for ten years, virtually any event—a spontaneous restaurant meal, a planned outing, or even just daylight saving time adjustment—was immediately fielded by the eating disorder and processed as a threat.

After the acute ear and sinus infection subsided, my cold symptoms persisted and I knew that something was off. Until then, my immune system had always proven hardy, allowing a stuffy nose for only a day or two before it quickly resolved, and often a houseful of sicklings left me unaffected. This time, however, I couldn't kick it. I could feel my body splintering. But we were leaving for a beach vacation in a month, and I had always embarked on these unpredictable, restaurant-and-alcohol-laced trips with a soothing cushion of underweightedness. I forced myself to drop a couple more pounds, until I was just three pounds shy of the lowest weight I had sustained during my worst years. Even my tiniest pants were a bit loose. I knew I had entered the zone where I did not look good, but I didn't know how to stop, to gain, to live. I finally recognized that the eating disorder was never satisfied and the trend would always be downward; I could only make myself shrink very slowly, one day to disappear. Desperate, I sought commiseration in eating disorder memoirs, such as Marya Hornbacher's *Wasted* and Portia di Rossi's *Unbearable Lightness*. I read them to unlock the code to freedom, but each of their recoveries read as an afterthought, a miracle unarticulated, a mystery I'd have to accidentally encounter on my own.

Despite my critically low weight, during our week in Key West I kept a close eye on the bottom calorie line. I could never truly heed my body because below the net of the cottage cheese and green tea and almonds was a black, yawning hunger that must be denied. My work to create a space—between my thighs, my joints, the folds in my brain—where I could feel free to consume what seemed excessive amounts, to take a vacation from anorexia, was futile. The nagging monster—which was really my body's survival instinct—screamed in my head to eat a half cup of the kids' peanut butter, to which I acquiesced because the voice was louder than any eating disorder chatter. I did it again two days later. My body was fighting back, but the disorder, like a fastidious accountant, ensured that I sufficiently restricted later to accommodate these "binges."

Upon returning home, I felt drawn and quartered. The eating disorder begged me to maintain the ultra-low weight or push it even lower, and my body was employing every physiological drive it could muster to force me to eat amounts significant enough to gain some mass. This reactive eating was becoming so extreme that I could no longer offset the numbers by even the severest restriction on the following days. That precarious balance between my body and the eating disorder was collapsing, and I had to negotiate a new dynamic before I had a psychotic break, before my body succumbed. I had been sick with a transient cold for almost two months, my eyesight had declined, my breasts were tiny pancakes, and I was on hormone-replacement therapy for my nonexistent periods. I couldn't stand to witness or exist in this crumbling body.

I spent two consuming days online and in my head. At first I continued to negotiate with the eating disorder, confirming the physical damage to a body at my current BMI and how much I could mitigate that if I increased to various BMI thresholds. I was essentially reassuring my eating disorder that I would stay with it, but we needed a place more sustainable. I was still bargaining with something that would kill me regardless.

Meanwhile, my body kept pushing back, commanding me to eat—and to eat some more. Since I hadn't yet mentally signed a new decree to eat only a certain amount or maintain a certain size, I was without a contractual defense against those impulses. And so I kept eating. And in that burst of energy, in that promise of nourishment, my life force heaved forward with possibly one of its last breaths and shoved me through that flimsy, cobwebby membrane of delusion that I could live contentedly and healthily enough with an eating disorder.

I couldn't. It had to end now, before I did.

I immediately began hunting online for motivation and a route to recover, to save my life. Within a day I landed at the somewhat new site of Gwyneth Olwyn, a patient advocate who had become increasingly involved in spreading science-based knowledge about eating disorders and recovery from them. Her well-referenced articles explained that my first attempt at recovery was unsuccessful because I had neither been eating significantly on a daily basis nor allowing my size to settle where it may. Simply reaching a BMI of 18.5 or 20 did not yield health. I learned how my early, obvious anorexia had merely shifted manifestation to a compulsion to exercise away my limited intake, and then most recently to a war with my body's need to ingest as much food as possible and save itself. I learned that these behaviors—anorexia athletica, subclinical starvation, and restrictive/reactive cycles, respectively—were all just facets of the same eating disorder spectrum. I was still as sick and doing just as much damage as in the early years of mercilessly starving myself.

The eating disorder had convinced me that for life I would have to micromanage my calorie intake and expenditure to maintain my weight, but Olwyn's information about each person's genetically determined set point rang so clear. It was true that until I was hit with anorexia at age twenty-three I had been able to eat whatever I wanted and stay virtually the same size. And then I read extraordinary news. There was a way out, and it was the most delectable route I could imagine: I would eat, a lot, every day. I would respond to the deep hunger inside and then eat to hunger cues for the rest of my days, with my body and mind finally free of eating disorder chatter, which I had come to believe was my life sentence. It all sounded too good to be true, that I could eat what I want, temporarily bloat with fluid and have a less than perfectly flat midsection, and then settle at my natural set point and be cured. The eating disorder rejected such a protocol: *Who is this woman, anyway? No one who eats 3,000 calories a day isn't huge. You saw what happened when you increased your intake by just a little. She's just trying to make you fat.* But my mind, fueled with more food than usual, embraced the logic that such an attempt at brainwashing legions of anorectics would never work, anyway; if we feel ourselves getting larger but no happier, we'll simply fall back into restriction, as I had done during my first attempt at recovery. And members of the forums on her site claimed that it works. *There must be something here.*

I delved further into her site and read the article that changed my life,[18] which outlined the progression and accumulation of physiological damage to those with eating disorders. I could already recognize, after just ten years, at age thirty-three, the falterings of my immune system and vision, the distance between myself and my family. My deepest fears were confirmed, as evidence predicted that my body and mind would continue to deteriorate until I perhaps committed suicide, my marriage crumbled, or my dear sweet children were at best estranged from me and at worst eating disordered themselves—a prospect, even for a woman deeply entrenched in this mental and physical hole, that was far too painful to risk. I recognized that if any of my kids eventually fell into a similar pattern, and there was one major thing I could have done to prevent that—namely, to recover—I would probably indeed kill myself. I could never live with the pain that I allowed the most cherished beings in my life to wander down the same horrific path that I would not wish on my worst enemy.

The article also explained the cognitive dissonance common to anorectics, that nagging feeling that I was in fact acting self-destructively as I rationalized it as healthy eating and exercise—an easy excuse, given the normalization of such behavior in our culture. Further, I had reasoned that I had forever altered my perception of food and physical movement as a necessary mathematical equilibrium, that I could never "unlearn" the calorie content of everything, and that I would just have to manage it for the rest of my life. *Well,* I had thought many times, *at least I'll never be fat, and for that I'll always be praised.*

---

[18] "Is It Too Late for Me to Recover from Restricted Eating Behaviors? (Ages 26–52)," *The Eating Disorder Institute*, accessed October 11, 2017, https://www.edinstitute.org/blog/2011/9/17/is-it-too-late-for-me-to-recover-from-restricted-eating-behaviors-ages-26-52.

While that article spotlighted my behaviors and justifications and delineated how the situation was unsustainable on physical, mental, and social levels, it also offered something more powerful than a name for my condition and a horrifying peek into my future if I allowed its continuance: absolution. I now had the promise that my body would forgive, that I could indeed go back home, that it's never too late to recover, repair, reclaim. There was a roadmap, and it was the easiest, most natural thing I could do. I would honor my hunger and rest, allowing the physical recovery from which the mental recovery would flower. The first time I had approached recovery incorrectly and ignorantly, but this time I could do it right.

I barely slept that night, rattled and exhilarated by what I'd been offered, but by morning the pill I had been trying to throw down my shy throat for years had finally passed the choking point of the eating disorder. I had made my decision. And by lovely fate—which I've always sensed invisibly turning the steering wheel at critical moments when a certain direction must be taken—my close friend Jennifer and I had already planned a breakfast date for that morning. During catch-up chatter over coffee and tea, nervousness roiled in my chest at the thought of divulging what had been my darkest secret and now perhaps my greatest endeavor. Between laughs and bites of toast I debated whether I was ready to speak the words that would make it true, to turn the prospect of recovery from a concept into a trajectory for which I would be accountable. Then she disclosed that she had suffered another crushing miscarriage. There was my invitation to share my own pain. The word *eating disorder* tripped and fell out of my mouth. I told her everything in broad strokes and she responded with the sympathy and gentleness I'd come to expect from Jen during our five years of friendship. Still, I feared my history would be perceived with some scorn, that I would be judged as having vainly chosen such an existence. I felt like I had removed all the flattering clothes I had so artfully assembled and was showing how ugly and broken I was inside. But I could do it because she not only knew me well but herself understood deep psychological pain. As I swiped many tears off my cheeks and we continued to talk, she repeated that I would need professional help—one of many things that went wrong the first time. I knew she was right, but I needed more than that; I needed a community of support. I ate that cathartic breakfast of buttery eggs as food, not caloric values, and I left the café relieved and resolved. Now that I had told Jen, it was real, and I would have to indeed pursue recovery.

However, approaching Alex the next day with the truth and the plan was more delicate and daunting, because I felt like I was also identifying our failures: mine for donning the guise that I had recovered years ago, and his for not recognizing how I immediately relapsed and simply became thinner, more anxious, and more depressed as our family grew.

"Kerrie, I truly didn't know that it had come back." Alex exhaled and ran his hand through his overgrown hair. "I'm so sorry I never noticed, but I haven't been here much to watch you eating, and I guess I attributed your moods and you becoming a little thinner to how crazy life has become with all the kids and that I'm just not here at the house to help enough. I'm so sorry. I feel like I let you down in a big way." He grasped my forearm, and in the exhilaration of recovery I accepted it, not considering placing blame right then.

"Well, maybe you didn't see it, but I was also doing a good job of hiding it this whole time. I also didn't know that it was all the same, that I was still starving myself and stuck in that same loop, even if it didn't seem quite as bad as it was at the very beginning. But now I understand that I didn't feel better even at higher weights because I have this neurobiological condition. And I now know there's a way to recover from it, and I'm really excited about eating and finally being free, even if my body gets a little out of whack as it repairs itself." I opened my laptop and showed him informative articles about the science behind the condition and process upon which I was embarking.

Tears sprung to his widened, soft brown eyes. "I'm so embarrassed, and I'm so sorry. But I'm so proud of you. And I can't wait for you to return to the woman I met eleven years ago."

At first I only waded my toes in the water of unrestricted eating, with meals and snacks no longer calculated but still merely what I typically consumed. Any overwhelming desires to eat more were satiated with only enough to cut the worst manifestations of hunger. I knew that a very deep void was lying in wait underneath, but in my apprehension I sought to create a solid, safe springboard for that real plunge. I would inform a significant number of people about my history and what to expect in upcoming months, unlike my first attempt at recovery, during which Alex knew some basic facts about my struggle but most everyone else was left to guess the reason behind my physical changes. This time I wouldn't let such worry about external judgment hamper my efforts. I banged out the following letter in an hour's time at my computer and e-mailed it to seemingly everyone—old, faraway friends; new friends; my kids' babysitter; my parents; my in-laws; anyone I would encounter on an even semi-regular basis—before I could change my mind.

I'm writing to you about a personal matter that I would like to make public, as a key part of what I believe will be a successful recovery. You are a close family member, a dear friend, a local acquaintance, or a friendly regular fixture in my life, and depending on where you are in my social circle you may find the following to be disturbingly candid or still not enough information. I imagine that some of you may be upset that you're learning all this through a general e-mail, but please try to understand that the prospect of broaching such a number of separate conversations is extremely overwhelming and anxiety inducing, and possibly enough to compel me to retreat. If you want to know more, just send an e-mail, or call, or talk with me in person, but I need to throw a brick through a window first.

As you may already know somewhat, or have suspected, or have imagined not in the least, I've been living with an eating disorder for the past decade or so. Prior to that, during high school and college, I maintained a normal, healthy weight and the exact proportions of my body were of negligible interest or concern to me. The condition was sparked by my mental destruction by a verbally and emotionally abusive manager in a job I could not escape; I sought refuge, control, and a faulty sense of self-esteem in my power to adjust the needle on the scale, an obsession spiraling to full-blown anorexia and starvation to the point of virtual emaciation. Later I wanted so desperately to start a family, and so I forced myself up to the lower end of my previously natural weight, but not (as I know now) through properly consistent nutritional means and without the support of a therapist, and so neither my body nor my mind actually recovered. At any weight I continued to use the control of food (even at a seemingly normal intake) as a coping mechanism. Facing myriad stressors, crises, or periods of chaos over the subsequent years, I've found excuses to drop further pounds, believing that this slimming will make me feel better, to the point in the past month when I was only a handful of pounds shy of my absolute lowest weight from the darkest days, neither looking nor feeling good in the least. The picture isn't pretty, but please, please know that there was absolutely nothing that any of you could have done or said to change anything. Not only does an eating disorder maintain an iron grip on any person, but, as most of you know, once I get an idea in my head, I cannot be convinced otherwise. I so stubbornly insist on deciding things for myself.

And so I am here to tell you that I am resolved to fix myself correctly, once and for all, for myself, my family, and my friends. If I were to stay on this path, my bones will continue to deteriorate and I will begin breaking them by the time my children are in college. My brain will shrink; my eyesight will continue its decline. I will be forced to eat like a sick bird because my metabolism will crash as I age. I will not only fall apart physically and mentally, but I will never be truly happy again. I will never be able to enjoy my family and other pursuits unfettered, as this illness, and the resulting anxiety, isolation, and depression, consumes probably about 50% of my conscious thought. I have quite a list of further reasons why I must make this change, but perhaps the most compelling is that, if I do not, I am likely to pass this terrible existence onto the most precious beings in my life, my children, two of whom are impressionable little *girls who are and will be looking to their mother as a role model. I will absolutely talk to them about this issue and share my journey with them when the time is right, but in the meantime, when they are such adorable sponges, I must be a healthy-looking, -behaving, and -functioning woman in their eyes.*

I am no longer restricting my eating (wow, is my body hungry!) and I am seeking a regular therapist who specializes in both eating disorders and cognitive behavioral therapy, which is a proven method for "rewiring" the brain to return to normal, healthy thought processes. If you know someone who may help, please point me in that person's direction. When I am soon completely ready to begin formal recovery, I will be eating substantial amounts of food consistently, which will allow my body not only to gain weight but (unlike my first attempt) to trust the intake enough also to repair its cells, organs, and systems. Unfortunately this necessary route is likely to make me look and feel quite bloated at the beginning, and then possibly at first seem to gain the most weight around the middle, but this will subside and my renewed body's fat will redistribute in a normal, attractive way that some of you remember. And through this e-mail, I'm approaching recovery not in secret but with the understanding and support of those around me, without the worry and anxiety that people may wonder if I'm pregnant, or "letting myself go" (though, in a sense, I am, for the better), or enduring some mental or physical condition that is compelling me to gain weight. If someone asks me why I suddenly look so good, I'll briefly tell that person the truth. I encourage you to do the same if someone happens to ask about me. The embarrassment and raw shame, which kept me from divulging my struggle to so many of you who are otherwise very close to me (and for which I've always felt terrible and am so, so sorry), is steadily fading. I'm immersing myself in the thrill of becoming whole again, and I will look back at the past decade as merely a chapter (in an otherwise full and happy life) precipitated by a constellation of forces out of my control but finally closed by my own courage, perseverance, love for myself and my family, and support from those around me. And I hope to be able to help others struggling similarly, even just through listening and sharing my own experiences, so please never hesitate to talk with me about yourself or put me in touch with someone you know. And, as I encouraged at the start, you can ask me any questions about restrictive eating disorders in general or my own journey so far, which I know I've presented in only broad strokes here.

Thank you for reading this, and thank you for always supporting me.

Immediately after I launched that missive into cyberspace, I slapped shut my computer and scooted to the car with my grocery list in hand. I felt like I might have a heart attack, vomit, or both. I couldn't bear the thought of so many people in my life staring at me psychologically naked. I couldn't imagine what responses I would receive. I comforted myself that, on a sunny Sunday afternoon, replies would likely only trickle in. *Most people probably won't even see the message until tonight if not tomorrow morning when they turn on their computers again.* Nervous energy rushed me through two stores to fulfill my list, and when I returned to my car, I couldn't wait anymore. I wanted to read any first reply in solitude. I accessed my e-mail on my phone, and I saw that not even an hour after I broadcasted my plight to the universe I had ten messages—one-third of the recipients had not only read it immediately but did not in fact dismiss me as an exasperating, self-indulgent basket case who could be dealt with later. They seemed to have sensed how cold and exposed I was, and with great compassion wrapped me in a blanket of support, understanding, a twice-recommended therapist, and compliments on my bravery for both tackling the disorder and sending such a letter. Tears of gratitude, the tears of receiving overwhelming love, flooded my pinkening face until I couldn't focus on the screen anymore. I spent the rest of that day and the next fielding these replies, my relief growing, my soul increasingly buttressed.

Of the approximately thirty recipients of my e-mail letter, two women told me about their sisters' struggles; a handful about their friends, at least one of whom required hospitalization; and three about their own battles with eating disorders. All three women had been quite close to me, but I'd had barely an inkling that they might be similarly starving. One had been struggling for longer than forty years and resolved to pursue a true recovery because of what I had written. Suddenly the finding that approximately one out of every three dieters becomes eating disordered[19] didn't seem so padded; we were everywhere, suffering silently. I was outraged at the misinformation and invisibility, and then my destiny was sealed: I would recover, and I would write about it.

---

[19] C. M. Shisslak, M. Crago, and L.S. Estes, "The spectrum of eating disturbances," *International Journal of Eating Disorders* 18, no. 3 (1995): 209–19.

2

To recover, I would eat at least 3,500 calories every single day, supplying enough fuel both to restore my weight and to reverse ten years of damage throughout my body—from the pilfering of muscles and bones and organs that had kept me alive to the shutdown of my reproductive system. Dedication to that hefty daily intake was formidable; I would have to eat approximately twice what I'd been consuming. But all that food would ensure that I supported not only healing but my unavoidably active lifestyle,[20] according to the recovery guidelines outlined on Olwyn's website. This recovery process involved psychotherapeutic support, re-feeding, and remaining sedentary[21] to rest what was ultimately a full-body injury. Although the demands of childcare might hinder my physical progress, I imagined that the prospect of modeling for my kids a fully conscious, freely eating person would keep me motivated, and their sweet selves would buoy my moods. And I was so very eager for all the foods that I not only finally could but in fact should eat every day. I began fantasizing about meal possibilities—pancakes with syrup, pasta with oily tapenade—and wrapping my head around the practice of conceding fully to hunger while reluctantly continuing to count calories to confirm that I had eaten at least the minimum each day.

I was optimistic for the true plunge, but then I fell ill with a debilitating combination of my children's stomach virus and a rebound of that cold I hadn't been able to shake for two months. I wondered if finally unwinding

[20] "I Need How Many Calories?!!" *The Eating Disorder Institute*, accessed October 11, 2017, https://www.edinstitute.org/blog/2011/9/14/i-need-how-many-calories.
[21] "Phases of Recovery from a Restrictive Eating Disorder Part 1," *The Eating Disorder Institute*, accessed October 11, 2017, https://www.edinstitute.org/paper/2012/11/23/phases-of-recovery-from-an-eating-disorder-part-1.

myself from the secret and shame of the eating disorder allowed not only my mind but my body to exhale, and this collapse of my immune system was the first reveal of many layers of damage cloaked by denial. And ironically, just when I wanted it most, I had very little hunger. Nausea derailed my body off my carefully laid tracks to healing. Even more menacing was the eating disorder voice, which I could finally recognize as a foreign, destructive impulse, as it swelled through the unintentional calorie deficits: *This not eating is good! You can lose the few pounds you gained last week. Your smallest jeans could fit again. This illness will give you a few more days of Skinny You.* Because I was eating to satisfy my hunger, I could still feel like I was recovering, but because my appetite was limited, I could still be thin. Here, at the tail end of those torturous ten years, I was finally granted such a sublime state—right when I wanted it all over.

The eating disorder was pleased by the illness's effect on my proportions, but the real me—the recovering me—framed that pause as an opportunity for further mental preparation for the long road ahead, as time to work through misgivings and address likely culprits for relapse. Although I was no longer afraid to reenter my optimal weight range, I could sense that the impending water retention, which I read online served to facilitate repair but could be extreme during the first month or two, could be so disconcerting that I might turn back during that early phase, when giving up would be easiest. I could recognize that the eating disorder had charmed me not only with a mode of control but also the tactile sensation of thinness, of walking through the world with a little less physical baggage, which also lent the illusory ability to slip through a crack if I needed to escape. Dropping a few pounds always felt so good during a crisis period, like a morphine drip against my life.

I needed insurance against that mechanism, affirmations from a staunch place that reminded me what I will gain, why I'm fighting, and how those reasons are more compelling than any future decades spent in size-zero clothing. I wrote the following in a file that I kept at the ready on my computer desktop as an antidote to any uncertainty that may strike along my path of recovery. With this simple list I was grasping that scared, doubting girl by the shoulders and commanding that this is what we're doing now. *We're going to live.* I wrote:

I want to live my life in FULL, not in HALF.

I WANT TO BE HAPPY (because I will be healthy). I WANT MY FAMILY TO BE HAPPY (because we will all be healthy).

I want the bulk of my brain activity to focus not on food but on enjoying the moment, whether with family, friends, or work/recreational pursuits and handling stress and adversity head on. I cannot wait to rewire, and thus free, my brain.

I want to eat intuitively, feeling satisfied always, with no reactive eating.

I want to want to be intimate with my husband.

I want boobs again.

I want to live the seven to twelve years that continuing on this disordered path will take off my life.

I want my eyesight to improve.

I do not want my bones breaking at age fifty-five.

I do not want to have to eat progressively like a bird because my metabolism steadily declines as I age.

I do not want my brain failing at age seventy.

I DO NOT WANT TO PASS THIS AWFUL EXISTENCE ALONG TO ANY OF MY CHILDREN by setting dangerous physical or behavioral precedents.

I want to get my periods again, so that I won't be taking hormone-replacement therapy for twenty years. I want my daughters to understand from my example, well before they hit puberty, that menstrual cycles are a normal part of a healthy woman's life.

Being unattractively thin, no matter how much I think I enjoy that nothing jiggles or rubs together, is NOT AT ALL WORTH anxiety and depression and the physical and mental deterioration that awaits me if I do not make this change.

I have proven that I can be any weight/size/appearance that I want; I am choosing to rest at my natural weight because this is where my body and mind will be most HAPPY, HEALTHY, and ATTRACTIVE.

I WILL NOT LET THIS ILLNESS CHARACTERIZE MY LIFE.

Although I never had the dedication to maintain a daily diary, a friend convinced me to keep a record of my experience. There I delved into what I must mourn and leave behind. First were the many clothes that would no longer fit me. To this I wrote that I could begin searching online for pieces that accentuate and celebrate a curvy, sexy woman, the hourglass body I would once again have. I could find images of women with similar shapes to my natural one—even celebrities—and note their radiant beauty as I let myself be inspired by their flattering clothing styles. I believed that, with enough exposure to fashionable figures who are not runway models or whittled starlets, I could retrain my brain to acknowledge that my natural proportions are at least as desirable as the artificial ones I'd been sporting.

The second item on my list was the loss of my identity as an ultra-thin person—not only my self-perception but others' impressions that I'm extraordinarily "put together," with my three well-groomed and well-behaved children and my body befitting a sixteen-year-old. I had loved being regularly revered for the show I put on, because it had indeed required so much damaging effort. But what would happen to all of that, now that I would be stripping it all off, appearing as myself rather than a superhuman, ironically as I tackled something that would prove even more difficult? I wasn't the only one who would be looking at my changing body.

Against that concern I already had some armor in the form of that e-mail explaining my condition and intentions for recovery, publicizing that I was beginning to actively fight this condition for both myself and my children. I knew that this, not a number on a scale, was an accomplishment worth praising. Pushing that notion further, I committed myself to publish a chronicle of my recovery, both funneling my newfound mental focus into writing and instilling the journey with even greater purpose. I figured that if an e-mail could inspire healing in a silently suffering friend, perhaps an entire book could alter the widespread misconceptions about eating disorders and possibly change or save numerous lives. I was no longer thin and empty; I was a warrior and a writer.

Now both mentally bolstered and with my stomach acids normalized post-virus, I was ready for the food. I consulted a friend who was a nutritionist, and she helped me brainstorm delicious meals dense in calories and fats as well as easy ways to incorporate extra nutrients into many types of dishes: cheese melted into sandwiches, avocado on top of almost anything. Later that day, I took my first trip to the grocery store in this new mode. For many years I'd been composing meals from the lowest-calorie and often highest-protein items I could find, seeking the biggest satiety bang for my calorie buck, so doing exactly the opposite was surreal. I stood in front of the salad dressings, which I intended to start using liberally, my eyes grazing with disdain over the "lite honey mustard"—my watery, low-calorie standby—before picking up a hefty bottle of Caesar. I noted the significantly higher calories per serving not with horror but with enthusiasm, and then I stared at the whole lineup of full-fat dressings: the green goddess, the creamy ranch. *When foods are no longer numbers, what do I truly want?* I was a child with a realized fantasy of running through a supermarket and filling a cart with all the cookies and sugary cereals she desired. I was high on the freedom of eating without fear.

And eat I did. As I learned through Olwyn's science-backed articles, my history and current medical status put me at low risk for re-feeding syndrome[22] if such intake is not slowly increased, so I decided to move directly to full recovery levels. I began my day not with fifteen to thirty minutes on my step machine in front of the TV, which for years I felt necessary to feel energized and "kick-start my metabolism," but sitting in front of my computer with a half cup of trail mix. I regularly ate two large breakfasts, snacks between meals, and everything that appealed, but I directed my attention toward fats—often oils and nut butters—in which my body was severely deficient and are critical for the repair of the central,

---

[22] Re-feeding syndrome consists of electrolyte and other imbalances that result in extreme nausea, dizziness, weakness, and swelling in extremities; it requires immediate emergency medical attention to prevent fatal cardiac arrhythmias.

peripheral, and enteric nervous systems. I kept a daily tally of my intake, but after I hit my personal minimum of 3,500 calories, which was often by midafternoon, any more was simply extra fuel for the fires of repair, for accelerating recovery. My overachieving nature was coming in handy, and I was fortunate not to have lost my hunger cues like many others with eating disorders who struggle to reach their intake goals. I was lucky; I felt so famished that I couldn't avoid exceeding my daily minimum. Dinner and dessert, which had long been a logistical puzzle to consume only the remaining allotted calories for the day followed by a willful resistance to the hunger driving me to the pantry to "borrow" calories from the next day, was now a calm place of true intuitive eating. For years I had assumed that I would eat the entire kitchen if I allowed myself free access, but instead I experienced a sensation so remote it felt like a fable learned and forgotten in childhood: physical satiation. After meals my stomach was full but not nauseated, and my body just wasn't interested in any more. My mind was not compelled to think about food. And there was no guilt. None. What a contrast to my former "binges"—which were merely my body's life-sustaining reaction to starvation—after which I would feel either still hungry or overfull to the point I couldn't get off the couch. I would be overrun with shame for what I had allowed myself to do and dread of what must be accomplished to erase the mistake. Although I had never induced vomiting, I would employ steep restriction and extra exercise that would leave me teetering on the edge of passing out.

But this was not bingeing[23]; rather, great quantities of calorie-dense foods were preferred. As my eating behavior shifted, so did my perception of food. The long upheld hierarchy of safe, known, water-bulked items down to the fat- and sugar-laden forbidden foods collapsed to an even plane. Chocolate cake, which once carried such mystique as a rare reward for losing a certain number of pounds or restricting for days in anticipation of a birthday party, suddenly lost its ethereal sparkle and became just that: a piece of cake. With equal and guiltless access to anything I wanted, sometimes I opened the cupboard to the cookies and other times I prepared apple slices with almond butter, depending on what my body seemed to be requesting in the moment. For whatever reason I happened to want anything in particular, I would, for the rest of my life, simply eat it. Food was no longer an enemy, nor was it equivalent to Christmas morning. It was delicious fuel for my health and happiness, and in the short term it was required in abundance to repair a decade of damage.

I was finally truly honoring my deep hunger—which began when I rose in the pre-dawn hours and often didn't ease until I dragged myself from my

---

[23] "Binges Are Not Binges," *The Eating Disorder Institute*, accessed October 11, 2017, https://www.edinstitute.org/blog/2012/10/31/bingeing-is-not-bingeing.

bedtime reading to eat a hunk of cheese—and I ate approximately 5,000 calories every day for the first month, at least 3,000 more than what had been standard for me. Recovery became as much a full-time job as restriction had been. I didn't worry about exactly what I would be eating, but I worked to arrange each day so that I would be home, at a café, or near a bakery at the hours when hunger typically surged, which was challenging among preschool shuttling and errands. At this early stage, when slipping into old patterns could be quick and simple, I sought to avoid opportunities for the eating disorder voice to coerce me, as it did one evening in bed when my stomach was grumbling but I was too tired to go downstairs for a snack: *Remember how well you slept when you went to bed on an empty stomach? You'd sleep so much better tonight if you just stay in bed and don't go into the kitchen.* Then the familiar warmth, the fluttery anxiety, unfurled in my chest and reached for my throat. The eating disorder no longer felt like an embrace, but a death grip. I had to defy it, to roar *No! WHENEVER I am hungry, I will eat.* My legs swung out from beneath the blankets, and I had won the moment. The eating disorder might still be lurking in my head, but I was the soul in charge of the body seeking energy to restore itself.

That night's sleep was indeed restless, as so many had been lately—not from doubt about my recovery, but from my body's incessant processing of all those calories. My heart was beating rapidly at all hours, and I felt like a furnace. In late February I was sleeping not in flannel pajamas but T-shirts; otherwise I woke up in a slick of sweat, kicking off all blankets and even opening a window to cool me down while Alex shivered but tolerated my needs. In my restricting days I would rarely wake up in the middle of the night, probably because my starved body needed so desperately to remain in deep repose, but now I was not only waking numerous times per night but rising bright-eyed and bushy-tailed before 4 o'clock. I pranced through the days, but I also noticed the occasional heart palpitation,[24] which may have been a symptom of progressive damage to my heart—like all organs, it had been plundered to keep me alive.[25,26] I ceased my afternoon neighborhood strolls to avoid straining it, and instead I dove inward, turning to my journal each day as realizations about bodies, weight, calories, and eating disorders flooded me, now that I was open to truths about these issues.

I felt betrayed by the socially reinforced notion that a person's weight is

[24] Damage to the heart from restriction is multifaceted. Palpitations, or tachycardia, are often the result of nerve damage due to restriction making the signal for a strong, steady heartbeat inconsistent at times.

[25] G. de Simone, L. Scalfi, M. Galderisi, A. Celentano, G. Di Biase, P. Tammaro ... and F. Contaldo (1994), "Cardiac abnormalities in young women with anorexia nervosa," *British Heart Journal* 71, no. 3 (1994): 287–292.

[26] R. A. Cooke and J. B. Chambers, "Anorexia nervosa and the heart," *British Journal of Hospital Medicine* 54, no. 7 (1994): 313–317.

determined by the balance between the calories consumed and those expended through essential biological functions and deliberate exercise. That convenient message bleated from every angle—magazines, healthy living websites, diet programs—and I had absorbed it as common-sense wisdom. It had all been so neat and appealing to a mind soothed by math and logic; I could simply plug in my height and ideal weight into online calculators to determine how much I should eat each day to slide down to that weight and then maintain it. Chain restaurant menus had recently begun prominently posting calorie content next to each item, and the implication had been clear: *We'll hand you the numbers. If you supply the willpower, you'll get whatever body you want.* But since diets commonly fail, I thought, what was wrong with these people? They had seemed too lazy to do the damn math and stick with it. And by contrast—I used to believe—I was a paragon of self-control. I may have been utterly obsessed and physically weak, but I had been winning the fat race. I had been proud, and society had applauded me.

As I continued to read articles substantiated by cited scientific research, I learned that the masses of perpetually failing dieters were simply people without an eating disorder, whose bodies would not sustain calorie deficits and would quickly and inevitably expand to return to natural set points[27] as well as roar back with even greater fat stores.[28] I was blown away to learn that the dreaded so-called "obesity epidemic" was due not so much to a growing population of lazy overeaters but to the warped lens of society's fetishization of thinness and its terror of the larger sizes that have roamed the earth for decades.[29,30] Even someone at a BMI of 30—which is typically derided as obese and unhealthy—can in fact be optimally healthy if it is that person's genetically determined size, not one compounded by years of dieting. I learned that this dieting, against all my logic and personal experience, is in fact what makes people—non-eating-disordered people, that is—fatter than they need to be.[11]

I, on the other hand, was the lucky recipient of a heritable genetic variation that can activate the neurobiological condition of restrictive eating, a handy trick in the hunter-gatherer days that would have allowed my mind to suppress normal reactions to starvation—listlessness, physical weakness,

---

[27] R. B. Harris, "Role of set-point theory in regulation of body weight," *FASEB Journal* 4, no. 15 (1991): 3310–8. Albert J. Stunkard, et al., "A Twin Study of Human Obesity," *JAMA* 256, no. 1 (1986): 51–54.

[28] "Gaining Weight Despite Calorie Restriction," *The Eating Disorder Institute*, accessed October 11, 2017, https://www.edinstitute.org/paper/2015/6/13/gaining-weight-despite-calorie-restriction.

[29] "Obesity Basic Facts I," *The Eating Disorder Institute*, accessed October 11, 2017, https://www.edinstitute.org/paper/2013/12/4/obesity-basic-facts-i.

[30] "Obesity Science in Context," *The Eating Disorder Institute*, accessed October 11, 2017, https://www.edinstitute.org/paper/2015/1/21/obesity-science-in-context.

foggy-headedness—and present a false sense of energy and calm so that I could head into the wild to find or hunt food for myself and my tribe.[31] By natural selection, many with such a capability survived to reproduce, and studies estimate that about one-third of the general population carries this genotype.[32] Today food is readily available in many countries, so instead, a diet, or physical or emotional trauma leading to undereating, or even a stomach virus often activates that genetic variation; online I met a woman whose thirty-year eating disorder was sparked when she fell ill with a gastrointestinal bug at thirteen years old. For those with that genetic variation, a substantial enough decrease in daily calories generates in the brain's amygdala a fear of food, which the logic center of the brain must rationalize.[33] This is a testament to the brain's power; how can food, this necessary fuel for our bodies, be a threat? In our modern society the rationalization can draw from the socially enforced repulsion of fat. In previous centuries, eating disorders were often shrouded in a pursuit for religious purity.[34]

I was fascinated with the science and history of eating disorders, and there I found solace. After years of berating myself for squandering so much time and energy on the excruciating and ridiculous task of not eating, I was absolved of guilt. I was not narcissistic. I was not self-centered. I was not a masochist. Under it all—after adolescent years of accepting and sometimes even celebrating my body's curves—I was not just another superficial girl who would do anything to be stick thin. Instead, I had experienced emotional trauma that cut down to the inborn crack in my gray matter, through which anorexia could bloom.

My perceptions were adjusting fast and furiously, likely facilitated by the energy that all the food was supplying to my brain. Each new realization warranted another journal entry, up to four in one day during those initial weeks. I was so high on the rushes of physical energy and this expanding, colorful mental space that I didn't mind that my weight increased by eight pounds in the first week. I was mentally present, truly engaging with my children and being much more patient with them. Jen and another close friend commented that I was noticeably "unwound" and "lighter," the latter

---

[31] Shan Guisinger, "Anorexia Nervosa: A Guide for Anorexics and their Loved Ones," *Dr. Sarah Ravin*, accessed July 7, 2014, http://www.drsarahravin.com/web/pdf/AN-Guisinger-article.pdf.

[32] Jennifer M. Jones, et al., "Disordered eating attitudes and behaviours in teenaged girls: a school-based study," *Canadian Medical Association Journal* 165, no. 5 (2001): 547–552. C. M. Shisslak, M. Crago, L. S. Estes, "The spectrum of eating disturbances," *International Journal of Eating Disorders* 18, no. 3 (1995): 209–19.

[33] Andreas A. B. Joos, et al., "Amygdala hyperreactivity in restrictive anorexia nervosa," *Psychiatry Research: Neuroimaging* 191, no. 3 (2011): 189–195.

[34] Walter Vandereycken and Ron van Deth, *From Fasting Saints to Anorexic Girls: The History of Self-Starvation* (New York: New York University Press, 1994).

descriptor ironic, since the water retention was pumping up at an alarming rate. Quicker than I imagined possible I was outgrowing jeans buried in drawers from fleshier times. By the end of the second week the scale revealed that I had gained a total of thirteen pounds, and once again the eating disorder threw in its two cents: *You're gaining a pound a day! See?! You knew this approach would just make you fat! You need to stop—you'll be HUGE in another two weeks!* But now I could distinguish that manipulative voice from my own true one, and I reminded myself that almost all of this initial weight gain was simply the temporary edema often experienced with re-feeding.[35] I figured I needed to buy one or two new pair of cheap jeans to get me through the next handful of swollen months, after which I could buy my new wardrobe for the rest of my happy life. Recovery didn't seem all that difficult, at least so far.

Still, I made my first appointment with a recommended therapist who specialized in eating disorders. I worried that, like the previous therapist, she wouldn't know what to say about my particular history, or perhaps she wouldn't understand or approve my method of recovery, or, most distressing, she would corral me to a scale at the beginning of every appointment. I had read online accounts of eating disorder therapists insisting on monitoring weight, especially if a general practitioner is not, which was also the case for me. I prepared myself to assert that I preferred not to be weighed, that I felt my time in therapy would suffer—as my mind would surely be rolling the new number around like a marble between my palms for the rest of the therapy hour—that my body would already know when to stop if I kept submitting fully to hunger, that I intended therapy not to police my physical recovery but to guide me through any rough patches and teach me coping skills that I had not developed during the years when the eating disorder laundered everything I wanted to avoid. I was so resolved that I was prepared to walk out if this woman said that I must be weighed. When I entered her office, my eyes swept desperately around the corners of the room, but there was no scale. There was a couch, but Sil—sweetly short for Priscilla—directed me to a pillowy chair across a matching one where she would sit. We were to talk like equals. As I sunk into that chair, I felt my jeans, loose a few days prior, cut into my waist, but all my apprehension floated away. I felt as light as her gauzy scarf.

In that first session, I enjoyed talking about my journey thus far, and Sil validated my experiences and conviction. On the intake form I had listed my weight history, but in her office we didn't discuss numbers then or ever—not pounds, not calories. We never even talked about my food experiences. For me, the return to eating was the easy part of recovery and

---

[35] S. Ehrlich, U. Querfeld, and E. Pfeiffer, "Re-feeding oedema," *European Child & Adolescent Psychiatry* 15, no. 4 (2006): 241–243.

virtually irrelevant after it had been achieved. I told her that I imagined all my physical and emotional symptoms and anxieties sorting themselves with the consistent caloric intake to which I was committed. I was confident that my recovery would be impressively quick and dramatic.

The next day my hubris was challenged. Although it was early March, the temperature was forecasted to hit seventy degrees and the day was crowned that first truly warm one of the year that previously summoned relief and joy as I abandoned my cumbersome coat and constricting socks and flounced around in the pleasant air, wearing a favorite short-sleeved shirt staled by many months in the closet. Especially in my eating disordered years this annual event had been a source of solace, the first escape from another endless winter of chronic shivering, so miserably cold in my lack of body fat. But now, just a few weeks into recovery, that glorious peek of spring felt like an oppressively hot day, with my water-swollen feet red and bulging out of my ballet flats. I chose what seemed a loose-enough shirt, but the cuffs surprised me, snug around my arms, and the bottom hem barely covered the fleshy gap above my jeans' waistband. In the mirror, I saw a Gretel having gorged herself on all the candy and cookies and was now overflowing her clothes, and I feared that everyone I encountered at preschool and elsewhere would see it, too. I threw on a draping sweater that seemed to conceal the worst parts. As I sweated through the day, doubt crept in: if recovery meant that such springs of happiness became sources of misery, I didn't know if I could do this. Eating whatever I wanted and feeling fullness without guilt was lovely, but this lightning-fast transformation, my thighs catching on each other, my body radiating like the sun, all on display for the town, was too much. I was grateful when the next day's temperature returned to a seasonable range and I could again conceal myself with my coat, even if that, too, was becoming a struggle to button fully.

However, the weather wasn't finished with me yet: an extraordinary string of those seventy-degree days stood in formation on the ten-day forecast. But this time, instead of panicking, I went shopping. Previously I had purchased only maybe five new clothing items each year, since I had a whole closet of things that always fit well, thanks to the restriction that maintained my body at a precise size. Back in those days, when I had entered a store I felt like a ghost, sometimes finding the smallest sizes hanging off me. But now I was a fully fleshed person, knocking low-hanging skirts off the racks because I didn't sense anymore where my hips ended. I brought into the dressing room a range of sizes appropriate for someone who had never seen her own body, which wasn't so far from the truth. For the first time since my recovery commenced, I had to face myself in a full-length mirror, an event that had once emitted gasps from me in dressing rooms as I registered how truly emaciated I was, before a twisted pride set in. This time, however, my eyes fixated on the parts that had changed most: the hips, thighs, and butt having expanded exponentially, the stomach flesh that exceeded anything I'd had since toddlerhood. My general size was recognizable as close to my natural one, but the proportions weren't quite right, and I didn't feel that this appearance was much better than the ultra-thin one. I tried on the skirts and pants, and I was stunned to discover that the size smalls fit just fine. My self-perception had become so warped that I truly believed that I might fit a large, especially since I had grown so dramatically in less than a month.

Buoyed by the reassurance that I was not in fact suddenly massive, I approached my packed closet not just to find space for the new items, but also to take what had seemed an unthinkable step: to permanently remove all clothes that would never fit me again. I had been dreading the day, imagining I would lie with them on my bed and cry that I would never be that thin, that pretty, that victorious, and my abridged closet would stand bare of enticing options. Instead, I pulled out the smallest pants along with a few shirts and skirts, and I noticed that many had been either worn to threadbare death or weren't all that stylish, anyway. I wasn't nostalgic or otherwise sentimental about the pieces; I wouldn't miss them that much after all. And with those items out of sight, I was delighted to excavate some jeans and shirts that could probably now be filled out again.

I also found novelty in the world of meals not painstakingly planned and prepared by my own hands. I recalled how holiday dinners had once generated high anxiety, but I could anticipate them, preparing myself with careful extra restriction for a week or two in advance. Restaurants had been pure terror, with plates of only somewhat evaluable foods and waitstaff frequently topping off my wineglass, prompting acrobatic mental math to tally all those calories. Rather than enjoying the meals and atmosphere, I had been a fidgety calculator. If friends had proposed a last-minute dinner plan, I often feigned a headache or minor stomach upset. I lamented that I would miss out on the conviviality, but restaurants were the scourge of the eating disorder. But recovery changed all that. My first such spontaneous meal out arose on a Saturday when Alex suggested that we shake it up and take the kids out for dinner. I uncharacteristically allowed him to select the restaurant, and his final choice neither launched my mind through a list of potential strategies to eat as few calories as possible without anyone noticing nor steered me toward my computer to locate an online menu to scour. Instead I said, "Oh, that sounds great! We haven't tried that place yet." And I meant it. That's how a non–eating disordered person might react, and I was delighted to be doing it naturally. Then I was tested even further, when the restaurant plan shifted to a movie outing and thus dinner would be a popcorn and candy affair. Previously I would have scoffed at such a "meal" not only for myself but for my children, but this time I was able to let go and let my kids experience the joy of exception. My focus was no longer on controlling meals; it was on having fun.

Even activities I didn't particularly enjoy seemed easier, such as participating as parent helper at the preschool. Until then I had been reluctant and a little resentful to relinquish those hard-won hours of freedom when I could accomplish some freelance work or errands in silence. On those helper mornings at the preschool I had been listless, unfocused, and unmotivated, often checking the minutes until we could leave and I could eat whatever meager lunch awaited me. But a few weeks into recovery, I was present and at ease among the chaos of play, and, although my pants were a bit constricting, the three hours flew by. The diminishment of the eating disorder afforded a shift to a life more manageable—sunnier even. When that weekend we turned the clocks ahead for daylight saving time, I was happy to go to bed early and awake at whatever hour my body chose. I no longer puzzled out that an extra half hour of sleep would require that I eat less that day; I could recognize that once-precious concern as a waste of mental space. Instead, I enjoyed my super-hearty breakfast, did a bit of work at my computer, and pushed forward with a day that concluded with my savoring the extra sunlight in the evening, its beauty unquantifiable.

I was astonished by the startling ease of this first phase of recovery, how quickly I returned to a healthy perception of food after a decade of obsession and disorder, like I could have done it all along but didn't realize it. Now I could see that for those ten years I had held the pill of recovery in my mouth, occasionally throwing it to the back of my throat as I tried to forget all the numbers, only to find it at my teeth again. Clearly I had needed all the pieces—recognition that my body couldn't sustain the anorexia; clear, detailed information about recovery; and listening to hunger cues—before my tongue could launch it down my gullet for good.

I also began to perceive the range of body sizes as normal variations of the human form, not ubiquitous examples of lack of self-control or victims of the supposed obesity epidemic. While working at my laptop in a café, I noticed all the young and middle-aged adult bodies finding seats and returning coffee mugs, people who during previous visits had disgusted me with all the "fat" that they seemed to think was acceptable to let hang out and, worse, feed with cinnamon rolls, which I had eschewed. This time, as I ate an iced lemon muffin, I merely observed the variety of body shapes, grateful to be among people who could honor their hunger and then move onto mental pursuits more valuable than what they will eat, or not eat, and when. I felt embarrassed and foolish that television images of willowy nutritionists had duped me into believing that if one ate correctly, one would be healthy and enviably thin. If only I had known that many of these supposed experts are likely eating disordered themselves,[36,37,38] often driven by their food obsessions to enter this field and justify their own behaviors. And perhaps the doctors I had encountered during those ten years, who saw my protruding ribs and had known I had lost my period long ago, had projected their own fat phobia onto me. Maybe they didn't want to pry too much and offend me. Maybe they didn't know enough about eating disorders. Maybe they were tired of lecturing "overweight" patients and thought *finally, a thin girl* when their computers calculated my weight as barely medically stable. No doctor had asked if I was eating disordered, restricting my calories, throwing up, or exercising excessively. Not one.

The anorexia, the medical community, and the dieting culture at large had morphed my body from a tool through which I could accomplish satisfying mental and physical tasks into an enemy to be whipped, contained, controlled. My skin and flesh had become othered, and the touching of even intimate areas registered as neutral as the smoothing of my hair by a stylist. Reproductive endocrinologists' transvaginal wands left me neither aroused nor repulsed. Even on those rare occasions in bed with Alex, he had been touching not an extension of my soul but merely a mound of clay that I had been perfecting. I had been utterly dissociated from my body, which had become my most prized possession. I hadn't realized how I had not been experiencing true sensual, sexual pleasure until, during that first month of recovery, I was suddenly compelled, quite fiercely, to satisfy myself. I was shocked that there was something screeching to be satiated, and then I relished this intimate reunion with my body, exploring and appreciating.

I girded myself for my son's preschool evaluation, dreading how my eating disorder may have muffled my parenting. However, miraculous to me, the teacher celebrated his development into a well-rounded and solidly confident child who was more than ready for whatever kindergarten would bring in the fall. My vision was smudged by tears of relief—*I'm not a monster after all*—as she emphasized that Alex and I had done an amazing job as parents for Charlie to exhibit so many outstanding qualities on a regular basis. I wanted to soak up the praise and approval, but I felt like a fraud in

[36] G. Kiziltan and E. Karabudak, "Risk of Abnormal Eating Attitudes among Turkish Dietetic Students," *Adolescence* 43, no. 171 (2008): 681.

[37] D. Drummond and M. S. Hare, "Dietitians and eating disorders: an international issue," *Canadian Journal of Dietetic Practice and Research* 73, no. 2 (2012): 86–90.

[38] F. Gonidakis, A. Sigala, E. Varsou, and G. Papadimitriou, "A study of eating attitudes and related factors in a sample of first-year female nutrition and dietetics students of Harokopion University in Athens, Greece," *Eating and Weight Disorders-Studies on Anorexia, Bulimia and Obesity* 14, no. 2–3 (2009): e121–e127.

that room. I knew I'd been intervening in matters large and small typically less often than other parents, and usually because my attention had been too scattered among three children or I had been just too exhausted to pick so many battles. The teacher claimed that I seemed to let things roll off my back, but I knew it had not been due to some wise calculation, but rather because I usually had bigger fish to fry, and that shark had often been the calories to restrict. I had always been regretful for what I could have accomplished in those lost years, including what kind of mother I could have been if I had parented more consciously. I worried most about Charlie, who had lived for more than five of his youngest and most vulnerable years with an eating-disordered mother and upon turning one year old had limited his repertoire to bread, cheese, plain pasta, and peanut butter. But he was still eating, growing, and happy, and his teacher confirmed that his essence—his warm, whip-smart, hysterically funny self—had weathered the storm, and both he and his sisters were thriving in their preschool groups.

With this assertion that my children were not broken, I had amassed enough fortitude to cease weighing myself. Until then I had watched the numbers with fascination, with confidence that the gain was pure fluid that would recede before the needle hit any alarming point. But the edema was mounting, and I saw that I had gained to the highest I'd weighed in a decade. I couldn't bear to see the number rise any higher, so I resolved not to consult the scale anymore; I would simply allow my body to do what it wanted, investing in the faith that it wouldn't be outrageous as long as I kept eating at least my minimum each day. I drew upon my waterlogged experience of pregnancy and rationalized that my body may tend to bloat but would settle back soon enough. Meanwhile, I was running out of clothes again, finding pants to be less and less flattering on my expanding lower half, so I searched online for wrap skirts, which could adjust to whatever shape my body took. As I burrowed in my sewing kit for the measuring tape for my waist and hips to determine my size, I gave myself a pep talk: *Don't worry about the numbers. You're swollen. They don't matter. They probably aren't even that bad.* But the tape showed I had gained more inches than I ever imagined possible after four weeks of re-feeding. I was appalled, and something—perhaps the eating disorder—compelled me to double down. I tried on a pair of pants I had worn in the pre-anorexia years, certain they would fit fine, but no, they were too tight. In that instant, my eyes caught up with the gain I couldn't comprehend escalating at such a rate, and I saw myself larger than I'd ever been. With my puffed arms, soft belly, and inflated thighs, I didn't even recognize myself. Although Alex regularly reminded me that I was still beautiful, that this was so much better than skin and bones, I was horrified that this is what recovery entailed.

My normally clear enough face had erupted in dozens of pimples, my hair was thinning, and that precious gap between my thighs—which I had always checked, with feet together, in front of the bathroom mirror before I stepped on the scale to assure myself that I was not actually fat no matter what the number—was sealed. For my entire life my thighs had never more than occasionally brushed when walking, but now they reluctantly squeezed by, sometimes catching on each other when I was damp after a shower. The flesh and skin of my legs were so swollen with water that I couldn't comfortably cross my legs. I was constantly aware of my proportions, especially in motion. The only place I could transcend my body was in my bed, where I could spread my arms and legs so that nothing touched and I could let the covers fall so that I couldn't discern the outline of my body. There I read for escape, avoiding everyone. I had shifted from excitement to disgust over my rapid transformation and I didn't want to let anyone, even my husband, see me more than necessary in daylight.

I had been planning a springtime weekend in Manhattan, but walking was too awkward and meeting up with old friends while in such a physical state mortified me. I longed to return to the city, where I felt whole, free, and stimulated, but I had to accept that becoming truly whole and free required me to sit tight for a while. Instead Alex and I began planning a return to Paris to celebrate our tenth wedding anniversary at our honeymoon spot. We giddily booked a plushly furnished, parquet-floored apartment for a week three months down the line, which seemed plenty of time for the edema to recede, my face to clear, and shopping for new clothes to fit a refurbished body and mind ready for carefree eating and uncontrived lovemaking. A honeymoon do-over was the perfect denouement in the narrative arc of the eating disorder, soon to perish, with romance and happiness to emerge for the next chapter, as I envisioned it.

But first there was more work to do: I had to peel away layers of coping mechanisms. As I skipped my morning and afternoon sessions on my step machine in front of the television as well as most daily walks, I didn't miss them as much as I expected; rather I was relieved to abandon that compulsive activity, walking only when the weather was pleasant and I was truly craving that meditative motion. Digging deeper, I noticed that I was using my freelance work somewhat like that exercise: I had believed for years that I needed that quiet, focused brainwork as reprieve from the spastic nature of motherhood, but I had also been using it to cope with the eating disorder. Even short blocks of time in front of a screen, evaluating or editing material that rarely mentioned food or weight, had been a respite from the otherwise incessant mental yammering about what I could eat and when, and how I couldn't eat, lest I get fat. Further, through professional achievement and income earning I was attempting to assert myself as more than an eating disorder and a mother, similar to how the eating disorder had given me the false sense that I was asserting power—the ability to be as thin as I desired—when my professional self-worth had been deteriorating under a manager who utilized tyranny perhaps to bandage her own deep emotional wounds. But the anorexia had become my chief mechanism, my religion for coping long after I had dismissed Catholicism for being as viable as Santa Claus. Without a sense of ultimate justice or predetermined purpose outside of myself, I had placed my faith in the hands of calories and pounds to make the world controlled and right, and now I was shedding it all to look deep and discover who I really was and what I truly needed.

My first test didn't wait for me to gain my footing. I had been depending heavily on a part-time babysitter to watch one or all of my three children on most mornings while I drove one or two to preschool, grocery shopped for the hungry horde, or tackled some work. If she called in sick one day, the remaining week felt strained; when a sitter quit, my whole life seemed to crumble. When our current sitter announced that she had accepted a full-time salaried position elsewhere, my heart sunk into my stomach, which turned sour as I imagined the daunting and time-consuming process of interviewing potential candidates and eventually training someone who would, if luck blew my way, turn out to be decent. I congratulated her and absorbed the jarring news right before lunchtime, but I still ate all the rice-laden sushi and ice cream I had planned for that meal. I no longer needed to funnel my problems into the eating disorder, laundering my anxiety with restriction. I had to fuel my mind and body so that I could post some childcare advertisements online that afternoon. I was dealing with life head on.

Feeling triumphant, I returned to Sil for our second session. We began exploring my past, discussing my relationship with mother, which I characterized as mediocre but not destructive, and certainly not a contributor to the onset of my eating disorder. I explained that I had excelled in school because I enjoyed the material and was naturally successful academically, not because my mother ever pushed me. I described how, starting in middle school, I began retreating from her influence, once our attitudes diverged by the usual forces of adolescence. I was adamant that the starvation was roused by the hurtful words of my manager when I was twenty-three, not anything related to my mother, who had diminished to a background figure in my life.

Crossing her legs draped in soft jersey and propping her grayish-green glasses on her notepad, she invited, "Well, think about that. You didn't have a mentoring relationship with your mother, especially during the most important years. So you attached yourself to mother figures elsewhere. And when that boss did anything but nurture you, you didn't have the foundation not to be unhinged."

It was so simple, yet I was stunned. Much like when I first read about the body's set point and the calories required for recovery, here I was hesitant to shift my understanding of my experience and to embrace a new paradigm. Tears drenched my face as I defended my mother. "But she hardly ever commented on my weight or made me feel that I wasn't beautiful. And she called me the day after I sent that e-mail announcing my recovery . . ." But the tears kept coming, because my soul knew that there was some truth in it, even though my mind was resisting. After my eyes dried and my breathing calmed, I gathered and shared with Sil what I knew about my mother's difficult childhood—her adored father's sudden death, her mother's depressive episodes—and Sil helped me arrange the pieces in a new, more complete way. I began to suspect that the tragedies and weaknesses in my mother's early life may have derailed her own growth, that her adolescence had looked nothing like mine. Of course my mother loved me and had tried her best to connect, but in the end I withdrew because I most needed the wisdom of a woman who empathized with my struggles. Up the family tree were "motherless daughters," as Sil called us, and she explained that my inexplicable, copious tears at that moment were the compounded sorrows of the matriline. She suggested that I may be the point of overflow and perhaps would prove the strongest and most courageous among my female family, the one to look it all in the eye and stand it down so that my children could be the first in the line to be truly mentored and then fly free.

At home I was looking more to those delightful children, the eldest not even six years old, admiring how they inhabit and move in their bodies unaffectedly, how they yank off their clothes and race each other around the living room with full bellies leading the way. The only body comparisons they made were matter-of-fact remarks about the presence or absence of a penis as they learned the differences between girls and boys. They simply ate when they were hungry and stopped when they were full, which I was finally able to do myself. Why should I not also adopt their instinctual body acceptance? Studying them, I noticed how much my refeeding and repairing body resembled my two-year-old daughters': the pliable arms; the sweetly puffy feet, thighs, and calves; the protruding soft bellies filled to capacity to fuel growth. These forms were ephemeral shapes accommodating and reflecting a particular phase of development, as was mine. I had similar scaffolding—the water retention, the congregation of fat on my midsection—which served to regrow my withered organs and depleted bones. I noticed that the acne breakouts were subsiding and the skin around the remaining blemishes and dry patches was a new color, glowing and even. On a grocery errand I was startled by the reflection of my face in the glass of the car door. For years my angular, sallow visage in a mirror had registered for that first flashing instant as alien and ugly before I turned away to the food or weight preoccupation of the hour, but now the mental images of my face finally matched what my eyes perceived. In the bedroom I lingered in the mirror, noting my eyes brighter, cheeks filled out, just prettier. *Oh, yes, there I am.* I even looked younger, becoming one of the "lucky ones" asked for identification after ordering a drink at a restaurant with friends, even local wine shops I'd frequented.

But that wasn't sufficient to distract me from my broadening body. I was no longer weighing myself, but I could no longer zip or button a pair of baggy pants I had purchased a week prior. I couldn't stand the sight of myself in any pair of pants I owned, never mind allowing anyone to see me like that, so I jammed them all back into the closet, resigning myself to a skirt, tights, and flats that choked my bloated feet. I began to fret that my consistently robust eating wouldn't in fact move me out of that swollen phase quickly, that perhaps the unavoidable exercise in my daily life— chasing around three needy children—was lengthening my recovery timeline.

Sil recommended an acupuncturist, who pricked my tight skin and promised relief after a series of sessions. That night I also massaged my feet and legs toward my center, and I went to sleep hopeful that I would wake many times to urinate the excess water. In the morning, I eagerly assessed my body, but I couldn't discern any change in my body's interstitial fluid level. Later that morning I felt like I had reached a new fashion low, hunting a store for loose yet stretchy black pants that I would indeed wear out in the world. Since the beginning of my recovery, each shopping trip had ended with at least one item that let me feel decent-looking, but this time nothing was flattering, and I could see clearly that I was now larger than I'd ever been. For me, I was overweight.

For an anorectic, this was the supreme nightmare. I returned home with what I deemed my "fat pants" and cried. I bawled regretfully that I had done this to my body, that my atrociously sore and puffy thighs were my due punishment for the years of jogging in place in my bedroom to work off a cookie. I cried because I didn't know when this was going to end, especially since every hour that I was running errands or chasing after my children was probably not only one more hour of water retention but amassing another thin layer of it. Recovering and mothering seemed incompatible, but I couldn't stop either train; I was never returning to restriction, and my children weren't going anywhere. I was already so tired of it after not even six weeks, and I wasn't sure if this stage would end before I lost my mind. I sobbed because I feared that Alex might resent taking over some of my duties whenever he was home. I wanted to lock myself in my bedroom, resting and hiding from the eyes of absolutely everyone until it was all over.

The next day, Alex agreed that I could and should spend the upcoming weekend lounging, that he would do all the cooking and child-wrangling—

what sweet relief. That evening, I noticed that my feet, which had been puffiest at the end of the day, were hardly swollen at all, and that symptom had been replaced with a cool, lightly tingling sensation in both my feet and hands, which a little research revealed was likely peripheral neuropathy, another common sign of damage from restriction.[39] I didn't know if the acupuncture, self-massage, or something else had triggered the shift, but I was very grateful for that sign of progress and repair.

An hour later I had a new reason to cry, and this time out of joy, relief, and disbelief: I got my period! I was bowled over. This had not happened spontaneously in longer than a decade. To think that instead of years of attempting to restore my fertility through various means, including harrowing months of hormone injections, I just needed to fully honor my hunger for a while to signal to my brain that I was physiologically fit to be a mother. Less than two months into recovery, entrenched in water retention, muscle aches, and now tingling extremities, here was my period, which often takes many months to return to those on this journey. This miracle demonstrated to me how loose the timeline is, that our bodies simply do what they do, in whatever order they do it, in order to get us where we need to go, and that we just have to trust the process. Suddenly I loved this process. Perhaps my body also seemed to know when I was desperate for a pick-me-up, too, for I was flushed with motivation to push on. As I herded the kids to bed, I carried extra-tired Eliza extra tightly up the stairs, and my eyes welled with the knowledge that I can show her and her sister, from the age of two, what a woman's body does—that it is beautiful and powerful.

I recalled, as a young girl, the jolting image of barging in on my mother in the bathroom as she dropped a bloody pad in the wastebasket, but I couldn't recall how she explained periods to me, which I wanted to pilfer for my own with my daughters. I figured I had plenty of time to develop a script, but, like for most aspects of parenting, there was no dress rehearsal. Just two days into that first period, I was sitting on the toilet and the bathroom door opened to Josie hobbling in to show me how she banged her foot while rollicking with her siblings. I panicked and tried to convince her to leave the room so I could finish my business, but she had already spotted the bloody pad. Josie immediately pinned me with her brown saucer eyes. "Mommy got a boo-boo?"

Part of me wanted to completely avoid the issue for when I had it all figured out, but another part pushed forward. *The time is now.* I said, "Yes, but it doesn't hurt."

I awaited further inquiries into this mysterious wound, but she merely asked, "You okay?"

---

[39] "Exercise II: Insidious Activity," *The Eating Disorder Institute,* accessed October 11, 2017, https://www.edinstitute.org/paper/2013/2/26/exercise-ii-insidious-activity.

I crouched down and said, "Mommy's okay," and squeezed her to me, which elicited her signature giggle-sigh. I continued, "Mommy's okay . . . Mommy's okay . . . Mommy's okay," and pressed us even closer. Tears rolled down my cheeks because I was, for the first time in far too long, okay. I prolonged that hug, feeling our bodies meld, letting myself become her, feeling hugged by my own body. I was feeling the unconditional love of the mother inside me, my body telling me that I can always come home, that it will always forgive me, that we can always return to this, a mother comforting her daughter. I cried with such relief and gratitude that my body could forgive the incredible crimes I'd committed against it. That moment with Josie revealed that the return of my menstrual cycle was more than a reclamation of womanhood; it was another layer of self-forgiveness. After years of starvation and dissociation, I was experiencing a communion of the self.

3

I was bleeding with proof that I was healing, that this re-feeding protocol was indeed the way to rebuild my body. I hadn't experienced a natural period for twelve years, no matter my weight; only when I let the hunger take the lead did my body trust me enough to allow the possibility of reproduction. I was elated—approximately 5,000 calories per day had done some kind of magic. But my body, increasingly exhausted and sore through every limb, was telling me that cutting out exercise machines and walks outside was not enough. I needed to really, truly rest my body.

Without complaint Alex cooked all the meals and wrangled all the kids for two days while I lounged on our bed, remaining as still as possible. As a mother of three, a woman who had not spent a day in bed for illness since her firstborn entered the world almost six years earlier, this was hardly imprisonment—it was luxury. My supine body sank into the mattress and pillow, my legs and arms spreading slightly, every muscle and bone quieting. I found the hours gliding by smoothly, unlike during the eating disorder years when the mere half hour before I would permit myself to eat felt like an eternity. With restriction behind me, time unfolded differently. I nodded off for twice-daily naps, and as I staggered to my desk to write in my journal, my thigh muscles creaked and seared, begging me to stop moving so that my body could continue to repair all the decrepit tissue. The pain and fatigue regularly drew me back to bed to read and sleep. The kids occasionally joined me for a snuggle, and Alex offered to deliver snacks to me. Lying there, I placed my hands on my quadriceps, feeling through the thin fabric of my loose pants a startling heat emanating from my thighs, perhaps the burning of all those food calories to restore the muscles and fat that for years I had starved myself to keep in check. I marveled that I could come back, like a starfish, and that I could actually welcome it, even sheathed in water, much of my skin as tight as on a pregnant belly.

In those hours of penance for overtaxing my muscles and drastically under-fueling them, I worried about the edema, which did not show any sign of abating. And I now had plenty of time with my laptop to scour the Internet for stories of distressing levels of fluid. I uncovered reports from anorectics in inpatient facilities that were prescribed thiamine supplements, as that B vitamin may assist in curtailing the body's hoarding of water. Some claimed that they had little to no edema while taking those supplements. Curious, I continued to dig, uncovering the mechanism of thiamine in processing carbohydrates, which tend to be consumed in hefty amounts during aggressive re-feeding: if this thiamine becomes depleted from the body's stores, tissue begins hoarding extra water, presumably to help digest those carbohydrates. With further research, I came across the dangers of thiamine deficiency, which can manifest in the cardiovascular system as wet beriberi, a bundle of symptoms including extreme edema, tingling extremities, increased heart rate, shortness of breath, and even heat radiating through the skin—all of which I exhibited.

Naturally, I was convinced that I was thiamine deficient. But I felt I could handle the situation, and I didn't want to see my doctor and be led to a scale. Later that day at the health food store in town I procured supplements, since wet beriberi can escalate to heart failure. *Recovery could have killed me, but I figured it out in the nick of time.* But the next morning, with a few thiamine doses in my system, I felt no different, I noticed no change in the tightness of my skin, and my feet still couldn't slip into my shoes. I was still breathless after climbing the single flight in our house, and my heartbeat felt even faster than the previous day. I distracted myself with a short proofreading job, but then I descended into concern that the thiamine was not working fast enough, that my deficiency was progressing too rapidly toward a cardiac event. I tried to calm myself with a few errands, driving from the post office to the grocery store. As the clerk ran my credit card through the machine I leaned against the counter, breathing fast and shallow, heartbeat to match, a shooting pain in my left shoulder, and the world was sparkly and slow. *Oh, please don't pass out right here.* I swallowed my panic so I could drive home and make an appointment for later that morning with my general physician, Dr. Kelly. I didn't want to alarm the whole household—especially since self-doubt whispered that nothing was really wrong—so I told our babysitter, who was entertaining the kids across the house, that I just had an appointment and she could reach me on my cell. I called Alex at work in the city and explained the situation, and he kept me on the phone to try to relax me, but after a half hour I couldn't wait anymore. The symptoms were just as bad, if not worse. I suspected that I was on the verge of a heart attack, if I wasn't experiencing one already.

I could have called an ambulance, but doubt pulsed through me: these extreme symptoms, just one day after uncovering a possible thiamine deficiency, seemed almost too sensational, too coincidental. I drove myself the fifteen minutes to Dr. Kelly's office, struggling to stay in my lane as I frequently sipped the water that kept me calm enough to proceed. I was on the verge of hyperventilating as I shuffled across the parking lot. I leaned on the receptionist's counter and explained that I thought I was having a heart attack. Immediately I was ushered into the room where on every visit the nurse had taken my weight, height, and blood pressure before I could see the doctor. My life seemed in the balance, but my brain still had the capacity to worry that I would be asked to step on a scale, and I wasn't ready to announce to strangers that I was recovering from an eating disorder and could not handle knowing my weight. I was greeted by the same nurse who had seen me twice a few months prior, when I was struggling with an ear infection. I avoided eye contact, worried she would remember me and comment on my altered appearance—I had gained probably thirty pounds since then. Fortunately she overlooked the scale and instead reclined me on a table, lifting my shirt to expose my soft, sloping abdomen for the ECG leads. I suspended the shame of my alien body so I could focus on deepening and decelerating my breathing, and I was already feeling calmer by the mere vicinity of medical professionals who would know what to do. I was still unsteady as the nurse led me by my shoulders to an exam room, where I waited for Dr. Kelly. He sauntered in and with his thick hands placed the cold chest piece of his stethoscope against my breastbone. Then he glanced at the test readout. "Well, the ECG is normal, and I don't detect any kind of cardiac problem."

I exhaled; I was not on the brink of death by eating disorder recovery. Yet my symptoms indicated to me that something was very wrong, and I was eager for his opinion on the possible thiamine deficiency. I explained that I was recovering from anorexia, the first time I revealed it to someone with whom I did not have an emotional connection, someone whom I feared would judge me. My gaze remained downward while in a small voice I described my recovery process so far and what I had read about the role of thiamine in early weeks of re-feeding.

Dr. Kelly seemed unmoved. He tapped his pen on my chart. "You might be deficient, but there are a lot of things out of balance while you are recovering from an eating disorder. Just keep taking the thiamine and that should be fine in a week."

My chest and throat flushed with terror that I could have a real heart attack before the week is over. "So . . . there's nothing else I can do? What if this happens again?"

"Well, if you find that this is all becoming too much, I can prescribe you some anxiety medication."

I furrowed my brow and looked past his balding head to the sunlit evergreens out the window. "But I'm seeing a therapist, and I've been doing great with all the mental and emotional parts." The tears were racing down my cheeks. "I j-just thought I was having a heart attack. I haven't had much anxiety about recovering. I was just scared today that something awful was happening to me." I was bewildered at both what he was suggesting and the calm way he had discounted my symptoms.

He surveyed my face steadily, like I was a child or a stupid adult with whom he had to figure how to communicate. "If you feel that this is too much, I can prescribe you something. Often just a little bit of anxiety medication can make a big difference. Just think about it. And when you're home you'll probably find that you feel a lot better." He closed my chart, nodded with a weak smile, and left the room. I was still on the examination table, stunned.

Dr. Kelly hadn't explained why I felt like I was having a heart attack. *Did he think I was making it all up?* I felt humiliated. I sensed that I was being dismissed as crazy. So if I ever again felt my heart and breath racing, if I ever had another sinus infection, I couldn't return there. I had been pushing along so well in recovery without medical monitoring, and the first time I recognized that I could not treat myself and reached out for help, I did not feel cared for. Doused in disappointment I cruised home slowly along the smooth curves, noting that my hands effortlessly held the steering wheel, that I didn't need frequent sips off my water bottle. As he had predicted, I was in fact calmer, which I didn't understand, if the thiamine issue was just as present as it was fifteen minutes ago.

Oh. I had an anxiety attack.

There was no wet beriberi. There was only the lathering of myself with the stress of the potential deficiency. Maybe Dr. Kelly had assumed that I was familiar with those symptoms as a common reaction to extreme stress and that soon enough I would recognize to what he was alluding. But neither he nor I knew that was the first time my body had absorbed and expressed the strain of a crisis, the first time I hadn't responded to tension with a jerk on the eating disorder reins. I didn't yet have sufficient coping skills to consciously manage a life much more intense and unpredictable than the one I checked out of in my twenties.

I spent the rest of the day curled on the couch, breathing deeply and crying. Of course I hadn't wanted to be diagnosed with a life-threatening heart attack, but I began to understand that a scared, tired part of me wished to be carted to a hospital, to just lie there and let my body heal like the sick thing that it was, monitored by nurses and doctors who would ensure that I wasn't deficient in any vitamins. I wanted to be somewhere I wasn't expected to run the workweek marathon of eating, resting, editing, and caring for three children, among school, babysitters, preparing meals, doctor visits, diaper changing. I didn't want to be the caregiver of me, too; I wanted someone else to be in charge and ferry me along. In flashing moments I wished to be childfree, just so I could enter inpatient treatment without the guilt and heartbreak of leaving my kids behind. But I had to carry it all.

I fumed that no one bothered to stop me from running myself into the ground during the week. Perhaps to an outsider, my condition and the recovery from it didn't seem more than a matter of eating and going to therapy to deal with my changing shape, but that wasn't even half of it. I was enduring a full refurbishment of my body, including my brain, plastic enough to now forge new neural pathways—I was learning to think differently. Every organ contained haggard cells that my formerly starved body hadn't the energy to replace. I was exhausted and in pain as every part of me was under renovation, yet I was expected to continue to perform the already overtaxing duties of my daily life, as if recovering from an eating disorder required no more time and energy than an extra load of laundry every day. Steeped in indignation, my anger eventually settled and turned toward the only person who could truly help me: my husband.

Alex took a train home from the city early that afternoon so that I could be relieved of the post-nap dinner and bath grind. He was sincerely concerned about me, but as I lay on our bed I knew that this break was only an emergency, that I was granted a few hours' reprieve because my body had short circuited with anxiety symptoms but I would be expected to pull it together for tomorrow and all the following days without compromising our regular schedule. That anxiety attack was a sign that something had to change but I couldn't put my finger on how to do it, and Alex was not offering any suggestions. I wept into the pillow, feeling very alone and growing bitter.

Later that evening, I discussed with him what had happened that morning and how my body was feeling now. A fight churned in my chest. Through my wet, flushed face I wailed, "I'm . . . so . . . broken!" Howling like this was the little girl inside, the frightened and overwhelmed soul who just wanted someone to take care of her, to at least share the burden of asking the questions and persistently pushing for the answers.

Alex's voice fell low and soft. "I just don't know what else I can do in this situation. I have to be at work during the week, obviously, and when I'm here I can deal with the kids and make all the meals. I think I've been doing everything you've asked . . ."

I had to concede that he was correct, but I just grew angrier. After a decade of marital arguments, I knew that asking him to notice a dirty floor or misplaced toys was futile—he could react only to specific requests—but in the critically important case of my recovery, I needed him to do more than what I asked. I was so drained by all the asking, by all the strategizing to fit recovery into my life. I had always considered myself a very self-sufficient woman, so I had to swallow my pride and admit that I just couldn't do it all. I had to brush off my guilt that he already had plenty on his plate. I gasped out my need: "Yes, you're taking care of these children and things, but you also need to take care of ME." I felt so childish, so helpless, but at that moment, with a subtle shift in his gaze, I saw that he understood. I soaked his shoulder with tears and he soothed me in his arms, stroking my back.

I had recognized my needs, honored them, and asked for help. Tapping a little deeper into myself, I concluded that I was simply too tired to sit at my laptop and focus deeply on the detailed manuscript evaluations that for years had been an escape from household life and proof of my ability to be a superwoman: a mother and an editor, back and forth all day long. But to recover, I would have to move past guilt and be a bit less of each; I would have to spend some of that mothering and editing time instead resting and reflecting. Alex agreed to take on all the household and child duties every weekend going forward, and, with gratitude that we were financially sound enough not to depend heavily on my freelance income, I informed my main client that I was entering a sabbatical to write a book. I exhaled and settled back into my pillows.

In those new idle hours, my food-nourished brain began to ruminate on painful aspects of my past, which the insistent thump of meal planning had been suppressing. First up was my strained relationship with my mother. That discord commenced when I was eleven or twelve years old, as my hormones rose and my body morphed. Like most children that age, I was struggling both to eke out an acceptable social standing in middle school and to assert my independence from the authority of my parents, which was not well received by my mom. Typical mother-daughter squabbles about unsupervised afternoons at the mall and slightly revealing clothing escalated into trials for my inexcusable "attitude." Of course I didn't like when I didn't get my way, but most infuriating was how many of those arguments shook out. Usually my mother would not engage in debate about topics ranging from curfews to college tuition; rather, she quickly deemed me "defiant" and "ungrateful" before bursting into tears and retreating to her bedroom, concluding the proceedings. If my father was home and informed of the conflict, he would rush at me, widen his aquamarine eyes and, close enough for his spit to pellet my face, accuse me of cruelty toward her, insisting that I must have said something horrible to make her cry like that. Such episodes often ended with my apology to her—somewhat sincere, because my aim hadn't been to upset her—and an unsettling sense that I hadn't been advised, or even heard. Although as a snotty, righteous teenager I relished my victories, on a certain plane I was disconcerted that my mother was often forfeiting simple disputes that, as the adult in the scenario, she should have had the experience and wisdom and strategy to win. I could see now that deep down I had felt that she was supposed to be showing me how it's done.

I had gradually withdrawn from her. In high school I sought answers to life instead in books, friends, romances, and the rich inner world I cultivated, the last of which manifested in notebooks of overwrought poetry and other introspective writings. I performed exceptionally for teachers who inspired me and appreciated my efforts and insights, and I now understood what Sil had explained, that these authorities slowly became mirrors to my self-worth. Later, while attending NYU, I found my professional home in book publishing, thriving during an internship that not only utilized my editorial talents but was dominated by knowledgeable, compassionate women. After graduation, that internship was upgraded to an enviable assistant editor position supervised by a seasoned editorial director, and she let me fly with whatever I was willing to take on, which was everything I could get my hands on. At twenty-one years old, my career was already at full tilt—I was acquiring and developing new books—and my confidence and fulfillment primed me for falling in love with Alex, the man I would marry. However, too soon the publishing house downsized significantly, and I was left to find a new place for myself, a new guide. By luck or fate, I landed under Valeria, a female manager with not only little to give but everything to take, with unpredictable, brutal criticisms and threats. The starvation, which began as seemingly benign calorie cutting to trim down before my wedding, had kept the barometer of my dignity hovering just above excruciating levels.

Continuing to rest on my bed, my mind then flashed to photographs from my parents' wedding and years when I was a baby—my mom had been so very thin, appearing much like how I looked with anorexia. I began to postulate from where I had inherited the predisposition for an eating disorder. I wondered if a conversation with her about possible food issues on her end as well as the factors that seemed to have led to our maladjusted relationship would not only enlighten me but finally allow us to connect on a soulful level. But I bridled my hope: her reaction to the mass e-mail about my eating disorder centered on the hormone-replacement therapy and why I never told her that my eyesight had been declining. As a nurse, she had remained in what seemed her comfort zone, focusing on only physical effects, not inquiring into the deep and complicated emotional aspects of my condition. I can't say I had been surprised, but I was disappointed, since that had seemed an ideal opportunity for her to face so much that had gone awry, to acknowledge and embrace everything about her little girl who had traveled to hell but was now pulling herself out.

I e-mailed some questions to her and we talked by phone a week later, during which she was refreshingly forthright. I knew that her father had passed away when she was ten, but I learned that he was an admired firefighter in their coastal New York community and he had died suddenly from a pulmonary embolism. She had been, she said, the "apple of his eye," and, as she described him so favorably, he seemed to have been the same for her. She recounted how she had been devastated by his death, and with her much older brother in college she was left with only their chronically depressed mother, who was occasionally admitted to mental institutions and had once attempted to jump out a second-story window of their house, from which my mother, at only seven or eight years old, and her brother pulled her back to safety. I could only imagine the trauma of these experiences. The revelations confirmed for me that my mother had simply not experienced the engagement of a mentoring mother, so she simply couldn't be the one I wanted for myself. I felt sympathy and compassion for her—both of us had been sidelined by circumstances.

Then I asked if she had ever been eating disordered, mentioning those photographs of her when she was in her twenties. She explained that during those times—planning her wedding and years later the stress of moving to a new house mere weeks after my birth, the first of her two children—she had simply been too stressed to eat much. She claimed that she had never felt obsessed with not eating or with losing weight, that any resulting thinness was temporary and simply a symptom of anxiety that regulated once life became comfortable again. I knew that she was not a chronic dieter; I could only remember her at average weights and eating freely, at least to my eyes. She seemed never to have been ensnared in a full-blown eating disorder, but I wondered about a connection between her under-eating and her anxiety, as eating disorders fall under the category of anxiety disorders. I kept to myself that perhaps I had inherited from her a menacing tendency.

I considered the genetic contributions of my father, too, as I recalled how he had once lost a significant amount of weight with the Atkins diet and then developed a preoccupation with bicycling and frequent sessions at the gym. During a visit home from college I had been startled by his gaunt physique, his face having aged ten years in two months, suddenly lacking any fat around eye sockets and cheekbones. My mother had divulged to me her worry that he might have gotten caught up in the weight loss, and at the time, when my knowledge of eating disorders was limited to after-school specials, I left any interventions to her. Fortunately his state proved to be a short phase; however I would never be certain what had truly been happening with him. So I found myself wondering about my dad, too, but also why I needed to wonder, as I already knew that restrictive eating is highly heritable. As I sat with it all, I grasped that I wanted to spread the blame and exonerate myself as much as possible from falling prey to the lure of thinness. I was yearning to hold further proof that I was born to fail, that something foreign and corrupt had entered my body and all I had needed to land on my face was a diet and emotional trauma to strike me simultaneously, as they did at age twenty-three.

Instead I had to deem my entire self—even if there was indeed an ounce inside that really just wanted to be skinny—worthy of the clemency I was bestowing upon my changing body, to sink into myself and love every bit. And this was no small feat, as I had always assumed I would be merely average, nothing special, without the self-reproach that would allow nothing less than superhuman excellence, academic and otherwise. It was the same fiery thing that had prodded the eating disorder along; self-criticism drove me to believe that extreme thinness was making me exceptional. But by reading Kristin Neff's *Self-Compassion: Stop Beating Yourself Up and Leave Insecurity Behind*, I learned that, counterintuitively, self-criticism precludes success because self-doubt stifles our potential, and thus for my entire life I had actually been holding myself back. But now I could free myself, by continually forgiving and accepting myself, and grow into my true capacity—much like how I had already reclaimed the mental space owned by calorie micromanagement. Again I looked to my children, whose example had already taught me intuitive eating and body acceptance. As maddening as caring for three young children could be, I didn't have to dig deep to behold their beautiful range of delightful and frustrating traits, and each day, no matter what any of them happened to do, to me each little person was an exuberant, extraordinary individual worthy of my deepest love and kindness. To be self-compassionate I merely had to transfer that perception of my children to myself, to be as gentle and nonjudgmental with my own soul, to accept, despite the whys and hows of my turn into anorexia, that my soul was always beautiful and flourishing.

And like my leap from restriction to robust eating, my brain accommodated the shift more easily than I imagined. A week later, for his kindergarten registration screening, Charlie was rigorously evaluated for a full hour as I sat in a plastic chair and cruised the Internet on my phone. A teacher called me into a room to share with me that overall he scored slightly above the average incoming kindergartener. Although his scorecard was full of achievements, I zeroed in on the missteps—apparently I had neglected to show him a clothes iron and explain what "at least" means—which in a knee jerk I perceived not as his but my own lapses. If I had still been eating disordered, I surely would have berated myself endlessly for being too wrapped up in self-starvation to teach my child everything his peers' parents had, then both punished and soothed myself with restriction to lose just one pound, driving myself deeper into obsession, perhaps so much that I neglected to work on those kindergarten concepts I had sworn I wouldn't let fall through the cracks before September. But in recovery mode, the self-compassion cavalry galloped in to discern that test designers are not arbiters of good parenting, that many kids missed more items that he had, that I was not at fault for rarely ironing clothes. If he picked up those ideas by the start of school, then great, but I wasn't buying into that kind of guilt anymore.

I was more quickly spotting my pitfalls and, with the energy of food and rest, I was learning to walk around them. Key to this burgeoning self-awareness was therapy with Sil, a safe space lush with compassion, which bolstered my courage to gaze into those parts of myself that were dark and confusing, feelings that seemed ignoble or inconvenient: an impromptu longing for an otherwise forgotten ex-boyfriend, or the realization that I had wanted children as a chance for happiness great enough to snap me out of the eating disorder. In my teens and early twenties I had been on my way to knowing myself, but anorexia extinguished lights in my mental living room, and since then I had been merely feeling my way around. But Sil walked into that room and guided me to the light switch. Once I gathered the nerve to flip it, the objects were illuminated to high relief. I immediately ascertained the room's emotional design, drawn from honest human needs—a lovely place to live, not just an area to stumble around and feel ashamed about.

I put up my feet and absorbed it all, my new mental home. Soon enough my survey fell on the closet of my broken hearts, more specifically the hurt accompanying the sense that certain boys had deemed me unworthy to be wrapped in the kind of devotion and sometimes infatuation I had bestowed on them. Even during my years in the dark, I knew that closet was there, but I dared not open it, fearing it were overstuffed with disappointments, a precarious stack of board games piled so high and hastily that I would be pummeled by those wounds, a rush of attachments that could smother my marriage. I had been most intimidated by the memory of Matteo, a statuesque geek with whom I had spent three late-teenage years fixated, and with him I tossed off my virginity and believed I was in love. I had been confident that he would truly love me, too, if he could pull himself away from his computer animations and other intellectual pursuits in order to devote more energy to the noble cause of romance. During our freshman year of college we attempted a long-distance relationship, but both the arrangement and our emotional tie were far too weak to survive that, and my conflicted feelings were too strong to maintain any friendly contact after we broke up. A few years later I met Alex and henceforth barely thought of Matteo, only occasionally of his California blond hair when I caught the warm whiff of a vanilla candle, which had often been burning in his bedroom. In those moments I found myself not so much yearning for him as simply curious about where he was. But I retreated from any urges to contact him, out of dread of the contents of that closet.

This time I typed a short greeting to test if the e-mail address I found for him were functional. I couldn't guess if the note would ever reach his eyes, much less if I would receive a response, but nonetheless I felt invigorated and triumphant for turning the doorknob. *I'm facing things now.* I spent the rest of that morning reevaluating that relationship more objectively than I ever had, stripping away the self-criticism that had convinced me that I had simply failed to rise to his level of appearance and intelligence. Instead, I saw that I had fallen for someone with many positive qualities, but I had mistakenly believed that intellectual intelligence included or implied emotional intelligence, which discussions during therapy sessions had shown me was a separately cultivated skill. I had subsisted on rare glimpses into his heart—"love" at the end of a handwritten letter or his watercolor and ink portrait of me walking toward a sunrise—a slit of an opening into which I jammed my hand, determined to prize it wide open, but all my straining was futile. I had assumed that such a bright person would see that I was extraordinary; and when he didn't, or at least didn't show it, I felt judged as unworthy. But from my new place of self-compassion, I apprehended that I had simply extended a fully open, loving heart but he hadn't known how to receive or return it.

With growing confidence, I dug into mental shoeboxes of moments with him. I recalled sitting cross-legged on Matteo's plaid-covered futon bed at his parents' house as he recounted a telephone argument he had minutes earlier with his girlfriend, who had just become his ex-girlfriend.

"I told her that I had to hang up because you were coming over," he said, moving notebooks so he could sit at the other end of his bed. "And then she said she wasn't worried because you weren't that pretty, anyway."

I flushed with mortification. My eyes fell to my loose gray-blue corduroys, from which I picked some imaginary fuzz. My upper back was being scratched by the bulky wool sweater that revealed nothing about my tiny waist.

Matteo must have sensed his misstep, for he quickly followed up. "I told her that wasn't true. I think you're beautiful, and I told her that. She's just a bitch." I only half-believed him, conjuring an image of her, ruler-thin in her pompon uniform, towering on her long legs, topped by silky lengths of brown hair, conventionally attractive. I knew I had appealing physical qualities, too—baby-fine, shimmering blond hair draping past my shoulders, steel blue eyes, swollen lips often curving into a lopsided grin—and my body was average height and of an hourglass shape inconducive to jeans shopping but seemingly attractive to some boys. She and I were apples and oranges. But I had to concede that my looks did not harmonize with his—six-foot-two and with minimal fat; a chiseled chin; could have been a runway model—nearly as much as hers. On the surface I didn't care much, reminding myself that this was out of the mouth of a girl who couldn't manage her first two weeks at college without cheating on him, a girl who couldn't appreciate what seemed to be devotion to her. But still, I had tucked away her comment, like a tiny acorn in the sole of my subconscious shoe, a pinching reminder that no matter how much I could ever convince Matteo to care for me, to find me irresistible, people might wonder how someone so mediocre was with someone as striking as he, and that maybe he would wonder if he could do better. That sense of inadequacy quietly hindered my relationship with him, but worse, I unwittingly began carrying self-doubt, a chink in my contentment with my body, another deeply planted seed from which the eating disorder would grow six years later.

When I checked my computer on the morning after I had sent Matteo that shot-in-the-dark e-mail, I saw that he had responded, enthusiastically barraging me with peculiar details about his life on the West Coast, in prose festooned with trademark witticisms that would have left my teenage self swooning but the new me interpreted as silly affect, fool's gold. I needn't have feared slipping down the rabbit's hole of his charms; I felt nothing more than a cool pang of nostalgia. I replied with broad strokes about my career, husband, and children, feeling proud of myself for my nonchalance in the exchange.

But his return message clocked me in the head—he had been doing more than making videos of himself snowboarding and deciphering the universe as an astrochemist: Matteo had a daughter, just about eleven years old already. Sophie had been accidentally conceived just a couple of years after he and I stopped communicating, and he married Sophie's mother, but the tumultuous relationship was doomed and they divorced when Sophie was a toddler, and Matteo took primary custody of their daughter. I was astonished that within a few years he had accelerated from an emotionally unavailable person to a man raising a child alone, investing his love and attention so fully as a single father, beginning in just his mid-twenties. I had experienced how much a baby can unexpectedly open the floodgates of the heart, but still, as I gleaned from his words his deep adoration for Sophie, my chest fluttered with the longings of years before, and I felt rejected. *Why couldn't he have loved me like that? Did he always have it in him, but I wasn't enough to ignite it?* I wanted to feel like I imagined Sophie in his arms: fully seen, fully loved. As a teenager I had patiently pined for Matteo to hold me in a total, unreserved embrace, the one for which, I understood now, I had ached from my mother. Analyzing that longing and applying my new skill of self-compassion, I could now see that, like in my employers, I had sought that unconditional love also in romantic partners, those boys unequipped, who always left me wanting.

I revealed to Matteo my eating disorder and my recovery process—the edema, the exhaustion, the gratifying sense of collecting my emotional pieces, my book—and he responded to that vulnerability with both gentleness and an affirmation of his high opinion of me. He wrote, "I hope that this challenge alone doesn't overwhelmingly define how you see yourself. The quick-witted and defiant young woman I remember from growing up was (from my biased opinion) a particularly special person that is distinct from the survivor of great physical and emotional adversity." His words crystallized what had been bubbling in me, that I was indeed more than a former anorectic, and right then more than a woman fishing compliments from an ex-boyfriend. I was someone willing to examine her emotional body of injuries neglected. Recovery was revealing itself as the soul's unnumbing, the enduring of pins and needles before we become ourselves again. Matteo and I e-mailed only few more times after that, and with each contact I reread his message fewer times and deleted it faster as he left my focus more quickly. He was a god turned human; I was a little girl growing into a woman.

With my mind and heart open to thinking and feeling, with restriction no longer numbing me, I was maturing through these experiences of deferred pain, but I also began discovering new joy in unexpected places. On my many drives per week around town to run errands or shuttle children, I noticed that I was turning up the radio music, singing along to the local classic rock station, tapping the steering wheel, letting the familiar beats and melodies fill my body and become me—what a contrast to the eating disorder years when songs had been simply background noise to all the meal calculations. I was also returning to the visceral pleasures of food. When my friend Amanda suggested weekend lunch plans, I embraced the prospect of a delicious meal I didn't have to prepare. Although she hadn't seen me since I began recovery, we chatted on the phone almost daily and she knew all the details, so in her case I could swallow the embarrassment of others observing my changed body and meet her. My chosen restaurant, the Garden Café, had always been one of my local favorites, but the generous portioning and myriad ingredients in every vegan dish had once spun my head with guesstimates and calculations, and typically I had spent more time striving to eat almost nothing than enjoying my companions. However I knew this time I would have fun, and for days before our lunch date I fantasized about all the menu items that had called my soul and stomach for years but I had deemed too calorically expensive. I was ecstatic that I could now order anything I wanted, eat it all, and truly taste it.

But on our walk from the parking lot to the restaurant, Amanda was waffling. "Ugh, I ate a really huge dinner out last night and now I'm feeling too guilty to eat a lot today. I'm not sure if I can do Garden Café."

I deflated, glancing at her jean-clad thighs that didn't touch when she walked, while mine rubbed together under my loose skirt, mourning the body that would never be mine again. Still, I could no longer relate to feeling guilty over food, and my growling stomach was king now. *I am going to eat all that amazing food, enjoy it, and continue to get better.*

As I was about to recommend she go with one of the appetizers, Amanda piped up, "But that place is so great. I could always order something small or just take the rest home for lunch tomorrow." Soon placed in front of me was what they called an Indian enchilada—a thick wrap stuffed with potatoes and chickpeas and spices expertly chosen and balanced for sublime taste and texture—along with a glass of dry Riesling, for this was a personal celebration and I no longer concerned myself with the calories in alcohol. I ate and drank, closing my lips around generous forkfuls among our zippy conversation, feeling like I were laughing louder than anyone in the room. I felt free in the company of both food and a friend, each of which had long required my exclusive attention—the former for constant calculations, the latter for maintaining the façade that I wasn't so miserable. I had arrived at that elusive center, completely present and open with a treasured person in my life, eating to my hunger and delight without a single number running through my head, not even an estimate.

The milestone of two months in recovery came and went. The water retention had expanded my body undeniably beyond what I recalled as its natural set point, and the only thing that had begun to dissipate was my patience. I invested in a special lymphedema massage—a trying experience, both explaining to the therapist that I was retaining water due to recovery from an eating disorder and allowing someone to see and touch so many of my bloated parts—but that attempt to drain my body ultimately relieved nothing. As the disappointment waned, I began to apprehend that this was another aspect of recovery that could not be circumvented or shortened, that it was simply necessary to repair my body. Still, I was jealous of online accounts of very young women and men who ate recovery minimums for just a few weeks before the edema disappeared literally overnight, the belly fat redistributed to other areas, and they skipped off into the sunrise of remission, even if they had slipped and restricted for a day or two along the line. I was indignant that these teenagers, many of whom had deliberately chosen severe diets to be admitted to the cult of thinness, had easier recoveries than I did.

From childhood through college I had almost never dieted, apart from a couple of curious and short-lived high school dips into what I thought women of all ages did all the time to "maintain their figures." But I hated hunger more than any part of my body I might wish to pare in order to look thinner in a prom dress. At nineteen years old while standing on an NYC subway platform with my Three Musketeers bar and Pepsi can, waiting for the N train to usher me to my internship at a literary agency, I recalled an earlier conversation with my roommate about her friend who had fallen into anorexia. At the time I thought with such certainty: *I could never be anorexic. I feel so sick when I'm over-hungry. And food is so good! I don't understand making yourself starve. My body is fine enough. It just doesn't seem worth it. I don't get it.*

My attitude toward food and my body had been solid until the daily battles with Valeria, and now I was certain I was doing absolutely everything I could to piece it back together: eating well above my caloric minimum every single day; resting my exhausted, aching body as much as possible; making tremendous mental strides in therapy and in my journal. I was as strong and stubborn in recovery as I had been in anorexia. *Haven't I earned my medal by now? Don't I deserve to walk off the field?* The hitch was that biology would never care how brave and dedicated I was. My body would need more than just a few months to resolve that many years of damage.

It would also need to expand further. One morning at my closet I chose a pair of recently purchased pants that had been fine a few weeks ago, but now they were too tight around my hips for me to wear comfortably and confidently in public. In a fury I tugged them off and pulled on a skirt that had been fine a month earlier—but now the cotton fibers were straining. My second period was due any day, so I reasoned that premenstrual bloating could have been compounding the existing water retention, but I could tell that this was more than a couple of pounds. The accumulation of edema, fat mass, or both had clearly not yet stopped, and I couldn't take much more of it. Also, the weather was warming, and I was fed up with lying in bed so much—I just wanted to take regular walks, which since childhood I had enjoyed for the fresh air, scenery, warm sunshine, and meditation. I wanted to chase balls in the yard with my children and simply feel "normal." I had kept my head to the grindstone for two months with the notion that by now I would be turning the corner, leaving behind the pain and edema, watching the new mass redistribute to my natural shape. I thought by now I would have a body almost healed, wearing sexily snug jeans, boarding that plane to Paris with my husband in July, celebrating ten years of marriage as well as a ten-year eating disorder now in the past. I wanted to recover like those teenagers and, after only a few months of re-feeding and rest, have a revitalized body to fill with all the cheese and baguette it desired, walk with strength, and make love with confidence and emotion unfettered by an obsessive, starved brain. I needed that vision to pull through, but what if it didn't arrive on that schedule? I feared I would relapse if my body was not smaller than this when I shopped for clothes for the trip, if I ended up scuttling over Parisian cobblestones in the same fraying skirts. I had to do something about it.

I knew I had been doing very well in recovery, every day eating beyond my minimum calories, starting my second period exactly thirty days after the first, never reacting to external stress with urges to restrict. I had progressed more than I dreamed possible in merely two months. I wondered if taking a diuretic to flush away at least some of the edema so that I could look and feel a little more like myself would really be so bad. If I did so, my body would probably hold less interstitial water to move cells and would thus require extra time to complete repairs, but those likely additional weeks or months of pain and exhaustion felt like a small price to pay to unburden my eyes, which winced in full-length mirrors.

However, once the thrill of the potential result subsided, the concept of diuretics—even without a return to restriction or exercise—wouldn't sit straight with me. My ingrained drive to accelerate all processes, to be the first one to hand in her perfect test paper, to feel powerful, exceptional, and in control, was colliding with the essence of recovery: the surrender of the mind to the wisdom and needs of the body. My thighs needed that soreness, my arms and butt needed that water, my whole self needed that exhaustion so that I would remain as immobile as possible, allowing more calories to be used for internal repair rather than running after my children. I reviewed the remarkable changes that had happened in two months—the intense sweating and heat radiating off my body, the explosion of acne, the extreme muscle soreness, two periods—all come and gone, and there were two more months before our anniversary trip. Those upcoming weeks could hold the switch that released the water, or perhaps not, but I had to be patient, to act as a patient, for the best chance of getting there. To thoroughly recover, I knew I had to be brave enough to let the path reveal itself and guide me.

Feeling comfortable in this revitalized sense of teamwork with my body, I then realized how much mental progress I had been making in other areas. Since I began recovery I had been avoiding any celebrity or fashion magazines or websites, fearing that the images of ultra-skinny figures would "trigger" me—a perfect term, since slipping back into restrictive behaviors is as good as a gun to the head. But now, when those bodies occasionally crossed my vision, I noticed that I no longer idolized or aspired to those proportions. I no longer viewed them as a goal but a state I had left behind, with those drawn, sullen, pale faces, eyes without light, smiles without radiance. Nothing would touch them—clothes, tight doorways, and, likely, emotions. They were becoming increasingly invisible to the world and themselves, merely a mountain of poking bones. By contrast, I was now a place where my children dove in for a cuddle, where their weepy or sleepy heads easily found a soft, soothing spot to rest.

Minor crises were touching down more smoothly, too. As was inevitable a few times a year, Alex e-mailed to inform me that, because of a meeting the following week, he would not be able to work from home that Wednesday, as had long been our weekly schedule. That kind of news usually tipped me into a frenzy of despair about how I might not be able to switch around childcare to make it all tolerable enough, how I couldn't settle on an alternative day to suggest for him to instead be home because all the options felt like torture, how my life would just continue to be terrible forever, launching me into fitful tears. I usually also resented that he once again seemed to be avoiding a role in figuring out a solution, so I often countered with a nasty comment about responsibility that would stoke the tension and leave me feeling even worse. But this time I responded to the issue directly, writing, "I will wait for the second part of that statement, in which you propose a solution for the week." Alex replied that he would work from home on both Monday and Friday, affording me two days with him at home instead of the usual single one. His decisiveness was a delightful surprise, and I recognized how much more productive I could be if I faced even tiny adversities head on.

Meanwhile, my body's expansion slowed, my hunger was tapering down, the muscle soreness and heat in my thighs and backside were dissipating, and the extreme exhaustion was lessening—I no longer required at least one nap every single day. I believed I had turned that corner, that things would start to get better, that I had delved sufficiently into my past. The sessions with Sil had become lighter. One afternoon she and I were chatting lightheartedly about the kids, and at a certain moment I was neither thinking nor feeling much of anything when a pin slid imperceptibly into my soul, pricking an invisible source of anguish. Out of seeming nowhere, when I thought I was fine, I began to release tears that had been barricaded for a decade. Through my eyes poured the sadness and resentment that Alex had never been alarmed enough by my diminished body to do something about it; that he didn't insist that I quit that awful job under Valeria, even though we'd struggle financially; that after I first told him about my anorexia, as I embarked on my failed recovery attempt, he didn't want to discuss it much, mention it later, or seemingly research it enough to realize that I had relapsed so soon and steadily through the years until I was almost as skeletal as I had been at my worst. How could he not have seen all this? Did he not care to really look, or to do anything about it? Did gender conditioning suggest to him that I, as a woman, will fret about my weight and sometimes not eat much? I didn't know the answers; I was only uncovering the questions. I sensed that this was just the beginning. The totality of my emotional pain was a long sheet of bubble wrap, with so many matters still to pop.

I had been donning the mental armor that I'm okay with whatever shape my body takes both during repair and afterward, but that mindset soon exposed itself like a pair of pants I could wear weeks ago: it just didn't fit. I couldn't fake it 'til I made it. I agonized that this would drag on, that I wouldn't be any smaller when I held Alex's hand as we crossed the Pont Marie over the Seine. I needed Paris as my finish line. The diuretic idea tempted me again, but I wondered if I could find a method that could accelerate the process in a healthier way. So I further investigated the physiological mechanism of the edema, learning that the water facilitating the movement of cells in and out of damaged areas while immobilizing those parts of the body was much like my swollen foot after I fractured it in high school,[40] but now my entire body was covered in a layer of fluid, and most dramatically in areas I had once shrunk the most. I uncovered methods for reducing this kind of injury edema, like soaking in Epsom salt baths and then wrenching medical-grade compression garments onto my legs, butt, and arms. Disappointingly the garments did not make me appear smaller, but the tight material of the bike shorts, leggings, and sleeves pressed the areas enough to smooth away the worst lumpiness and allowed my thighs to glide past each other when I walked. If nothing else, I "felt" a little smaller. After a week I noticed a reduction in soreness both during and after wearing them, and I surged with possibility that they were speeding the internal reconstruction and I just might dry out in time for Paris, which was now just six weeks away.

I was still spending weekends on our bed, sometimes backward with my feet propped at the top of the wooden headboard, hoping that gravity would draw the water from my feet, legs, and hips down to my kidneys to be excreted. Through the window behind the bed I observed the graceful maple develop brownish-pink buds, and then tiny green leaves, unfurling and converging over the weeks. I believed that if I just kept my feet up, or at least did not carry my new weight all over the house for endless hours, by the power of magical thinking my body would progress like that tree. I believed that by June, when the leaves reached the full glory of a canopy of green over the deck, my physical struggles would be over and I, too, would revel in the summer of my body. How badly I wanted to feel that summer, to head outside on my own with music through my headphones as I propel my body through the world, caressed by the air and sun, my eyes resting softly on the trees, the sloping lawns, the curve of the asphalt, as my mind

[40] "Edema: The Bane (and Blessing) of the Recovery Process," The Eating Disorder Institute, accessed December 12, 2017,
https://www.edinstitute.org/paper/2012/5/22/edema-the-bane-and-blessing-of-the-recovery-process?rq=bane.

delved into my inner world of emotional problems to be sorted. Even as a teenager I thrived on those meditative walks; and when stretches of rain or the pit of winter precluded those escapes, I became prone to depression.

Since beginning recovery three months earlier I had been for the most part stuck in my house, a cacophony of noise and crying and whining and other chaos. With no guaranteed moments to recharge, I could feel myself approaching something dangerous and terrible. I had been laboring to rest and eat as much as possible to encourage my body to complete the repair phase, and I had been swimming so steadily and deeply in my heart and psyche to rework the pathways of my brain and truly heal from this, but I knew I could never achieve happiness and balance if I ignored my other needs. As more weekends unfolded and the windows opened to the tweets of birds and scent of cut grass, the conflict heightened. I knew that any exercise would at best exacerbate edema and at worst precipitate a relapse, but I could sense that the depression, which would only grow if I continued to imprison myself in my house, would surely take me down.

I'd had enough self-denial. I put on my compression shorts, ate a lunch a bit larger than usual, and strode beyond the mailbox. My body felt so much heftier and jigglier than the last time I'd walked our road. My legs and feet were a little stiff and sore and unable to shuffle quite as fast and fluidly. I felt self-conscious and awkward, but after a few minutes I was enraptured in the warm sunshine, my body inhabiting the world, with no little ones tugging at my clothes, and, best of all, that behind my filmy gaze I was not calculating the next meal or the snack I will have "earned" through those precise minutes of walking. After ten minutes I knew it was worth it. But after about twenty minutes of my arms naturally swinging, my rings and watch felt tight and my hands tingly; the centrifugal force had drawn the water in my arms to the extremities, and it was becoming painful. My feet became quite sore, too, and by the end of that half hour I just wanted to get home, eat a substantial snack, and lie down. I spent the rest of afternoon on my bed, recuperating.

That walk demonstrated how much further I had to go, but I also acknowledged how far I had come. I treasured the focus and creativity I'd gained by responding to my body's demand to eat and rebuild. Further, my size seemed to have stabilized, my hunger was tapering down, I had two periods under my belt, and the muscle soreness was receding. I wanted to be unequivocally pleased with my progress as well as overwhelmingly grateful that I wasn't battling the triggering family and friends, digestive issues, and unsupportive therapists that others in recovery often endure. But the undeniable fact was that I was drowning in that water, both physically and emotionally. I was now almost as obsessed with the edema as I had been with restriction—it was my first and final thought of each day and so many in between, with much anxiety and depression sprouting from it. I became exasperated with wearing the same few "acceptable" outfits, not recognizing my body in the mirror, feeling hot under the sweaters I still wore in late spring to conceal my upper arms. I couldn't pretend that navigating Paris—merely a month away—would be fine, with my hands swelling up after not even a half hour of walking, my feet puffy and pained after just moderate exertion.

Out of panic I chased diluted dandelion tincture with gallons of water. Then I finally swallowed those over-the-counter diuretics I had tucked in my closet. But the edema still did not budge.

Desperation drenched me. I was no longer sure if I could continue with recovery if this is what it meant.

4

"I can't go to Paris like this," I sobbed to Alex. "Please, is there a way we can cancel it?"

I didn't know which was worse, the sense of bitterness that the eating disorder would mar that trip like it had done to our honeymoon, or the deep disappointment of abandoning that delectable opportunity to reconnect, celebrate ten years of marriage, and briefly breathe a life away from the demands of three young children. I was trapped between recovery and relapse; I was torn between carrying all the grief and asking Alex to share it. So I put the decision on him.

"I don't think we should do that. We can't just get a refund. We'd lose a lot of money." The dams in my eyes broke. "But Kerrie, we're going to have a great time no matter what. We don't have to do so much walking. Even if we just stay inside the whole time, I'd be just as happy—as long as I'm spending time with you."

His sweet sentiment felt genuine, and I willed myself to be content with it. But I had already written in blood the narrative of recovery, that this summer trip would be the perfect final curtain on the entire struggle. I knew I wouldn't be satisfied merely lounging in the small apartment we rented for our stay. My dream was shattered, along with control over my tear ducts. Alex came closer and held my face.

"You know you're beautiful, right? You're way sexier than you were before, even if you don't feel comfortable with how you look right now. And this isn't our only trip together without the kids. As soon as we get back from Paris we can start planning a trip for next year—maybe we can go to Italy. It will be a whole new adventure. But this time we'll just take it easy and focus on being with each other, not doing anything in particular."

Somehow that was enough for me to back away from the ledge. I had needed to be reminded that, like the swollen body I was inhabiting, this trip wasn't close to the only one I would ever have and I needed to widen my perspective. I exhaled the expectations, the crisis. He wiped my slippery cheeks, and I fell into his chest. Alex had made a convincing point. Ten years ago we had stomped all over Paris, and this time we could choose which spots were special enough to revisit and which new places really excited us and fit whatever level of activity my body could handle, and we would travel by Métro whenever possible. Maybe the scenario wasn't storybook, but it was better than not going at all. And it was certainly better than returning to the eating disorder for the rest of my life.

Still, I wondered again if the edema and exhaustion could be improved, just a little. Amanda had recently recommended her naturopath as a resource for bringing my body into better balance, so with cautious optimism I made an appointment. In her office in her bright, modernized farmhouse, this holistic doctor compassionately probed my history. She paused to smooth her curly hair behind her ear and marvel at how far I'd come, inviting me to do the same. But by then recovery had seemed just the natural course of things—what else to do after a decade of ravaging my body and mind than to rebuild it all by necessary means? But she encouraged me to reflect on my courage and determination to pursue and persist, especially among three young kids and a freelance career. I longed for a rush of pride, but I felt like a humble hero; I had done simply what anyone would.

I left with a list of liver, adrenal, and other tests I could request from Dr. Kelly and notes about Chinese herbs and foods that might help with the swelling. I was hopeful that the included acupuncture session and homeopathic remedies and herbs would offer relief, but days, then a week, passed with no discernible change in my body. Plus I had a new symptom: my hands, arms, feet, and legs ached even while resting, and these areas had almost overnight become more swollen. I couldn't force on my wedding rings and watch anymore. The bones and joints in those more active parts of my body were clearly inflamed, begging for the immobilization necessary to repair what starvation and exercise had worn down.

This fresh pain was shocking—*isn't this naturopath supposed to make me feel better, not worse?*—but also was my swift acceptance of it. I was recognizing that my journey to homeostasis was not simply a matter of eradicating individual symptoms. Here I began to trust my body, integrating that the exhaustion, pain, and edema were all in the service of caring for me, not a cruel universe's twist of fate designed to ruin my vacation. Holistic medicine was indeed accomplishing its mission to prime the body for healing, and I knew that mine would require many stages and layers of it. In those hours each day when my body seemed to burn, tiny fissures may have been healing within my depleted bones, but the mending that was palpable to me was the one between my physical and emotional selves. I was not only comprehending but appreciating that my body was on my team, not an "other" to be controlled with willpower. With each steady breath I could feel that old catastrophic split, the one that had allowed the eating disorder to sprout like a weed, begin to narrow.

Beyond the respite of my bed, however, household matters inevitably demanded attention, including the expiring lease on our family car. We intended to trade it for another three-row vehicle commodious enough for our growing children, but once we examined our target choice at the dealership, we knew the trunk space in that one would be inadequate. Alex pointed across the lot at what we should consider: the minivan.

I'd always been as certain as death and taxes that I would never, ever, ever own a minivan. Even with three children, I was determined never to be engulfed by a massive hunk of metal that might as well have *MOM* airbrushed on the sliding door. But peering inside that very roomy car, and checking our original option again, I knew it was what we needed. Through the drizzling rain I shuffled defeatedly back inside the dealership. At the salesman's desk I was silent, with my clenched jaw damming the flood of tears behind my eyes. *We came here just to get another car and I'm leaving without my dignity.* Alex was giddy about the minivan's interior space and automatic doors, and I was nothing short of devastated, which felt absurd yet justified. As my face reddened with tension, Alex offered the alternative of taking the smaller car, or even renewing the lease on the one we already had and letting the kids be a little cramped for a few years.

I felt ridiculous scooting to the bathroom to cry and then pull myself together after the ruddy-faced salesman joked that the minivan came with a soccer sticker. This wasn't how I expected recovery to change things. I was supposed to be this newly hatched, sexy woman who could be and do anything, but at that moment I felt like simply a mother of three who appeared like she couldn't get back to her pre-baby body and was about to purchase a car that would complement that image. In that bathroom mirror I could see how I looked to that salesman. But as I continued to stare, my gaze penetrated beyond my blotchy face and discerned all the parts he would never see: the brave warrior against a neurobiological condition, the writer, the compassionate friend—which, along with me as mother, was my true, aggregate reflection.

With a paper towel I dried my tear-stained face and returned to the sales floor. I sat next to Alex and choked out, "Let's just get the minivan. It makes sense."

"Wait—are you sure? We don't have to . . ."

"Yes. Let's do it."

I was able to concede what my eating disorder–riddled self never would, to surrender to what needed to be done, as I had with hunger, weight gain, exhaustion, and now, as trivial as it may have been, a car. As appearances lost their grip on my self-image, I understood that a minivan would not make me older, uglier, fatter, or any more a mother than I already was. That car would in fact make my daily life easier, with less physical energy expended and less stress accumulated as I wrangled children in and out, leaving more calories and headspace for my body and mind to recover. Like my body, that new car was a vehicle for what I wished to accomplish, not a manifestation of who I was. To wade into the prismatic ocean of myself, I was releasing my fiercely held, stark identities.

Without food restriction and without a body I felt comfortable exposing in a swimsuit even in my secluded backyard as June opened its wide, balmy arms, the languorous summer hours belonged not to the sweat of exercise in the sun, but to me. Inside the house I began writing the first chapter of my book, I absorbed some traveler's French for our trip in a few weeks, and I flagged guidebooks for sites, restaurants, and shops to visit in Paris. I also needed to procure some new clothes, as the same few outfits had been in heavy rotation for months, and they were neither very stylish nor summery. I visited a few local stores, but many clothing cuts didn't flatter my odd proportions, and glimpses of my partially naked self were even more disheartening. The slog of traversing parking lots and department stores left me extra exhausted and pained, so as a last resort I turned to the Internet and ordered many skirts, shirts, and dresses—more than I would truly need, but I had to assume that most wouldn't fit adequately, especially when I was guessing sizes. I braced myself for the usual shopping disappointment as well as shame and frustration with my body, but after the packages arrived and with trepidation I tried item after item, I could have been knocked over with a feather: everything fit just fine. I even looked beautiful. The universe had thrown me a bone.

I couldn't wait to leave the diapers, messes, and whining to my in-laws, to be in a place with no one to take care of but myself, no one talking to me but my husband, with whom I had been yearning to spend such extended time, to share with him the expansive landscape of my freedom from anorexia. Although recovery had lifted me out of obsessive mental loops and low libido, I had been grappling with my resentment toward Alex for not intervening during those years of starvation, along with my ambivalence about my clothed body, which heightened to humiliation when naked, and I wanted to work through all that. During those first four months of recovery, he and I had sex only once, a blue-gray predawn quickie under the sheet and with my shirt still on. Like in the old days of restriction I had summoned any scrap of desire to make it tolerable. That was no way to be with my life partner; I wanted to feel unselfconscious of my shape, fully engaged with the man I loved, affixed to him by the old sexual energy that had resurfaced and was surging through me, directionless.

By fantastic luck, the bedroom in our Paris apartment had just one narrow window onto a gloomy air shaft, and by closing the heavy brown drape the room was as blind as I could ever hope. After a fitful post-flight nap, we stepped out to meander our beloved Ile St-Louis, the island in the Seine where we had also stayed for our honeymoon. We relished sunlit kirs along the hustling sidewalk and then dinner at the quirkily festooned restaurant that charmed us on our first night there ten years ago. I helped Alex order his preferred number of escargot, then we sipped our first glasses of heavenly French house red. Alex was awed by not only how far we'd just flown but that an entire decade had passed since we last sat there. To me it felt even longer, since with an eating disorder each hour of not eating feels like a day. Still, I was astonished that I could eat and drink freely, a perfectly natural behavior that six months ago I didn't believe I'd experience ever again. I rolled buttery scallops on my tongue as I listened not to anorexia chatter but the conversations among the Parisians and Americans packed close. If I hadn't pursued recovery I would have calculated a steep restriction for a month to "save up" for the trip, leaving me skinnier and more starving that I may ever have been, knowing that even with many thousands of "earned" calories available to me each day I would still guesstimate and tally each bite of macaron or shred of baguette that crossed my lips. But there I was, my eating driven by the harmonious desires of my stomach, tongue, and mind, without anxiety or regret. I didn't need the wine to feel intoxicated.

In the fading twilight we giggled and staggered on the cobbled streets back to our rented home for the week. With a swoosh of the thick drape, the bedroom was instantly inky and swirling with tingly sex. I pulled off my tight compression shorts before Alex found me in the black—I didn't want any reminders of my swollen body once I turned on full blast the lust and confidence that had been bubbling for months. I pleased him in ways I had never, and we engaged every which way. I allowed him to brush and grasp and kiss me in places that had never been so fleshy, and he said that he loved every part of me, that I was the sexiest woman alive. I could almost believe it, in the dark. We flopped all over the bed, initiating various positions, and I waited in vain for one to rub me the right way, to push me onto the unstoppable escalator to orgasm. Something was in the way.

The next morning, I stepped out of the shower, and as I reached for the towel I forgot about the mirrors lining every wall of that sadistic bathroom, and I caught a full view of myself, a chubby girl in limp arabesque. I had been avoiding glancing at my naked body, as if those foreign proportions didn't exist if I didn't acknowledge them. But this is what Alex had touched, what I was pretending was sexy. *What a joke I am.* Disregarding the warm weather forecast, I wrapped myself in a loose cardigan and ankle-length skirt, and we ate herb omelets and stretchy croissants at an airy café at the foot of the bridge leading to the Ile de la Cité, from where Notre Dame loomed. Alex glowed with gratitude for the night's sensuality, and as he thanked me I hid behind my teacup and drank down my fraud, willing the burgeoning tears to slide back into my eyes. I, too, wanted that night to be the rekindling of a healthy, robust sexual chemistry between us, and the wine and darkness brought me close, but I sensed that I'd been trying to force something. I watched the young French families pushing up the hill and tried to catch their conversation as they began their day—anything to drown out the truth, that my body was holding me back, along with something intangible, insidious.

The bright day was perfect for walking without sweating or swelling too much, so we proceeded down the wide-sidewalked Boulevard Saint-Germain toward the Musée Rodin. I was delighted to be there again, spotting cafés that appeared familiar. Through the leaf-dappled shade we walked less than an hour before my feet and calves began screeching at me to stop, and soon I was gasping for Alex to slow down. Wilting into awareness of my body, I began appraising others', noting the parade of thin thighs in shorts and bright pants scissoring past, tiny sizes that were mine for so long; I remembered walking those same streets with the air between my legs and seemingly limitless energy. Back then we had walked for hours and hours for days and days before I couldn't keep it up, but now I was ready to collapse before we reached our first tourist destination. *It wasn't supposed to be like this.* Rattling in my head like a trapped hyena was the wish that I had never begun recovery, or that I had indeed relapsed a month or two ago, enough time to drain my body to a manageable shape. As pain ripped up my calves with each step, in storefront glass I caught my reflection—lumbering, too large for this city of waifs—and I regretted everything.

Just a few minutes into my self-pity, she approached—a girl thinner than I'd ever been, with mere strips of muscle ready to give up on her femurs, the skin on her legs an inhuman grayish-yellow. In the breeze her loose shirt clung to nothing, and she marched with such determination. Her face confirmed this specter of anorexia, her skin that sick color, her eyes so dead. My arm quivered to reach out and grab her crumbling shoulders, to tell her that she could die next month, next week, next block if she didn't get help. As she passed I could hear an echo of the hyena, the relentless shrieking crazy in her head. I vowed that I would do anything not to hear it ever again. I'd take the thigh flesh squeezing out of the bottom hem of my compression shorts, the strain in my feet swelling out of my sandals, the exhaustion as we approached the museum, just so I could admire Rodin's sculptures fringed by roses with my brain no longer pathetically deducting from my next meal the minutes I spent on a bench, seeing mathematical calculations rather than art.

After three hours of walking and lunch, my body felt like I had backpacked across a continent as we approached the apartment building, and within minutes I collapsed on the velour settee facing the floor-to-high-ceiling windows that opened gloriously onto the sumptuous chestnut trees, over the Seine to the Right Bank. The breeze was exquisite on my stinging feet. Each late afternoon of that week I lay on that lovely perch, reading or dozing, unable to lift my hand or adjust the angle of my foot without a deep burn pulsing toward my center, as I attempted to minimize the damage of that day's exertions, honoring my body's cues, which I had only begun to trust fully.

Until that point, I had been tallying my calories to ensure that I didn't slip under my minimum and thus hinder my progress toward remission. The success of this recovery protocol was clear to me by the rise and fall of muscle pain, the floods of three regular periods, the way the hours unfolded so steadily and effortlessly, and my hunger directing me to consume more than my minimum, so I'd be damned if I would mess it up by accidentally undereating. Still, those reassuring calculations were tedious, and I wanted nothing more than never to attach a numerical value to food ever again. And I had grown concerned that a week in Paris—an overwhelming landscape of unpredictable hours trekking sidewalks and museums, of fish moated in butter and cream—would require far too much accounting in order to guarantee I did not walk off too much of what I ate; I knew I'd be as consumed by keeping score as I had been ten years prior. So, although Paris didn't in fact mark the end of recovery, I decided it could at least terminate the era of counting calories. I was apprehensive to remove those training wheels, worried that I would panic or undereat, but I was also exhilarated by the anticipation of simply eating, not only in that gastronomical paradise but at all the dining tables for the rest of my life.

Each evening we strode into the persistent sun to our dinner reservation, often at fancier places than what we could afford on our honeymoon. I drank however much luscious wine would bring me to the level of giddiness and liberation I wanted to reach; I didn't flinch when the garçon topped off my glass. I ended each meal when I was satiated, not when I had reached an arbitrary, self-imposed limit. At one restaurant, before our main courses arrived, I scooped my blunt knife into a ramekin and smeared the softest substance onto a slice of baguette. My tongue kneaded this sweet, smooth, salty thing—mild yet exceedingly luxurious. "This is incredible," I blurted across the table to Alex. "This is the most amazing butter I've ever tasted! You have to try it!" I was practically levitating off my chair, so ardent that he experience such divine matter, which I believed only the dairy-devoted French could create.

He bit into his bread and butter, considered it for a second, and declared, "Sweetie, it's just butter. It doesn't really taste different than any other butter . . . ?"

In the otherwise sedate restaurant I covered my mouth not to spit out my wine as I laughed at the absurdity: *I don't remember the taste of regular butter.* Our chuckles pierced the murmurs of the composed Parisians surrounding us, but underneath I was aghast, wondering what else I might find, in food and elsewhere.

I was willing to try it all. We spent many hours with eight-, even nine-, course tasting menus, plate after plate of masterfully mingled ingredients—some of which the translating program on my phone could only vaguely identify—which I ate with my entire soul. Like my ever-undaunted daughters, I shrugged and popped mysterious morsels into my mouth, trusting the chef to flood my body with something new, something I might really like. But unlike a child, I also savored the pairings and textures—even red meat, which I'd eschewed long before the eating disorder erupted—as a marriage of enduring tradition and inspired novelty. During those extravagant meals I was becoming a bridge between my old and new selves.

I was also experiencing a physical fullness I hadn't since the early recovery days, back when I believed that stuffing as many calories into my body each day would propel me beyond the edema in a handful of weeks. I had been both astonished and pleased at the caloric value I was squeezing into my stomach, imagining the odometer of my recovery whirling toward remission. But now, with my progress no longer ticked off by food consumed, and eons from the terror that a full stomach would metabolize into fuller thighs, I was simply full—of medicine, of fuel, of the pleasures of life. I was simply full of life.

Alex and I staggered back to our room, glittering with food and wine and the romance of bridges as we crossed the Seine sparkling in the moonlight, landing on the bed, a dark Paris of our own. Before the stimulation of the city and substances in our bodies tipped us into unconsciousness, we hastily made love, again forgetting, or just ignoring the interruption of, the condoms within easy reach. We had become so used to contraception as an optional formality, extra protection against my slumbering reproductive system, that it was easy to disregard. I also wasn't worried; my period was due any second. In fact, it was a miracle that I hadn't start bleeding the moment the plane landed, that we had squeezed in any such sex at all.

The next morning, when my period didn't show, I began wondering. Sitting on the toilet I noted some mucus that appeared more like what I might find mid-cycle than at the end, and my nipples were sore and sensitive as I strapped on my bra. I hadn't cataloged my symptoms of the three periods I experienced that spring, and I couldn't remember my body's natural rhythms before anorexia, before the birth-control pill, which was twelve years in the past. I couldn't confidently recall whether I had any ovulation symptoms a couple of weeks earlier. Drying my hair and brewing tea to soothe my slight hangover, I slipped into infertility mode, running all physical signs through the algorithms of potential pregnancy, and I concluded that I very well may be ovulating right then. With the luck and irony of those who had struggled so much to conceive three children, Alex and I had unprotected intercourse twice in the days prior.

A baby could be forming in me at this very moment. I was both terrified and euphoric. I wasn't eager to add a fourth child to our mini cavalry at home, but there was something so lovely and magical about emerging from recovery with a new being to show for it, proof of my health and fertility—essentially, a trophy. But any possible fertilization was mere speculation, so I let the idea dissipate in the warm breeze as Alex and I embarked on full day of touring and shopping. Like hamsters we ascended the escalator tubes outside the Centre Pompidou, an entrancing modern art museum we somehow missed a decade ago. Then we rode the Métro across the city so that I could salivate at the rainbow of macarons at the acclaimed confectioner Ladurée, one of which my teeth crackled through before sinking into the nuanced ganache as we proceeded to the Opéra neighborhood, which held the legendary Harry's Bar. When we visited it during our honeymoon, the bar was so loud and cramped that Alex and I enjoyed our drinks without speaking. This time, on a weekday midafternoon, the bar was not only empty, but as silent and dark as a tomb. Alex ordered the famous sidecar, and I chose a whiskey sour, my usual drink before the eating disorder struck, back when I didn't care about the calories in mixers. The bartender scooted to the end of the bar to chat with another patron, and Alex and I were in our own universe on those barstools.

"Do you ever think about having another baby?" I asked him after we began sipping our second round.

"What?! No. Three is more than enough." His stance was clear, but I may have appeared disappointed. "Wait. You don't want another, do you?"

I pulled my skirt further over my compression shorts and grabbed for the stem of the cherry in my glass. "No, I was just wondering, since I could actually get pregnant now, like a normal person."

As we reminisced early times with each of the kids, slowly I realized that I wanted not so much a baby but a chance to redo those laborious, tearful attempts at conception, the pregnancies riddled with fear of food and weight gain, the highly medicalized births of underweight newborns who didn't have the stamina to breastfeed right out of the gate. In the end I had three healthy and loving children, but I wanted a chance to do it the "right" way, much like how I was redeeming not only my honeymoon but really the whole ten years subsumed by anorexia, with unrestricted eating. I wanted to be a normal pregnant woman, a normal eater, and, deep down, I just wanted my normal body. I wanted to push recovery out of the spotlight with a pregnancy, a bulbous belly that would distract from my puffy arms and thighs. Just as I had longed for the conceptions of my children to obliterate the eating disorder, I fantasized that a new pregnancy would bandage the wound of recovery, and when it was finally removed I would see that I had healed effortlessly. That hypothetical baby and even this vacation were diversions from my ambivalence toward my body, which seemed at times a forgiving angel who would reverse all I had inflicted on it and later a vengeful punk who reminded me with every catch of my thigh on the other that I was being duly punished with measurements as too large as they had once been too small. The pendulum of my body's size had swung in the equally opposite direction, and as I waited for it to settle, my eyes had been darting around for something, anything, else to watch. But what I really needed to do was to just be.

After a few days, the ubiquitous thin French girls consuming only coffee receded from my focus and I began immersing myself in what I had, rather than what I didn't. At each meal and stop into a boulangerie I ate as much soft, stinky cheese and *pain au chocolat* as my stomach could hold, and our engagement of food and conversation was never abbreviated by the messes or whines of one of our toddlers. Alex and I spent hours simply laughing, at one point sidesplittingly joking about the overtly sexual pop music the cab driver thought we Americans might enjoy. I stopped worrying about where I was in my menstrual cycle; I was grateful that our days abroad didn't revolve around the associated restroom access. For a few days I was entirely present, breathing Paris and myself in a way I couldn't the first time. However, my mind was no match for the matter of my muscles and bones, which were further deteriorating under the walking. Our day plans dwindled as I needed additional hours in the afternoon to rest my whimpering calves before we headed back out to dinner, and each morning, on my numb feet, I pitched into walls like I were drunk. Whether moving or resting, I was in pain. I lost interest in sex, which of course frustrated Alex, who only wanted a little more of me before we returned to our normal, unromantic life. I cherished our time in Paris, and I was relieved to confirm that my husband and I still enjoy just hanging out together, but by our last morning I was ready to go home, see our children, and recover.

In the airport lounge I pulled out my notebook, taking a final opportunity to chronicle the exquisite food and other experiences before the smack of home life knocked most from my memory. After I jotted down "Bertillon salted butter caramel ice cream" my eyes wandered up to a very tall, very thin blonde walking with a mug and glass of water to another section of seats, slipping right through narrow spaces between people, her body barely grazed by clothes that would be choking mine. I didn't learn until later that we had been there during Paris Fashion Week of all times, but I immediately ascertained that she was a model. Her pretty face had those generic, flat features held in place by wide-set eyes that lifted my way as she sipped her ice water. I glanced right down to my plate of airport mini croissants that were dry and awful, nothing like the ones I'd had with soft-boiled eggs for breakfast that week. But I had to eat them—I had to keep eating no matter what—and I felt jealous that she could forgo food, that she could have the spindliness that I would never experience again and be, of all things, paid for it, while I felt like I was paying dearly not to look like her. I just wanted her to disappear, for all those women in Paris to get out of my sight so I could stop feeling so conflicted, so I could stop being embarrassingly envious of bodies that didn't ripple, like maybe I hadn't made much progress after all.

I popped in my earphones and surrendered to hammering music, berating myself for such superficial jealousies. Then I returned to my notebook, recalling the commuter train we rode into the countryside a few days earlier to finally meet Alisa, a friend I had made on an infertility message board before our son was conceived. We explored her enchanting stone village and ate a delectable lunch made by her talented French husband as their two boys romped in the enclosed yard and garden, all of us laughing as any traces of social awkwardness evaporated into the steamy, sunny afternoon.

Then, tucking my notebook into my tote bag, I studied Alex, who smiled at me sweetly, and I considered all I was lucky to have: a warm family, devoted friendships, and a book I would continue to write after I returned home. Maybe from the outside I would be no more than cute and curvy, but I wouldn't be thrown away when the edges of my body start to fray, when the lines eventually set into my face. I would be whole, happy, and distinguished as a woman, a mother of three, a funny friend, a wife, an editor, and now the author of a book that could make a remarkable difference, possibly in that model's faraway, illusory, ephemeral world, helping someone starving to reclaim herself, perhaps even her.

Back at home, I hobbled to the bathroom like an old woman for a week and a half. Using the handrails on both sides of the staircase, I slowly maneuvered down the steps as if my ankles were broken. They appeared almost so, with skin white and tight with water, swollen enough that no tendons could be detected. The once-intermittent pain in my limbs was now constant throbbing in my feet, calves, ankles, hands, wrists, and forearms, and I was immersed in agony, unable to walk beyond our deck.

For my physical recovery, Paris had been a huge mistake. No matter how much I had eaten to offset the walking, my body was still wrecked. And I hated every inch of it. I felt like I had simply traded one dungeon—the constant starvation, the thin body I didn't recognize—for one of pain, limited mobility, and a plumped body just as unfamiliar as the one I left behind, and it didn't seem to be going anywhere soon. My period had arrived the day after we returned home; the final wisps of a redemptive pregnancy evaporated into the July heat.

My liberal Parisian drinking habits continued well after we arrived home. I was having a beer or glass of wine every late afternoon, which normally occurred to me only once or twice a week, to lightly anesthetize my mind before the girls awoke from their nap. I suppressed memories of the sex that wasn't quite right with Alex in Paris by reaching for my vibrator almost daily and fantasizing about other men. I met with the naturopath and she knocked out the severest joint pain with her acupuncture skills, but I continued to plumb these distractions for the comfort and thrills I couldn't find in recovery and in myself, after the novelty of free eating had worn off. I knew I was derailing myself, so I promptly ceased these methods of self-medication. And then, with the distractions removed, what was left was depression.

The kids were out of preschool for the summer. I skirted pool invitations that would require a swimsuit and I divided my time between playground activities that allowed me to sit and hours of cocooning in our bedroom, silent and cool in our new central air conditioning. There I completed freelance editing work and did my own writing when mental energy sparked, which was not often. Rather I mostly just lay on the bed, calves and feet flooding with the wounds of the asphalt I'd stomped for hours innumerable, watching the leaves laughing in the bright breezes, wanting nothing more than to flutter through it, too, in the yard with my preciously young children, chasing baseballs and bubbles, teaching my son to swim. My brain was no longer tethered to planning meals for the evening or even the entire day ahead; my mind was so finished with that obsessive calorie strategizing that I often had no idea what I was making for dinner until I entered the kitchen to begin. It had other matters to tend, and I was only discovering what they were. During anorexia my skin had been my bell jar—too compact, choking me—but now the thick glass had expanded to the windows of my house, allowing me a few steps in various directions, gazing at the world I longed to join and questioning the limited space within, the adult life I had constructed.

Breathing that stale air again and again, I could no longer evade that the major decisions of my twenties—walking down the aisle to be married, bringing children into my world—were made mostly on autopilot, taking blind stabs at routes and identities that might ease the sadness and helplessness of the eating disorder. I charted a logical adult course that I suspected could at least prevent me from veering off the edge, and maybe with a little luck knock me out of my obsessive thinking. Unfortunately, a husband and children hadn't cured me. They now bolstered my recovery, but ultimately I alone had chosen between total deterioration and a full life with the body I was born with. And unlike the eating disorder, I couldn't renounce loving human beings, some so tiny and dependent, and abandon my life as I knew it, even if I had committed to it all unconsciously. I would have to choose them again, consciously and authentically.

Each day my busy brain and I spent hours on my bed, often with Tori Amos and other emotion-wrought music from my younger years surging through my headphones, at the sight of which Alex often joked that I was regressing into an "angsty teen." I was twice that age, of course, but he was onto something. Although I felt distressed by my cumbersome body, more than one stranger had guessed that its plumpness belonged to a girl in college. My mind was similarly reverting as it longed to return to New York City, spinning out my life if I hadn't met Alex and hadn't fallen into anorexia: quiet days in a tiny apartment with freelance work, and then the nights by myself or with friends, amid the dull roar of the city, growing steadily and properly along that abandoned path. My soul thirsted for a second chance at those lost years, and I was flooded with an alarming urge to walk out of my house and never come back—that is, until I remembered my children, so sweet and maddening and needy, as divine as I had been depleted when they somehow grew from the dusty rocks inside me, three little beings I loved more than anyone. I could never unchoose them.

But regarding Alex, I hesitated. I had once believed that our minimal sex life was our only sticking point, and that recovery, with all its hormone-restoring magic, would fix that right up so that he and I could skip into a passionate sunset for all our remaining decades of marriage. My libido was indeed restored, but I was aching for almost anyone but him, which pained me as much as my legs. I wanted to want my husband again. I tried to convince myself that I should and could. I tried by acknowledging his physical attractiveness, our playful rapport, the way he made me laugh more than anyone else, that I was drawn to his arms before the eating disorder set in and we'd just enjoyed such a fantastic time together in Paris. He had even hidden the bathroom scale that summer, perhaps sensing my dangerous curiosity to know just how "bad" it was getting. Alex's appeal was logical but, as I had been discovering, my needs didn't necessarily have a neat, convenient solution.

With incredible compassion and insight in therapy, Sil helped me acknowledge unreservedly how much anger and resentment I held toward Alex for remaining so removed from the eating disorder—not only at its various severities and after I had divulged it to him, but also during my dramatic transcendence over it. Mere weeks after I chose recovery, close friends had commented about how much more lively I had become and occasionally asked questions about the re-feeding process and my emerging symptoms of repair, but Alex remained a comparatively uninterested party, occasionally remarking only on how my body was sexier than when I was so skinny, as if recovery were only skin deep. One evening on the couch I asked him if he saw how much I'd evolved since I began the journey.

"Yeah, your boobs are a lot bigger," he purred as he stroked down my waist, against which I froze and elbowed him off.

"I'm asking if you think I've been acting differently."

"Sure. You've been eating more and whatever everyone else is having, so that's a nice change."

"No, that's not what I mean. Other people have told me that my personality has, well, shifted. Do you agree?"

He sighed and we soaked in silence for a few very long seconds. "I'm not sure what you mean."

My stomach dropped. *How could he not see this? I'm a totally different person now.* "Well, I feel so much freer in every way. Doesn't that come across?"

I met his eyes, and he shrugged. "Um, I guess so."

At that moment I could no longer deny that Alex wasn't seeing me, that he might never have truly known who I had been and who I was becoming. We both knew that he hadn't discerned that I was relapsing through the years of pregnancies and babies. And I couldn't get past my recollection of a July weekday morning during the very first year of the eating disorder, the day when I hit rock bottom.

The episode had begun the previous night, when Alex and I went out to dinner in Manhattan after work. I barely touched my plate of salmon and haricots verts before we walked through delightful summer evening sun to more drinks at a champagne bar in Tribeca. As we passed the Soho Grand Hotel, Alex, in his tipsy grandiosity, suggested we splurge and spend a luxurious night away. *Away.* That was all I wanted: to find a space away from that asphyxiating starvation and that abusive boss, who had been particularly cutting lately. I walked on begrudgingly, and once we were sufficiently drunk at the chandeliered lounge we cabbed to our Brooklyn apartment. As Alex passed out in front of the television I pinballed around the kitchen, the alcohol temporarily releasing me from the anorexia. Frenetically I consumed thousands of calories of cereal, cheese, leftover cake frosting, everything.

After the morning light cracked through my eyelids, when normally all seems right and possible, my world collapsed. I was horrified that I had done it again, that I had allowed my willpower to concede to my hunger and as a result for days and days I would have to immerse myself in damage control: all the ultra-meager meals, the extra walks. And I couldn't face that torture chamber of a cubicle. That day, I decided, I would stay in our bed, head pounding with dehydration and every cell begging for food I would withhold. I was never going to get better. I was never going to get out of my head, that body, that job. *There is no Soho Grand for me.* I sobbed to Alex that I was so utterly depressed, and I begged him to call in sick and stay with me. Normally my misery preferred solitude, but that day I was sincerely afraid, for the only time in my life, that I could seriously, even fatally, hurt myself if I was left alone in that apartment.

I still didn't understand that I was eating disordered, but I couldn't refute that my daily grind—dodging my boss's insults and threats, preparing for our wedding in three months, and all the starvation throughout—had become too much. I was drowning in myself and I needed help. Soothing my head on the cool pillowcase, I pleaded with Alex to find a psychiatrist who would see me that very day, because this was an emergency. Still in just his boxers from the drunken night before, he went online and I held my breath as he talked on the phone with one receptionist, but he couldn't get me an appointment right away. His search stopped there, not making further calls or accepting an appointment for another time. Desperate, I rang my mother, whom I had long ceased inviting into my emotional world. I wailed about how miserable I was, waiting for her to say something wise or comforting, or to find a professional I could see immediately, even if I had to take a train to my hometown to do so. I was too weak to do anything but whimper for help from her and Alex, the two people I wanted to recognize the gravity of my state and take some kind of charge. I needed a hospital, but I felt like they were just patting me on the head and telling me it would be okay in the end. Throughout that hot day I ate nothing and, as a distraction, Alex took me down to Coney Island, where we rode the Wonder Wheel and I pretended to be happy. We sat in a photo booth taking pictures that were nothing but lies: I was not smiling anywhere inside, and I didn't feel like I had someone truly by my side.

The next morning I cried in Valeria's office, explaining through my sobs that I had called in sick because she had torn me down so much. She was largely silent, seemingly perplexed as I pleaded for a healthy working relationship. Of course that dynamic never manifested, as I was ultimately asking my abuser to mother me. But it felt like my last shot after I wasn't saved by my own mother and my future husband, like I craved to be.

On another baking summer day, now almost six months into recovery, my brother and his girlfriend stayed in the car while I went inside to pay for the grilling charcoal that Alex requested I pick up on our way back from lunch. I hadn't been to that store in months; with Alex on weekend cooking duty,

I no longer needed to stop there for fish and produce for the elaborate Saturday meals I had spent hours planning and preparing but not so much eating. I knew that most of the workers there hadn't seen me since my body changed dramatically. Although no acquaintance who didn't know my situation had ever made a comment about how I was no longer enviably skinny—I was lucky that my social circle was so tactful—when I encountered such a someone I would still feel a hot bloom in my chest, stand straighter with my thighs suffocating each other, willing my clothes to hang more loosely, to make me seem smaller underneath them, seem the person I will be when this is finished rather than the puffy one I was right then.

Standing in line, I ensured that my dress and light sweater—despite the ninety-degree heat—was draping the right way before I heaved the charcoal bag onto the counter, smiling at the friendly clerk.

His eyes lit up. "Hi! How are you! I see your husband and kids all the time, but you haven't been here in so long!"

"Yeah . . . I know . . . I guess I've just been busy!" I tilted my head and shrugged, so very fake.

As he offered the change I watched his eyes follow a horizontal line from his handful of bills and coins to my abdomen, which I willed my dress not to graze as I moved through the store. I pulled my midsection in a bit, and he asked delightedly, "Did you have a baby?"

My breath caught, and everything I had planned to say to the first unaware person bold enough to comment on my body—that I was recovering from an eating disorder, that it's a fairly common condition, that no one should ever remark about someone's size, especially because you don't know what's actually going on—was a sand castle snuffed by a single wave. I didn't hear his attempt, as misguided as it was, to link my absence to my altered body, likely without judgment, to which I could have laughed or told him to screw off and mind his own business.

Instead, in that innocuously inappropriate question, I heard, *Wow, you got FAT.* And instead of acting the ambassador of eating disorder awareness, I shoved the change into my wallet and lowered my eyes as I whispered an ashamed "no." I hugged the bag of charcoal as I returned to the car, stomping down all the threatening tears, which would have drowned me if I didn't oblige myself to keep it together for my brother and his girlfriend waiting for me in the car.

Once we returned to the house and the kids were gleefully playing with our weekend guests, I sat on the toilet and grasped the outsides of my thighs, which extended beyond the seat so much more than they used to. The air streamed out of my self-confidence, now a deflated bouncy house. I had spent all those months assuring myself, with the help of friends' compliments, that I looked fine and normal, that maybe my change of size fell within the expected, almost unnoticeable range of adult human weight fluctuations. But it wasn't true. And apparently I appeared more postpartum than I did after giving birth to twins: I recalled bringing Charlie to his first day of preschool, the girls only six weeks old, where some of the other mothers gaped with astonishment at my thin body. I was so far from that now, and I was disgusted with myself for loathing that fact, as if my body should have been exempt from the inconvenient physical manifestations of all I had thrust upon it. I abhorred my shame at the clerk's question. And I hated most of all that a stranger's offhand comment knocked me so easily off my track of self-acceptance.

But I didn't have time to wallow; I had family to entertain and my daughters' third birthday party to execute. In the morning I felt less fragile about my body, enough to tell Alex what had happened, who of course denied that I looked anywhere near pregnant and insisted that I was sexy and perfect. To survive the day I donned that sentiment, along with a flowing white hippie skirt and well-fitting black T-shirt that made me feel concealed but attractive, and I gratefully fielded polite "you look great!" compliments from family as I buzzed around the house and deck, ensuring that my girls and their preschool friends were enjoying the kiddie pool and cake, and talking and laughing with all the kids' parents. Surprisingly, the next day my muscles and bones were not the sore mess I expected after those hours of activity. In fact, they felt no worse than usual, and neither did my body image. Somehow that overloaded weekend was a boon; it demonstrated to me that my capabilities and happiness were not reliant on my shape.

When I called Amanda on Monday to tell her about the clerk's comment, she reacted instantly. "Well, you do look different. You look healthy now." I wondered if I could start seeing it that way, too.

A few months earlier I had asked Gwyneth Olwyn, whose online articles and forums had been comforting me along the recovery road, how long my edema would likely last, and she suggested that I consult a specialized physician if it continued to six months. *Six months?! I'll kill myself before I reach six months like this,* I had thought. Yet there I was, with August winding down, approaching that semiannual mark as bloated as ever, with pain and exhaustion deep in my bones. On most days I couldn't stand how my body felt as well as the vague but very real disconnect in my marriage, which felt like a weak magnetic repulsion. Still, I was optimistic that I could take these issues by the reins and steer myself toward satisfaction. I made an appointment for me and Alex to meet with a couples' counselor and one for myself with an eating disorders specialist two hours away. I yearned for a diagnosis and a prognosis for it all.

Brewing was the fresh start of September, the release of stifling humidity so that I could breathe and create. Long after my life ceased to run on a school calendar, that palpable turn in autumn—which I once heard on a local radio program well described as the corner of the year—still ushered intellectual and emotional richness to me as the leaves fell. I was so alive then. I needed that pulse of energy, that sense of turning the corner in my recovery, especially after I smacked right into my thirty-fourth birthday.

During my early childhood, my mother ensured that my birthdays were filled with fanfare—a pile of gifts in the morning, a party with friends, a chocolate cake she made from a boxed mix but was nonetheless annual heaven—and the day was reserved for whatever I desired, sometimes as simple as catching a movie with my best friend and ordering my favorite kind of pizza for dinner. As an adult living on my own I quickly learned that I needed to craft my own birthday celebrations, often beginning one month ahead to narrow restaurant choices and request it as a vacation day of drifting around New York City and casually shopping for fall clothes. After the eating disorder set in, the day morphed into the promise of eating and drinking after a week of depleting my body enough to accommodate the wine, extravagant meal, and cake that I willed to expand in me enough to feel like the happiness I'd lost long ago.

Despite that summer's consuming physical and emotional pain, I had been convinced that by my birthday, a few days after the six-month mark in my recovery, I would energetically launch past the mailbox to canter into town like an excited dog and order a large pistachio ice cream cone for the return walk, with sunshine caressing the triumph of finally eating freely again and loving my body. That vision was so relentless and the magical thinking such a lifeline that less than a week before my birthday I still hadn't formed a plan B. I woke up, now thirty-four, and all my hopes smashed when my feet met the floor. I took that same stumbling walk across the bedroom to the light switch, feet stinging and numb, overnight in such deep repair they forgot how to carry me gracefully. Like how for a decade my first deliberate thought each morning had been the number of calories I could eat for breakfast, now I couldn't avoid the daily reminder, right after my legs swung out from beneath the sheets, that I was so broken. Alex encouraged me to choose a restaurant for a fancy lunch or dinner, but food was no longer enticingly mysterious. He ceremoniously presented to me and the kids a plate of cupcakes, one punctured with a lit candle, and I wished, as had been my wish for years, to be better by my next birthday, to let this coming year include the end to all the pain. But unlike the preceding years, my eyes didn't widen, and my mouth didn't salivate at the sight of fat and sugar calories concentrated and whirled into a taste and texture that would make my cells sing. It was just another cupcake, neither as rare as it was as a child nor as forbidden as it was as a young adult. I finally understood why many people don't care to do anything special on their birthdays; it was a day like any other.

I hadn't imagined the journey to be this excruciating, this interminable, this maze of stops and starts so far into a soul I had almost forgotten existed and never suspected to be so labyrinthine. Upon entering recovery, I had believed I had only to scrape off the scales of self-criticism and starvation, but in order to truly reclaim myself I had to remove the skin, the flesh, the muscle, down to the bone, which I was cracking open to suck the marrow of who I really was. I had to taste myself and accept that there was nothing else to be—but that knowledge was powerful. In our first session with the couples' therapist, I began revealing to Alex my dissatisfactions, especially my stockpiled resentment toward him for not taking care of me in the one way I had needed to be: to be kept from starving. Although what I did and did not put in my mouth was always my prerogative and at the time I wanted nothing more than to be left alone with that, in retrospect I wanted him to have at least tried to intervene or steer me toward help. I was no longer embarrassed or hesitant to admit that I expected that of my life partner. This descent into myself was rewarding me with an ascent that reminded me of climbing the final distance of Mount Christoffel in Curaçao with Alex several years prior. As my worn sneakers slipped on the smooth face, I tossed aside my fear and self-doubt along with the water bottle I no longer had a free hand with which to hold. Both there and in the therapist's office, I knew that I wouldn't turn back now, that I would pull myself up, up, and up.

I was riding momentum, and I wanted even more solitude to rest, ruminate, and write, the latter of which I had been approaching only when creativity simmered and the household grind hadn't already ground away my capacity to sit upright and string words together. I combed the Internet for local writers' retreats or a small, quiet space I could rent cheaply, and then I found what seemed like a dream—a house no more than ten minutes away that needed housesitting for one week. There I could sleep as long as my body needed, feed the owner's cat as my tea brewed, then sit down and write until the day's inspiration was tapped. I would try to keep their garden plants alive, and then my limbs, warmed and moistened under the sun, would lie limp and healing as I kneaded my realizations and metaphors into another journal entry after lunch. In the afternoon, when I'd had my fill of this active inactivity, I'd zip home to visit Alex and the kids for a few hours, and before the late-day madness set in at home I would skip off to feed their cat again, read for an hour, fall asleep, and do it all again. In my mind, it was perfect; I would be in another place sometimes, and at the house sometimes, just like Alex was, and my temporary second home didn't require rent. He could work from home that week or take some vacation time. The arrangement seemed reasonable and, to me, so delicious. I e-mailed him a link to the listing, which he ignored. The next morning I asked him about it.

"So, what do you think about the housesitting job I sent you? You didn't respond."

"Like you're going to leave here for a week? Yeah, I just deleted it." His attention returned to the steaming pan, my hope collapsing onto itself like the omelet he was folding. I was denied his blessing, but I didn't need his permission.

"Well, what if I just go ahead and do it? It's not like you wouldn't see me for an entire week. I would come back every day, but I would finally really get out of this crazy house and actually rest."

"No, you wouldn't come back, because if you leave I'm not letting you back in." My locked elbows and shoulders barely held me as I leaned against the counter for support. Recovery had essentially trapped me in the house, and now Alex seemed to be caging me there, too. "How could you abandon your family like that?"

I was so stunned I couldn't utter what I wanted to spit at him: *you get to be somewhere else four days of every week, which I would never call abandonment.*

I perceived how I was perceived—that is, the stark counterpoint to his breadwinning. Working in finance rather than publishing, Alex would always earn more than I. And as the parent primarily at home I had willingly assumed the job of ensuring that we never ran out of milk or toilet paper, but until then I hadn't considered our roles so polarized. I could see that to him my recovery and writing were extracurriculars, but to me, they were everything upon which my new self and my happiness with my family would be built. We seemed to be further in our separate corners than ever. I began to feel that maybe he should get off our mat altogether.

Perhaps he sensed a threatening shift in me because a couple of days later he booked for me a two-day solo retreat to the Mohonk Mountain House, a popular resort perched on a lake less than an hour away. At first I resisted because I would have to bail on some freelance jobs I'd just confirmed, and I didn't want to go somewhere known for its hiking, boating, and other activities too physically demanding for me. I wasn't enticed by the vision of sitting alone in a hotel room while the other guests frolicked in the late summer sun; I would probably just feel worse about my situation. And why did Alex believe that an expensive, all-inclusive mini vacation was a fantastic idea, while a week of local housesitting was outrageous?

I didn't ask, and I convinced myself to stop looking that gift horse in the mouth, because nonetheless this was an opportunity to finally escape the house for longer than a few hours. With the included spa credit I booked a calf and foot massage, and I packed my writing materials, camera, music, and book. I didn't care that I was probably the only guest without a companion in tow throughout the entire mammoth place, which was an amusing amalgam of the sets of *Dirty Dancing* and *The Shining*. I didn't care that I ate lunch and dinner alone at the bar. I was alone. Finally, blissfully, alone. There was no running around and no whiny demands, and with my most strenuous jaunt a wandering into the gardens to photograph the blooms, there was almost no pain in my legs, feet, and hands. From the rocking chair on my room's private veranda I watched the copper sun disappear behind the mountains, and I breathed more deeply and slowly as I returned inside, which was my own space, silent and organized. I awoke too early for breakfast to be delivered, but I had packed some trail mix to hold me during those two mornings as I finished the first chapter of my book, writing without the threat of squealing from the kids' rooms or the clock telling me it was time to jump in the shower. I was reclaiming my inner and outer landscapes. Under the right conditions, I could write, I could rest, and I could endure less pain. I grew hopeful that, with the right guidance, Alex and I could get our marriage on the right track, that it could be molded into what I needed it to be. After just two days of seclusion, the end seemed possible.

The day after I returned home, the final day of August, I drove two and a half hours under the assault of a ninety-five-degree sun to meet Dr. Mehta, the eating disorders specialist whom Sil expected could give me a prognosis for my ailments and possibly a strategy or medication for managing them. A week earlier, Dr. Mehta had ordered a half-dozen vials of blood drawn to test for vitamin deficiencies, thyroid imbalances, autoimmune disorders, rheumatoid arthritis, and more. On the long drive to the appointment I fantasized that she would read the lab reports and diagnose me with a rare complication of recovery, some minor quantity gone awry that was making my symptoms worse than they ever needed to be, something that could be easily corrected with a daily pill. I was sure that this was all coming to a head, that I was reaching the summit, and I just needed her expert knowledge and proactivity to nudge me over the edge. I was determined to begin the fresh September with energy and vigor and clothes that fit a body I recognized and accepted. This appointment would be the exhilarating climax of my recovery process. I was sure of it.

Since I was meeting a psychiatrist, as I trooped down the halls to Dr. Mehta's office I reminded myself to be honest but seem upbeat enough that she wouldn't push for an antidepressant. As despondent as I was about the state of my body and increasingly about my marriage, my current emotional state was nothing compared to the paralyzing hopelessness and perpetual mental loops of self-starvation. Having both survived and dragged myself out of anorexia, I was confident I could continue to handle the gnarly aftermath, which Sil was successfully helping me keep in check. Most of all, I had finally reclaimed every corner of my brain and wanted nothing dulled ever again.

But I would have struggled to seem sad and listless in Dr. Mehta's presence: she turned out to be one of the most jubilant, effervescent people I'd ever met, and not at all what I expected. I couldn't imagine how she could be so full of laughter and bubbling conversation in the middle of her day as chief of a hospital eating disorders unit, but I suppose that was her appeal—I was set immediately at ease, and I wanted some of her contentment. I would inch close to her, hoping to surreptitiously swipe a lick of that frosting.

Fluttering around her cramped office in her bright shawl and gold jewelry, Dr. Mehta grabbed her notepad and turned serious, asking a stream of questions to glean my history and current condition. She asked me to rate my anxiety and depression on a scale of one to ten, which I knew was helping her gauge whether I would benefit from medication, so I gave the former a three and the latter a five—as accurate a guess as any, really, when applying numerical values to amorphous emotional states. Then she examined my feet and calves, palpating different areas and then grasping gently for a few seconds, which was her test for the edema I was complaining about. Dr. Mehta pointed to the bright white areas that her fingertips left on my skin and identified the phenomenon as mere "blanching" but not true edema. Whatever it was, the square legs of the kitchen stool, around which I tended to absentmindedly wind my legs while at my laptop, still left deep indentations in my calves for at least an hour, and even gentle self-massage generated soreness. Maybe I didn't look like the Michelin Man, but I was still swollen.

Then she suggested I try Cymbalta to alleviate the joint and bone pain. The name conjured an old advertisement featuring a woman too depressed to play with her droopy-eyed dog, and I suspected Dr. Mehta was tricking me into taking an antidepressant. She insisted that, while Cymbalta was technically an SNRI—a serotonin-norepinephrine reuptake inhibitor, a class of drugs often prescribed for anxiety or depression—it has helped her own mother's arthritis pain, which sounded promising for my own flares. I politely replied that I would think about it, but inside I balked at altering, muffling, or distancing myself from my thoughts, emotions, and other mental processes, my reconnection with which was key not only to my recovery but to living authentically henceforth.

I was also worried about weight gain, which is notoriously associated with SNRIs, as I could scarcely tolerate the size my body already was. She claimed that this drug did not cause weight gain, that it probably wouldn't affect my weight at all. I was incredulous, since I knew that these drugs' mechanisms tap into the very delicate balance of receptors that are involved in fat storage. The other possibility flashed in my brain: This might be an antidepressant that facilitates weight loss.[41] *You can lose some of this extra weight and still be recovering! If a specialist says it's okay, then you should go for it!* The giddy hiss of the eating disorder was louder than Dr. Mehta's melodious voice, and I was appalled. Even after six months with no such thoughts, there I was, as tempted by the magic of effortless weight loss as a year ago I had been by the low digestibility of raw almonds. For a moment I was ashamed, but then instinctively I turned self-compassionate and reminded myself that I was walking on a road with only six months of tread, that just a step to the left was another that was ten years deep. For a while I might occasionally stumble over the edge of that crevice, but as long as I recognized that I had stepped into the wrong track and corrected myself, I was still moving forward. I cordially told Dr. Mehta that I would have to go home and think about the Cymbalta, but inside I knew that I didn't want anything knocking me off balance.

Finally she turned to the lab results, the sole peek inside my body since I began recovery, and one that could reveal I'd been suffering unnecessarily. She dug through precarious piles of papers and files, and after her "a-ha!" I held my breath.

"Good news! All your labs came back normal." I exhaled and everything in me slumped. "These values might not be entirely normal for *you*, but there's no sign of disease, so I'm just going to prescribe you some vitamins—some calcium, vitamin D, vitamin E—because no matter what these say your body still needs more as it recovers. Does that sound okay? Do you have any questions about that?"

And there it was: there was nothing "extra" that was wrong with me. My muscles, my bones, my layer of fat were simply doing what they needed to do, just repairing loudly and explicitly. But it couldn't last forever. "Yes, I do. From your experience, about how much longer do you think I'll be in this?" *A month? Three at most?*

"Well, there really aren't many people with eating disorders who recover like you have . . ." I knew she was right, that most sufferers simply manage the condition, choosing an acceptable weight to maintain but always restricting and obsessing for the rest of their lives. I was one of the few brave ones who would tear it all down in order to build myself up again. "You're in a special group, and the pain you're experiencing is what is sometimes called 'post-recovery syndrome.' I'd say you probably have another six months."

---

[41] M. Hasnain, W. V. R. Vieweg, and B. Hollett, "Weight gain and glucose dysregulation with second-generation antipsychotics and antidepressants: a review for primary care physicians, *Postgraduate Medicine* 124, no. 4 (2012): 154–167.

Six: the clank of a barred gate. *Months:* the smooth tock of a key locking it. I didn't hear much after that. Eventually she handed over my vitamin prescriptions and in a daze I pushed out of the hospital, into the late-afternoon inferno of the last-chance heat wave. *Yes, you're still in hell, kid.* I may have been released from the maximum-security prison of anorexia, but I still wasn't truly living. I could eat freely, not obsess over food, and not weigh myself or ingredients, but I was trapped in another body I didn't recognize, in another kind of pain. If I hadn't traded one prison for another, at best I was in a halfway house. Regardless, I was only halfway finished with my probation.

Driving home, I was demolished. Ever since I had passed the two-month mark of recovery with persisting edema, I had been banking on the seeming certainty that I was always closer to the finish line than I was to the beginning, that the worst was always over, that I just had to make that final sprint and I would be done. But the doctor who was supposed to take it all away with a pill or tell me I'd be in jeans by the time flip-flops went into hibernation for that coming winter had instead pulled that finish line further back than I'd ever felt possible. She had in fact told me what I wanted to hear—that I had reached the summit—but I hadn't considered the climb down, that it would take just as long. The past six months had been brutal, and I couldn't imagine what could befall me next. I couldn't sustain the surprise or grin and bear any new pain.

I was yanked to a place I thought well out of my mental reach: the undertow of restriction, the temptation to halt construction on my scaffolded body, which didn't seem any more difficult or destructive to my happiness than continuing the journey of recovery. I could simply take that Cymbalta, lose the aches in my legs and feet and hands and arms, possibly lose the weight that reminded me with every movement that I wasn't really myself, and put all that nonsense behind me. In my current state I couldn't even enjoy mini-golfing with my kids because the sun boiled the water under my skin and my mending feet cared not to hold me up for that long. Surged with guilt, I felt like I had barely played with my kids for the past half year because I was so busy resting, resting, resting. Waiting, waiting. Waiting to live.

But after I reversed six months of recovery, where would I be? At the pantry, a stick of a woman staring glassy-eyed at the cookies and nuts for which her body screamed, negotiating with the eating disorder for just one granola bar to get her through the night—that's where. Restriction had been and would never be sustainable, the physical and mental trend would always be down, and that path would end unavoidably with the complete decimation of my body and family, with decades of misery ahead, if I survived that long. Instead of writing my book I would be on my exercise machines every early morning, afternoon, and anytime I wanted to eat. I would have to tell everyone that recovery was too tough to continue, that I changed my mind, that my interim body was just too much to handle, that I'd rather increase the risk that my children would develop horrifying eating disorders of their own, simply by my example. I would not only toss off my throbs and edema; I would give up everything.

And that was too much.

I recalled that after a few holes on that mini-golf course I had grown hot and tired, and when I realized that there were eighteen rather than nine holes total I wanted nothing but to retreat to the car and sit in the air conditioning while Alex and the kids finished the game. I didn't think I could handle those unexpected nine additional holes, but I also couldn't walk away and let my kids believe that I didn't want to be with them. I stayed and dragged my body through, dreading that the pain would accumulate until I collapsed in tears. However, the second half was not more difficult than the first. There were moments of shade and benches, moments of laughter, and then the end came.

I recognized that the end of recovery would come, too, but only if I continued the path, as dark and cold and ugly as it may be. The only way out was through. But to survive it all I needed to move through the world as my new self, even if I was still becoming her. I acknowledged that the maddening frustration of my recovery resided not so much in the physical slog of it, but in the waiting, the waiting to live.

5

With my fingers so puffy, my wedding rings had been hibernating in my jewelry box since the spring. On my left hand I'd instead been wearing a lackluster thin band with miniscule faux diamonds that I dug out of the bottom of that box. I'd felt crestfallen that I had to wear it on our Paris anniversary trip, but I deemed it only a stopgap that would be over any minute now, much like the shirts I'd worn a hundred times already, the few pair of underwear that didn't pinch me, the shoes that did for the first few minutes, and my swollen body in general. Investing in new clothes and accessories had seemed like a concession to the potential interminability or at least longevity of recovery. I had been certain it would all be over any minute now, *any minute now*, right before I, or that old gauzy skirt, seared with one rip too many to mend.

But Dr. Mehta's prognosis released me from the holding pattern, from spending the second six months holding my breath; rather, I would live as it unfolded, as slowly as it may. Studying the contents of my jewelry box I noted that every ring had been purchased by someone else, that I had simply slid onto my finger and flaunted with my gesticulations something didn't necessarily reflect me, just what someone else thought did. For the first time, I would choose my own ring. Browsing online I was immediately drawn to my birthstone, green peridot, which as a child I found disappointing as I longed for October's pink tourmaline or February's regal amethyst. But that color of young spring leaves had already been penetrating my adult world—the color I chose for our bedroom, the mug for my morning tea—and when the sizable oval stone set in silver arrived in the mail it seemed just right on my finger, a reclamation of my birth month, my root, who I was. It better encapsulated my new self than my diamond engagement ring, at which I had once stared and stared, entranced by its crystalline perfection, but now appeared too contained, square, cold, empty.

The refurbished me, even still in progress, was—like my new ring—larger, softer on the edges, infinitely more colorful, flashier, more unique. The new me was worth celebrating. I had finally uncovered true pride in the recovery process. And, although it was only a tickle, I sensed that this new marriage, the one with the once-fractured soul within, had begun outshining the one I had with Alex.

September escorted the year through its dramatic turn into autumn. Alex and I shepherded Charlie to kindergarten. Somehow, during those six years when I was restricting and recovering, he had grown into a fully minted boy who could board a bus and follow directions for an entire school day. The next morning I was in an ambulance with Josie, rubbing her leg and arm and begging the universe for her to be fine after she ingested an ultimately harmless amount of our babysitter's blood pressure medication. Life outside my recovery bubble shot into high relief, refusing to be ignored, and I was right there, no longer too fragile to engage.

A week later, as Alex drove us home after our annual family apple-picking jaunt—with hay tangled in our shoes and a brief sense of contentment in the minivan—the girls champed on the spoils and Charlie recounted the adventure with glee. "Did you see how many we got? Remember when Daddy got that big stick and got the apples high up!" But Alex was quiet and fidgety, pushing his palm over his scalp and squirming in his seat, reaching for his water bottle twice a minute. I knew what was happening; it had been happening increasingly over the past year.

"I need to pull over" rushed out of his mouth, and we were swiftly parked in the road's shoulder. Silently he and I switched seats, and I told the kids that Daddy felt like he might throw up. As I drove us the rest of the way home, I wondered about these panic attacks. At first they had been hitting only when he drove at night on highways, and his explanation was that he was tired, that he was becoming entranced by the lines on the highway and afraid that he'd fall asleep at the wheel. But now they were also striking during the day on two-lane roads. So far he had been deft enough to stop the car until he was okay or someone else could drive, but I feared that one day he might not be so lucky, and some of us could be in the car with him when that occurred.

After the kids bounded into the house, we hauled bags of apples into the kitchen and I draped Alex with a gaze of concern. He exhaled. "I've just been staying up too late. I read that can make these things worse. I have a few drinks to unwind and read or watch TV after you all go to bed, and then I end up being extra tired in the morning. It's a bad cycle."

"Yeah, it's definitely a bad cycle and it worries me a lot, especially since this involves panicking while you're behind the wheel. I wonder if maybe we can get some help with this."

"No, it's fine. Just let me handle it. I can figure it out. It will be fine."

I hoped he could indeed get to the bottom of it, or at least this could be a discussion with Paula, the couples' counselor we had begun seeing once a month. He was clearly not open to substantial action yet, so I let the topic dissolve. I spent the afternoon resting my legs from their march through the orchard, and online I ordered a few more long sweaters and shape-concealing skirts and leggings to wear underneath, preparing for the long haul through fall and winter, which I began to perceive as a purposeful time. The inflammation was transforming from a torture mechanism into a mere reminder that my soul was still working through it all, that its job for the next six months—or who knows, perhaps even a year, which had become a tolerable prospect—was to delve and contemplate, sit and grow, do it thoroughly and right.

A couple of days later was the eleventh anniversary of 9/11. Every year I recalled my experience of that day: my first full week at a new job in Soho; emerging from the subway to New Yorkers pointing toward smoke further downtown and saying something about a plane, a terrible accident, the Twin Towers. Just three weeks earlier I had watched window washers ascend the sides of those skyscrapers through the tall window next to my former desk at my previous job on Cortlandt Street.

The second plane hadn't yet struck, and then it did. The first tower fell as I was returning to my cubicle from the wall of windows where so many of my new coworkers watched the burning buildings. The collective gasp was a rising, sick chord, and then there was only the staccato of wails. A woman announced to my floor that our building was being evacuated immediately, that we shouldn't worry about collecting our belongings, but I did, anyway, predicting I wouldn't be coming back that day.

In the promising, slightly cool September morning sunshine, weather that couldn't have been more incongruous with the day's events, seemingly all of New York proceeded with me uptown, away from disaster, not that I knew where I would go. On my portable CD player's radio I heard that the second tower fell, and strangers exchanged glances of condolence and horror: the world seemed to be over. I walked up to 14th Street in the hope of catching a subway far enough from the fray to still be running and take me home to Brooklyn, but all had been closed down. I found a less congested avenue, turned against the tide, and pushed south through the irony of approaching the smoke and fire that every teary, shaken face I passed was determined to escape. I was disoriented and needed simply to get off burning, falling Manhattan, so I approached the first bridge to the east I saw. Crossing the gray water and under the impossibly blue sky, I was more alarmed than ever. *They could blow up the bridges next. This could be how I die.* I wanted to run for my life, but I couldn't move any faster than the plodding wall of Brooklynites, my heart pounding twice for each step we all took. Not until we arrived on safer ground and I found myself among hatted and bearded men did I realize I had taken the wrong bridge and was in Williamsburg's Hasidic enclave. My bridge comrades quickly found buses to take them home, and I was left with the Jewish men who would not give me directions in English if they didn't outright ignore me. But I knew my neighborhood was south, so with the sun's orientation I headed in that direction until I stumbled upon some recognizable streets, spending a total of four and a half hours walking back to the apartment I had just begun sharing with Alex and Megan, my best friend of a decade but not much longer, once anorexia stripped me and she and I grew in disparate directions.

I was very lucky—I didn't know anyone killed that day, and I was able to take the subway to work not even a week afterward, but something in me, and likely many New Yorkers, had cracked. My sense of security in my city home was rattled. Going about my respectful day of working and throwing all trash in the baskets at every street corner and saying "please" and "thank you" to every clerk didn't in fact earn me safety. We were all dreadfully vulnerable.

Back at work the next week, Valeria was increasingly perceiving not my efforts and talents but rather an inflated severity of any mistake I made as I heaved myself up the learning curve of an unfamiliar role in a sprawling company. And sometimes she lashed me for missteps that weren't mine. I was in strange territory, indeed, as no matter how hard I worked, I was always in the line of fire, those planes. As I reflected on that time, I could see how anxiety had cemented in me. Even after Alex got down on his knee a month later to ask me to marry him and I elatedly said yes, I still didn't feel safe and loved enough. I had to be smaller, not only for my wedding dress but to dodge the things coming after me. And by divorcing my body from the rest of myself, I had numbed my flesh to the things that did, silently, hit.

Eleven years later, I pulled on one of the flouncy one-size-fits-all skirts that had arrived in the mail. But the placement of gatherings was strange, or the material perhaps not accommodating enough, because the wideness of my hips and butt seemed to be emphasized rather than concealed. I waited for my panicked eyes to simmer down and deem that I looked fine enough, that I wasn't suddenly fat, for goodness' sake. But my doubt wasn't waning, so I decided I better choose something else for the day. Scanning my closet, I missed the simplicity of pants—entering a car without loose cotton twisting and bunching around me and catching in the door frame—so I chose the one pair I had purchased and worn in the early spring. Back then they eventually became a bit too snug, but I was certain that my weight had remained stable, so those pants should fit as they had last. Stepping just my calves into the leg holes I knew that experiment was a mistake—my tactile memory told me that the material was already touching me more than it had before—but something, perhaps the last gasps of the eating disorder, encouraged me to continue. *C'mon, let's see just how fat you are now.* I tugged the pants by the waistband, but they wouldn't budge past the middle of my thighs. I yanked them off and trooped in a circle in front of my closet, breathing fast and shallow, tears streaming. Somehow during the season of loose skirts I hadn't noticed this slow, continued expansion, which seemed likely due not only to water for repair but also fat stores in excess of what my body naturally held. I had been somewhat prepared for this, having learned that some in recovery do overshoot their set points temporarily, not as a result of excess calories but the body's own mechanisms for repair, and they eventually slide down to their natural size without restriction.[42] However, as if the universe doles out life justly, I had believed that the pain and edema were enough of a cross in recovery, that I wouldn't have to bear an "overshoot," too. My mind had long written that my path was to rest as much as possible to allow my body to heal all the damage, and then the water would instantaneously release, revealing the "real" me. But now tacked onto that was the time my body would need to molt however much extra fat I ultimately gained. My immediate reaction was resistance and resentment, which I knew wouldn't help me. I knew I had to learn to embrace the slowness and unpredictability of it all, but I didn't know how. As I waited for wisdom, I turned to my writing.

With the additional time I reaped from the resumption of school schedules, and staying true to my September commitment to live as joyfully and productively as possible through the unknown duration of my transformation, I began writing not just when I felt energized—by which method the first draft of the first chapter took an entire four months—but every single day, for even just three hundred words, as Anne Lamott's delicious advice for writers in *Bird by Bird* presented as a perfectly acceptable way to produce. For me, these short bursts of writing were optimal, especially with such emotionally dense and intense material that often wore me out after just a half hour at the keyboard. Already a morning person, I simply shifted my sleep schedule a bit earlier, and well before anyone else in the house could possibly stir, I sat in the kitchen, tea and trail mix at my side, to bleed out a short section each black morning. Even if my body was

---

[42] "Frequently Asked Questions," *The Eating Disorder Institute,* accessed October 11, 2017, https://www.edinstitute.org/faq/.

debilitated with pain and exhaustion after getting myself and the kids ready and off for the day, and if after accomplishing a bit of paid proofreading all I could do was spend the quiet hours of the late morning and early afternoon lounging on the couch, reading, listening to music, and dozing, I felt content in my meager accomplishment, in the knowledge that each parcel of writing—each "one-inch picture frame," as Lamott brilliantly describes the focus—would merge with the next. In just a month I was printing out a draft of the second chapter to mark up with my red pencil.

In my writing I became a happy, confident tortoise, slow and steady, and my next task was to place that lens over the entire recovery process. I began to perceive that each day, as long as I ate and rested, my body was also writing its single page of repair, each day patching up another one-inch hole inside me. I unfocused my eyes, which had been trained on the agony of yet another day, another month passed, another season entered without a drop of balloons and confetti from the ceiling that signaled the end. Instead, I accepted that I had a prescription to swallow—eat, write, rest—and after the day's pill was down I tried to live as normally and cheerfully as possible. I knew from my logical brain down to my most intuitive, soulful level that I would get there, in my body's own time, if I kept moving forward in this way. This was not patience; that was the waiting to live. This was its darker sister, surrender. With her I was unclenching my stranglehold on uncontrollable forces, and I began living in the knitted space of what life could be and what life just plain is.

I was now reveling in my process, of which my social circle was supportive and encouraging, although the subject felt strained between me and my mother. During our weekly phone calls she often asked how recovery was progressing—not inquiring into my emotional healing, but questioning just the physical symptoms.

"So how is the fluid? Are you still puffy and sore?"

"Yes, pretty much the same, but I just have to keep doing what I'm doing and be patient. It's a slow process. There's a lot of damage."

"Well, this fluid retention really worries me, especially since it's been going on for so long. I know you saw that specialist and she said it's okay, but I'm still concerned. Maybe you need to drink more water?"

I knew she just wanted me to be healthy and not have to suffer any longer than necessary, but in that new place of surrender, this felt like a second-guessing of my body, of my entire self. These exchanges also confirmed why I hadn't until that point appreciated the beauty of process: I hadn't been taught it—not by my parents, or other adults, or even society in general. This nudging, watching, and unfolding was right in front of our faces, in every flower we stopped to admire, but when applied to our own growth somehow it was disregarded as an excessively snaky road that we could easily avoid by strapping on wings and traveling instead as the crow flies. But the slow, scenic, often confounding route is where we may find the real healing.

"No, Mom . . . it's not that kind of water retention. This is like an injury swelling, but on a full-body scale. It helps the healing along, and it will go away when everything is finished. Drinking extra water isn't going to do anything, and I've already tried that, anyway."

"I don't know. Maybe you should see another doctor about this if it doesn't go away. And what about the weight? Has it shifted yet?"

The weight. Has it shifted off me? This was a seemingly innocuous question, and one that I couldn't deny having asked a pair of pants, but coming from her it incited something inside me. At that smoldering moment, the necessary shifting was to another topic of conversation.

"Since any extra is mostly the swelling, and I don't weigh myself anymore, I don't know for sure but I'd say I'm pretty much the same as I've been lately. So, anyway, what did you and Dad do this weekend?"

Shortly we hung up, and I no longer had to wonder where I'd learned that my body was an "other," something in the way rather than a wonderfully functional vehicle and self-healing vessel for all I am and what I can accomplish. I didn't grow up with a scale in the bathroom, but my mother had often lamented her thighs, her belly, how she looked in a bathing suit—the relentless criticism of the body that our culture ingrains in so many women. And now she asked about the "weight," like a separate mass that she believed only burdened me, when in fact that extra had also been my freedom. The pain and exhaustion and swelling often made my body feel to me like a petulant daughter going through an adolescent phase so challenging that I had grown sick of her, but when another disparaged her, I ran to her defense, proclaiming us one and the same.

I could sense the pieces of myself fusing, that I was welcoming rather than alienating parts I had wanted to cut off. In my afternoon hours of convalescence on the couch, after flipping through dissatisfying television programs, I searched my heart for more of them. I recalled a moment a few months into my and Alex's dating at age twenty-two, when I could no longer pretend for the sake of protecting his ego fresh to the world of relationships that I didn't have a series of other romances behind me. I was falling in love with Alex and wanted to share all of myself with him, and in my youthful naiveté that included the knowledge of how many sex partners I'd had and with which of my male friends I had previously had other kinds of dynamics. Although at the time I didn't fully understand why I was compelled to share this information, I was trying to invite Alex into the center of me, where I engaged deeply with other hearts, where feelings lingered, morphed, dissipated, reappeared, where relationships were often not strictly romantic or platonic but slid along a continuum of positive regard, where he currently and perhaps permanently held the most amorous position but was never the only one. I didn't get far through my history; he cut me off after I described my very first boyfriend, Danny. I explained to him that after that early high school "relationship," Danny and I maintained a casual friendship, but less than a year before I met Alex, he and I also shared an intense sexual encounter at the end of a night of a few beers when we both happened to be home from college. That night was an unprecedented event for me, an act that on the surface was out of character but in the black, quiet well of my soul, which cares nothing for propriety, was a precise and profound expression of the connection Danny and I shared. Until that conversation with Alex, I had told no one about that only time I was with Danny in such a way, fearing that in the end I was really just a slut, or so desperate that I would sleep with anyone who could fulfill me in some way. I wanted Alex to know who I was and to embrace how passionate I could be, but he shut down the conversation, stating that he simply didn't want to hear any more.

It stung, but I brushed that rebuff under the heavy rug of the flourishing young love between me and Alex. After just three months, we had proclaimed that the other was "the one," so I convinced myself that my string of previous liaisons wasn't all that relevant, anyway, that he was probably just uncomfortable because he didn't have any similar stories to share, that I wasn't going to mar my first successful adult relationship with a likely immaterial past. So, when the eating disorder sunk in its claws less than a year later, it sought not only to lend control through pain I could turn up at will—like pinching the thin webbing between your thumb and forefinger to distract from the bleeding gash on your leg—but offer a way to eradicate the undesirable parts of me, to starve away the very human fleshiness and messiness of my fluctuating desire for others, the sense that no one person would fulfill me in every way for my entire life. The anorexia whittled me down to that supremely thin woman beaming in a glimmering wedding dress. I didn't understand at the time that I had been complicit in the denial of self, that I had submitted to what I interpreted as his desire that I be pure for him, to pay what seemed a small price for calling an end to the dating hunt and win for life the first young man, and a great one, who could commit to me. But the price was a woman not fully formed.

Now, without the eating disorder stonewalling me from my soul, I hungered for those long-denied affections for, affiliations with, and reflections of others in myself. I was driven to reconnect with these men when a hazy emotional or spiritual need gripped me, as had happened with Matteo. These were brief, nonromantic exchanges that resuscitated intangible parts that had been just as starving as my body; they were steps I had to take to become whole. Although they weren't really infidelities, I still felt obliged to keep these interactions a secret from Alex. I was fearful that he would at best not relate or sympathize and at worst feel threatened, rejected, angry, or hurt. But I also felt that, if he and I were ever to meld in all the ways I now needed to be with a partner, if we were ever to be truly emotionally and sexually intimate, I needed him to hear who I was, who I always had been, and accept it without judgment.

During our next couples' therapy session, Alex agreed not only to begin meeting with Paula on his own, which I believed would be more vital to reviving our relationship than the joint sessions, but also to listen to my relationship history when I was ready to describe it. I was jubilant. *Now we're going to get somewhere.* Whenever we both seemed ready for that moment, I needed for him to understand that, at least for me, relationships are not a disjointed collection of short stories in which the fires and moods of each tale are snuffed when the next begins, the figures inconsequential to the subsequent tales. Instead, since childhood my heart had been expanding like a slowly blooming novel with characters who might disappear for a long while, only to deepen and reemerge hundreds of pages later in a different capacity or angle to me. Although Alex might be threatened by that truth, I wanted him to know, if he was to really know me, there have always been, and always would be, others. This was not polyamory, but they were always lurking in corners of my heart that he would never touch, no matter how much he may eventually welcome all of me; they were representations of embryonic intra-selves that needed nurturing in order to develop and enhance the whole of me.

Meanwhile, the next Saturday I sat at my desk wearing no better clothes or makeup than what I would on any lazy day and took some snapshots of myself. I needed a photo for my brand-new Twitter profile, which I hoped would generate an audience for my writing. In the winning shot the morning sunlight cast glowing and dark areas on my face, brightening my eyes to a turquoise that contrasted their pensiveness within my dark red eyeglass frames, my lips slightly tensed, perhaps about to speak or kiss. It was an odd photo, really, and although I didn't think I looked all that cute, among all the angles and expressions I tried that morning it struck me as the most reflective of who I was at the time. I wasn't here to smile and be pretty for everyone, to keep life light and easy. I was writing about what was real, and with the half-blind bravery of diving off a cliff before considering what could actually happen, I was putting my words and experiences online for strangers, my extended family, and acquaintances. I was out there, and that photo fit me.

A few days later, Alex praised me for setting up the account and using hashtags and other Twitter conventions without his computer-savvy assistance. Then he qualified, "But I don't like that picture you're using."

I had received a few compliments from friends on the photo, so I was mystified. "What's wrong with it?"

He shuttled around the kitchen, putting away the previous night's dried dishes. "It doesn't look like you. Your lips—they're too red, or just too *there*. I don't know. Your skin looks blotchy. I just don't like it." He closed the silverware drawer and met my eyes. "It looks ho-ey."

He was telling me I looked kind of like a whore. I felt slapped across the face, admonished for being repugnant to him, embarrassing, unacceptable. The self-assured, recovery-fed me wanted to slap him right back by telling him to wake up, that I wasn't hiding myself anymore, from him or anyone else, so he better start getting used to it. I was growing to accept myself as neither Madonna nor whore, but Alex seemed to continue to perceive me as the pristine woman in the white wedding dress, with eyes and lips only for him forever. I pressed him gently to elaborate, to explain precisely how I was sexy and awful.

The jumpiness in his voice settled. "It's too sexual. I probably wouldn't mind so much that you're putting it out there like that if I were getting it from you myself."

It was true—I'd barely let him kiss me in the past three months, and he was understandably frustrated and maybe worried that I was searching for someone else. But I also sensed a clash between his yearning to see all of me and his wanting to continue to dismiss the parts that were disconcerting, the willingness to claim all of me for himself only by the threat of someone else snatching it, like children among toys. Or perhaps he simply wanted to be at least as emotionally intimate with me as I was now with friends, even strangers. Nonetheless, that photograph revealed a wall that had likely always been there.

I retreated to our bedroom and opened the file, bracing myself to see what he did, a desperate and grotesque hypersexuality. But the image was the same as I recalled it: just me, with a complicated expression both intense and distracted, both grinding a thought in my head and inviting the viewer in, all illuminated by a rich contrast of light. There was the whole of me, greater than my parts.

On October 13, our tenth wedding anniversary, I expected a rush of achievement and affection, an aftershock of the closeness I felt toward Alex in Paris, but instead I felt awkward and forced to pretend that everything was fine, and better than fine—that I should have sex with him, the first time since we had been drunk on French wine thousands of miles away from our real life longer than three months ago. That Saturday should have been special, and his parents were babysitting so we could enjoy a romantic restaurant dinner, but I wanted it to pass as quickly as possible. I spent hours at my desk, posting inspirational musings on recovery on Twitter and tinkering with the next chapter of my book. The thick white frame of the window behind my laptop screen was my blinder to the rest of the bedroom, the bed, the man I married ten years earlier, who stood over a small heap of laundry to be folded. He wanted to know what my problem was. I replied honestly, "It's a weird day to have when things aren't so great." He stormed out of the room and out of the house.

I was still organizing little socks when he shoved through the doorway, jacket still on, and planted himself a foot into our bedroom, eyes fiery with defiance. "Either you let me in, or you let me go," he boomed, his pronouncement suspending my gaze.

I was electrified by the panic of the options, the bolt of truth through my heart. These were indeed the choices. But neither of which I was yet capable of making. And I doubted he would go through with such an ultimatum. Beyond the frenzy of the moment I could sense we were only at the stage of pointing out the baby elephant meandering softly among the rooms, which would grow and eventually demand a reckoning.

As the alarm subsided, relief rinsed me: he felt it, too, that the current state of our marriage was certainly not acceptable and neither of us was willing to continue in a relationship that could not be made fulfilling. And I was impressed that he was capable of cutting it off. Alex continued, "I don't know how long I can wait for you to stop resenting me."

"Good, because I can't wait forever, either." I wondered if the course would be determined by impatience followed by resignation, now that both of us were focused on our requirements for the relationship—and mine was that he evolve into a man I might one day forgive for turning a blind eye to my near-destroying myself. I leaned against the bed, hand in a jumble of toddler pajamas, in a standoff with my husband, waiting for who would give in or walk away first. *So this is how it ends.* It was breathtaking, like a roller coaster paused before the first steep drop.

But it slid back as Alex slipped into the persona he sometimes donned during charged conversations: the little boy who wanted simply not to be rejected, so similar to the little girl in me who wanted all of her to be cherished. He searched my face with huge, trembling, soaked eyes. "Please . . . I love you, and I just want you to love me. Please don't leave me." He choked on his sobs. "Please, we need to make this work. If we can't, I don't know what I'm going to—"

His voice collapsed into heaving cries, and his body into the rocking chair. The mother in me wanted to scoop him up into my arms and soothe him; the wife, lover, and warrior wanted to tell him to grow up or get out. I held his slippery face and offered assurance. "I want to get there, too, and hopefully we will, if we keep going to therapy and working on ourselves individually. But we also have to remember that it's been only a few months, and we have to be patient. If there's anything I've learned in recovery, it is that these things are long processes, but we'll get there." I kissed the top of his head. "I love you, too, and I always will."

He asked if he could kiss me. I hadn't wanted that for months, but it was our anniversary, and I wanted to try, to push myself for the sake of our marriage. I nodded yes, and as he his head tilted and his lips approached mine I thought, *Just forget all this stuff. Relax. Let yourself feel something.* As our lips moved in their usual rhythm I waited for a tickle in my body or my brain, even just of warm companionship, but there was nothing—just an odd smooshing between myself and a man I wasn't sure about anymore. I felt indifference. From the pit of my soul blared a deep reverberation: *This isn't working; this isn't working.* It rose into my throat, seeping into my mouth. Invaded with disgust for the kiss and for him, but wanting no more drama that day, I pulled away gently. We exchanged shy smiles and I proceeded to the closet to choose a cute outfit for our dinner date.

This repulsion I didn't yet understand, especially since Alex and I did get along so well in many ways. A scratchy voice inside often advised me to just shut up and be grateful for a man who was an excellent father and generally very good to me, to stop questioning and criticizing it all to death. That voice made valid points, but it also wanted me to stop moving toward the truth, to stop reclaiming myself, to say this was enough, that the rest of the road was too dark and dangerous. But the body does not lie. I would have felt something when he kissed me. And I wondered if it was just coincidence that a layer of pain in my body lifted away so soon after I allowed myself to bathe in that truth. For many months I had started each morning with shrill pins and needles in my feet as I hoisted my body onto them, an immediate and harsh reminder that another day would consist of the agonies of recovery, and then I would stumble on those numb yet burning feet across the room to the light switch. But now that sensation dissipated after just a few steps and my shoes were no longer snug in the morning. The swelling was going down. The release had begun.

During one of our sessions, Sil recommended that I read Susan Cain's *Quiet: The Power of Introverts in a World That Can't Stop Talking.* I often took up her book suggestions, and in this case I looked forward to a boost of pride for what I suspected was my mild introversion or what I believed that meant—that I was more comfortable spending time with one friend rather than many at once, that I preferred individual to group projects, and that I generally thrived in solitude, often alone but hardly ever lonely. I considered it a social disposition and not one that debilitated me, since I could maintain a lively conversation with acquaintances and I was usually comfortable reaching out to others. But, as I learned in *Quiet*, this hardwiring has deep roots and great reach, since at the core of this temperament is a low threshold for overstimulation. I began to understand that my impatience with my children's unavoidable noise and messiness, along with my lifelong impulse to run away from a busy day and lie on my bed with headphones plugged in my ears, were simply my need for retreat to a calm, controlled environment. Ever since Charlie's birth six years earlier, I'd been cringing at the unpredictable cries and destroyed order of the house, which only escalated as he grew and then his sisters entered and intensified the fray. I'd been ashamed of myself as well as envious of other parents who could seemingly take all the kid chaos in stride, whereas anxiety frothed in my chest and I occasionally burst and hollered at my children, a desperate attempt to smooth the waves that were crashing relentlessly on the beach of my sanity. I adored my kids, but I was happiest when they were sitting on and around me as I read to them. I had occasionally wondered if I was perhaps unfit to be a mother, that if I truly loved them I would embrace not only their playfulness but all the accompanying commotion and disarray. In recent months I feared that my inflamed desire to hide in my bedroom to escape my children and husband was clear proof that, underneath all that undeniable love, I simply did not want them in my life. However, now my eyes were opened to my introversion simply being at odds with my life circumstance. I could see that with self-compassion and perhaps some strategy I could achieve a balance. So during frenzied moments I was beginning to stop and recognize the source of my agitation, and if I needed more than the awareness to cope, I could deeply breathe or walk away for a few minutes in order to center myself.

My self-forgiveness and self-love were expanding, and I began divulging my history and process to more acquaintances, such as my chiropractor, whom I'd been avoiding during recovery thus far, hoping my body would deflate first and I would never feel obligated to explain. As I girded myself for these conversations with those in my outer circles, I felt a nervous fluttering in my chest and a strain in my throat, but it was not embarrassment of the eating disorder itself. Rather, I was ashamed that I had been only pretending to be a thin, pulled-together, happy, laughing woman, that I had been committing a grave lie of omission. I feared that they would feel that they really never knew me at all, that I might be hiding something else, that maybe they should stay away from me, that I was likely wrapped in layers of deception. I explained the eating disorder in humble terms, implicitly asking their forgiveness, so that along the way I could forgive myself even more.

Reactions were sympathetic, and the word I heard most frequently was *brave*—for recovering, for speaking about it, for writing about it. Still, I worried that everyone, even close friends who had known for months, would shy from me, even just slightly, like I had a minor yet contagious disease. I had expected my friendships to suffer. But after I presented my own pain and struggles, after I had extended a hand for help, that hand of mine unwittingly became an invitation to others, a safe place for speaking, for understanding, for compassion and commiseration. Friends divulged to me not only their own battles with eating disorders, but other deep pain, such as troubled marriages and spouses with substance abuse problems. These issues had once seemed to me ones that happened to other people, those who didn't have their lives together—not me, not my friends. But suddenly the lights in the bar turned on, and we saw each other no longer candlelit and laughing, but lined and tired. We had all been pretending that everything was fine, but we were all as subject to life as anyone else.

In the shadowy early evening of a late October Sunday, Alex was in charge of the kids as I enjoyed my last hours of luxurious, waking rest on our bed. It was my time of the week to allow recovery to take center stage, remedy any damage the preceding active days had wrought, and push me an inch closer to remission. But I was also avoiding Alex; I was evading any opportunities for him to kiss me again or argue about our tenuous relationship. I didn't want to confront what may be happening. I wanted simply to be left alone.

The stretch from dinner through the kids' bath was always chaotic, but this time it was louder than usual—my peace was punctured by not only squeals from the children but also shouts from the television, since Alex was watching the Giants, his favorite football team. I stopped reading *Let's Pretend This Never Happened,* my latest distractingly funny book, to plug Arcade Fire in my ears, allowing predictable beats in my headphones to soothe my mind along with my reclining body.

Between songs and above winding instrumentals I caught sounds of the kids and the television, but then a third interruption—Alex, not simply talking, but yelling. During sports games he sometimes leaped to his feet to cheer or heckle the screen, immature but harmless behavior that I had come to ignore. But that evening something struck me even before I could decipher his words: a rising impatience on the cusp of rage. I pulled off my headphones and listened. I could hear the children chattering to one another, toy cars skating across the pine floor before clattering into a wall— nothing out of the ordinary, or even particularly annoying. They were understandably uninterested in continuing to watch teeny figures dancing around a green field, so they had made their own fun.

"Will you STOP?! I'm trying to WATCH THIS!" My heart jerked and curled into a protective ball near the back of my tongue. The kids' playing ceased. "GodDAMMIT!" Alex groaned, as the announcer described a fumble. "Go ask your mother if she'll give you all a bath."

Toddler feet softly scurried up the carpeted stairs, and then Josie was at the foot of the bed. "Mommy, you take us a bath?"

I resisted the urge to scoop up that tiny girl with wide brown eyes and take care of her. Alex knew how my healing body was taxed by three kids in and out of a bathtub, how much I needed those weekend breaks from it. I despised that he was putting a football game before not only my needs, but his children's. I kissed her on the forehead. "No, Josie, tonight it's Daddy's turn. Tell him he needs to do it." I also hoped that stepping away from the television would allow him to cool down.

I didn't listen for his reaction. I flooded the music back in my ears, over which I could hear his occasional shouts from the living room. After another half hour, the kids' bedtime was approaching, and they were obviously still not bathed. I was in my pajamas, dozing off and yearning for as many hours' sleep as possible before Monday morning began. I had to move this evening along.

I heaved off the bed, feet landing in a flash of pins and needles, and trundled down the stairs. *Don't be snarky. It won't do any good. Just ask him to give them a bath.* He was standing in front of the television, a beer bottle on the table behind him, and I waited for him to acknowledge me. My hands reflexively found their way to my hips; my eyes widened, as if my furious stare would penetrate his concentration on the screen, which didn't break as he grumbled, "I know, I know—there are just fifteen seconds left. Then I'll give them a bath."

I'd been around enough games to know that fifteen seconds could easily stretch into twenty minutes. Still in my clichéd nagging wife stance, I said what I knew I shouldn't.

"I think we need to talk about this."

His head and voice snapped in my direction. "No. We don't. There's NOTHING to talk about." His eyes were scorching with ire. Through his face was a fury I hadn't seen since the night he said that he hated me.

The girls had been only ten months old. I could tell that Eliza was the one yowling, her cat-like laments always more piercing than her sister's. I had been asleep only a couple of hours and Alex hadn't come to bed yet, so I let him fetch her. He plodded past our bedroom and down the stairs to the living room, murmuring to Eliza. I imagined him letting her silky head fall asleep on his chest while he resumed his reading on the couch, then returning her to the crib, next to Josie. I drifted to unconsciousness but, as if caught on a fishhook of sound, I was repeatedly drawn to the surface by

Alex's voice, ever louder and more conversational. I looked at the clock and realized that she had been downstairs for almost a half hour, plenty of time for her to become fully awake and want to be nursed off schedule.

Annoyed that he would keep her up that long, I tramped down the stairs. I was not immediately noticed; both of them were fixated on the basketball game on the screen, Alex's ears covered by the television headphones. Eliza was propped on his right knee and staring goggle-eyed and slack-jawed at the television, which must have been kaleidoscopic to her infant eyes. An empty beer bottle was on the table. I deduced from the scene that Alex had wanted to both return to the game and console Eliza—misguided, but not malicious.

"Here, I'll take her back to her crib." I reached for Eliza.

"No," he said, twisting her away from me. "We're having some bonding time."

Bonding time? Did he think this was like our son, three years older than the girls, waking early from his afternoon nap and catching the last half hour of the baseball game with his father? "Honey, she doesn't understand what she's watching. She's only ten months old. And if she stays up any longer she's going to get hungry, and I don't want to have to feed her in the middle of the night. I'll take her to bed."

Alex chucked the headphones on the table. "NO! You're not taking her away from me!"

Instantly I was wide awake, my body tingling, on red alert. This was not really my husband. I'd never seen this side of him. I imagined there must have been three or four more beer bottles in the recycling from that night. He was really, really drunk, and in no position to care for a baby. He could pass out on top of all thirteen pounds of her. In unknown territory, I treaded carefully as I moved close. "Please, just give her to me and . . ."

"And WHAT?! Let you take her away from me? Fuck you! You are a fucking BITCH!" His eyes were fire and rage. "You know what? I HATE you. You are a fucking cunt." And with that, I stopped registering his noxious words.

Panic pealed in my ears and a fight-or-flight response tore me. Our red-faced daughter screamed and cried, searching my eyes for safety, and in my peripheral vision I saw Alex's left hand, the one not holding Eliza away from me, clenching in a fist. I thought that it might be for me, although he had no history of threatening me like that. The mama bear instinct reared up and I was willing to risk a blow in order to get Eliza out of there. I tugged on her body, and Alex pulled back. I pleaded with the universe to let me have her without hurting her. Then she wailed even louder.

Either by a miraculous slip of his intoxicated hands, or because he just gave up, Alex's grip loosened enough for me to pull her to my neck. I scuttled toward the stairs, and then up. *I'll call 911.* I stopped halfway to check if he was following me, ready to hurt me, but there wasn't even a shadow. I heard sobbing.

I fell into shock. My body rejected reality and I fell asleep after only a few minutes, with Eliza already passed out on my chest. When I woke at five in the morning to feed the girls, Alex was next to me, snoring heavily. The memory was so surreal that I thought I might have simply dreamed it, but I recalled too many sharp details, like Eliza's unmistakable cries. In the kitchen I prepared my pathetic breakfast and waited for him to come down, tail between his legs and begging my forgiveness, with another round of promises to curb his drinking.

"Hey, good morning," he said, rubbing the side of his head. "I guess I was up too late watching basketball."

I couldn't tell if this was a joke or if he truly didn't remember. "Really drunk? With Eliza? And yelling horrible things at me?" I couldn't repeat what he called me, making those names real.

"Um, I remember getting her because she was crying, but that's it. I'm sorry if I said things, but I don't think I was that drunk and I don't remember."

"Don't you see? You don't remember because you *were* that drunk. You could have hurt Eliza, and I thought you might hit me." The sobs were rising in my throat, the tears spilling down my cheeks. "This can't happen again. Please, please stop drinking." I was numb and barely felt his arms, which I both did and didn't want around me.

"I'm so sorry for whatever happened. You're probably right. I should cut back."

At that moment, I had a choice. I could superimpose the monster I saw the previous night on the man I thought I knew—the reasonable, apologetic one in front of me—and demand that these images be reconciled, force the magnetic field, delve into the agonizing why. Or I could renounce the one that I didn't like, write it off as a bizarre aberration, and continue with my usual day of breastfeeding and baby food and feeding myself as little as possible. In my eating disordered state, I did not have the capacity for complicated, distressing emotional issues; my brain was too starved, and any unease was processed into further control of my body's size. So, along with a pound or two, I dropped the issue.

"Okay," I said, then headed to the refrigerator to grab the carton of milk for the kids' breakfast.

I hadn't told anyone—not a single one of my closest friends—what I saw and heard that night. I had squeezed that memory down the kitchen sink like a sponge soaked with spilled milk.

But on that evening years later, lying in bed with my book on my chest, with the squeals and splashes of bathtime rising to my ears, after Alex drunkenly snapped at the kids and then me, something smashed my internal emergency box.

I shoved the headphones over my ears to drown the alarm and push it all down, but like a baby's head crowning, there was no going back. I recalled not just the detailed action of that night but the pain of witnessing my husband, the person I felt I knew so well, morphing into someone unpredictable and angry, perhaps with potential for violence. It felt like betrayal. I hoped that after he tucked the kids in bed he would continue to drink and pass out on the couch, only because I didn't want him in bed next to me. I didn't want him even thinking about me, and especially my body, which I hadn't wanted him touching as that flesh was healing and I was reevaluating our marriage. As recovery progressed, his longing expressions and brushes along my waist were obvious signs that he was becoming frustrated, but I was increasingly flinching at his touch and sometimes simply his approach across the room.

Like a child burrowing under the covers and willing a quilt to protect her from the bloodthirsty monster poised to throw open her bedroom door, I sought numb refuge in unconsciousness. I rationalized that if I fell asleep immediately I would evade this fear of Alex, the man who had never laid a harsh hand on me but whose words and behavior could turn ugly when alcohol was involved. I hoped to wake up at my usual pre-dawn hour and hear him snoring away the threat.

I was safe for the time, but I did not sleep well after that, even when he was staying overnight in the city. I woke many times each night, breaching the surface of consciousness after each sleep cycle, often unable to slip back. Something was demanding my attention. For the next week I awoke many hours earlier than usual, my mind and heart seemingly pumping adrenaline—not thinking of Alex or his drinking in particular, but poised to fight something on the other side of the bedroom door of my soul. I was still eating robustly, but while resting in the afternoons as my daughters napped, my limbs once again radiated a shrill pitch of pain I had not felt in months. I told my therapist and close friends what had happened with the kids at bathtime and with baby Eliza years before, and each time I described the pair of events I felt a flutter in my chest spread upward and curl around my neck, a stranglehold of anxiety that had lain dormant for far too long and was now extra hungry for me. I cried and shook as I recounted how Alex had completely turned on me. That I feared he might do it again.

I was having with both myself and those I trusted a conversation I would have had years earlier had I not subsumed the agony in yet another day of restriction. Just as a starving body eventually rears up and demands to be fed, that deferred pain was rising from the earth of my soul and bones, like a brood of cicadas swarming me with post-traumatic stress until the crackly corpses fell to the ground. Then the world seemed oddly silent, my early-morning shuffle to the light switch again without awkwardness, in a way that felt final. Something significant had tipped. I was intuitively certain that the barrage of new or deeper aches had officially ceased, that my body had at long last reached and traversed the summit, and it would begin descending toward health and equilibrium. Although I had still not been granted the magical morning when the swelling and pain were completely gone and I was in roughly the same body I had at twenty-three when this mess began, I was no longer waiting for the transfiguration.

I was in this eye of the storm of recovery when Danny e-mailed. He and I had been introduced by a mutual friend on my fourteenth birthday at a church summer carnival. I was struck by not just his full blue eyes, floppy brown hair, and elevated status as a sophomore in the high school I was about to enter as a freshman, but a profound attraction I was too young to understand. The next week, on my first day of high school, my breath caught in my throat as Danny boarded the bus—crazy luck that we were on the same route—and as he walked down the aisle, smiling shyly at me, resounding from my gut I heard, *Of course he's here. I'm supposed to know him.* He sat in front of me and my best friend, Megan, and the three of us talked the whole way to school. Within weeks I had my first date, first boyfriend, and first kiss. In a few months I'd break up with him out of boredom or some other frivolous reason I can't recall, but in subsequent years we'd get back together briefly, or we'd hang out as just friends, or he'd try to kiss me when he was going with someone else, and he was my last sexual partner before I met Alex—the one Alex hadn't wanted to hear any more about. But our effortless kinship was strained and then lost when the eating disorder struck me down and I was no longer the self that fit so well with him. Plus we were beginning our adult lives, forging careers and serious relationships that turned into families. I came to think of him rarely.

When Danny e-mailed to invite me to take on a small writing job for his business, I was happy to be back in touch, although I would probably have some explaining to do—I noticed a few weeks earlier that he had begun following me on Twitter, where I was sharing quotes from my book and links to eating disorder–related news articles. I was a little embarrassed to reveal my condition and recovery to someone who knew me through all the years I was content enough with my body; once again I feared I would seem a fraud. I also presumed that a man wouldn't really understand how easy such behavior is fostered and hidden in a society that has normalized restriction, particularly for women. But once I broached the subject with Danny on the phone, I was at ease as he listened compassionately and gently asked incisive questions about how it all began and how my body was feeling these days.

He reflected, "Your personality was definitely different, but I thought it had something to do with being with Alex—like you were suddenly more of an adult in an adult relationship, and I was still a kid taking forever to just finish up college. It never occurred to me that you were starving yourself like that. And I just want you to know that it wasn't subtle, the change in your personality. Before it happened and again now I feel very connected to you. You've always been really special, you know." I dismissed any romantic undertones and noted with bittersweet realization that he clearly saw the fluctuations in my personality, and he was one of the few people still in my life who knew me before the eating disorder hit. I thought of Alex; I wondered if a possible problem with alcohol was truly sufficient to absolve him of not noticing.

As Danny and I continued to catch up, discussing careers, young children, and my East Coast versus his West Coast living, and even touching on our spouses' apparent struggles with substances, I felt us gliding down our comfortable groove of friendship. When we hung up almost two hours later, I felt different, like a tectonic plate in my soul had shifted into place. I sensed that Danny and I had to keep talking, and not just about the press release I would polish for him. Again I thought, *Of course he's here. We're supposed to help each other.*

I called him a few days later to delve further into both Alex's and his own wife's relationships with alcohol. I told Danny about the night Alex turned into a monster, my voice quivering as I recounted the awful names that came out of his mouth, my eyes watering as I described how the terror of that night roared back when he snapped at me and the kids for interrupting the football game. Danny and I compared experiences, methods of coping, and attempts at intervention, leaving me feeling less alone and lost in it all.

During another of the handful of phone chats we had after that, we discussed how each of us had understood from a young age what kind of work we would do, and do well and happily, for the rest of our lives. We both felt that our occupations are simply an extension of who we are, and that link is vital. Danny explained that he was bothered that his wife couldn't quite relate to his lifelong dedication to photography while she pinballed around various entry-level jobs. I felt invited to finally articulate the similar disconnect I had sensed in my own marriage.

When Alex and I began dating he had spoken of great political aspirations—we many times joked over glasses of Côtes du Rhône that I would be First Lady—and I was enthralled by that ambition, the future of inspiring each other. But no Democratic campaigns materialized, and his work in finance seemed propelled more and more about making impressive money. Unfortunately, dissatisfaction and depression around his job accompanied that course. He tested various hobbies to alleviate those feelings, but he seemed to resign himself to drinking into the late evening, and he appeared exhausted on most days. I knew Alex had great potential and I could sense his need for something more. Spurred by my discussion with Danny, I asked Alex what happened to that crusade to get involved and make a difference politically, what happened to the unspecified social convictions that I presumed had underpinned that desire, because I was wondering if they possibly be exercised in a different way. Alex was quick to reply that he never really had a driving cause, that it was really just about obtaining a position of power. I was stunned. Then he muttered something about what kind of turkey we should order for Thanksgiving, indicating to me that he would rather avoid the topic.

Until then I had hesitated to criticize his lack of passion for his career, since Alex worked hard to provide for our family to the luxurious extent that my income had become merely supplemental. I discussed with Danny my gratitude for that financial stability, but on the flip side, my marriage—the true soul-seeking depths of it—was suffering. I yearned to be with someone connected within, intricately and consciously. Since Danny unapologetically sought the same in his marriage, he was showing me, somewhat like a mirror to my *animus*,[43] who I was and what I really wanted out of life and with a partner, and that I should not feel guilty about seeking what I desire. He was yet another person helping me grow, holding up an arrow along the path of individuation. Through that handful of conversations between old friends, I confirmed the validity and nobility of my quest to find deep fulfillment with a man, whom I hoped would ultimately be Alex.

Driving the smooth, swervy road between my town and the adjacent one east, where only grass and trees flank the sweeps of asphalt and I feel meshed with movement itself, out of my periphery popped a kelly green street sign with thin, quiet white lettering: Happy Road. I had noticed it before and been tickled that a road so named was in the middle of nowhere like that, but when my eye caught it this time, it made sense: it does happen this way, settling into the ride, not knowing how far I'd come or how far was to go, that the happiness and contentedness would saturate me. I was nine months into recovery; I didn't know if I was halfway there, or less, or more. Even with the vestiges of exhaustion and pain in my limbs, the anarchy of a house with three young children, and my marriage increasingly in jeopardy, I was more peaceful and secure than ever. In the thorny space between disappointment and promise, I learned surrender. As I banished

---

[43] In Jungian psychology, the animus is a female's inherited unconscious collection of male traits, which is elevated to consciousness through love projection onto at least one male with those qualities. Males grow to wholeness similarly, through projection of their anima, or female traits, onto a corresponding female love object.

numbers from my consciousness—weight, menstrual cycles, weeks in recovery, months—I ascended into acceptance.

Until then, the state of my body had been something to grin and bear, and I had been convinced I would never be satisfied until I felt and appeared normal for me. Restriction had been hell, and recovery still largely a brutal means to an end, but after that interlude with Danny I could feel in the marrow of my bones, which still softly pulsed with ache, that if I had to keep that swollen body for the rest of my life, that if recognizable proportions never in fact emerged, I would still take it over the rest of my life or even just another day in an eating disorder, where I could never feel joy, never be myself, never truly connect with anyone at all.

I transcended, and I felt omnipotent. As I reinhabited both my skin and my mind, as I snatched the gold ring of mental remission from a decade of anorexia, I was pulsing with ecstatic energy. My calves, feet, and hands were in just a bit less pain—perhaps due the endorphins of newfound self-love, perhaps the physical manifestation of emotional healing. Floating in my interior retreat, I experienced true contentedness. *This*, I noted, *is the opposite of depression*. I was blissfully gliding so close to the sun that I forgot to mind my wax wings.

Unintentionally, I began undereating. At that point in recovery I had been composing and eating hearty meals intuitively; far behind were the days of counting calories to ensure that I did not slip below my minimum. I trusted my body, and I continued to do so even when suddenly I could finish only half my usual large bowl of full-fat yogurt, granola, honey, and fruit, when I had to put down my fork after only a portion of the pasta I prepared for dinner. I physically could not stomach any more, almost like I was sick with a stomach bug. Since I had never been one of the "lucky" anorectics whose hunger signals shut down—I was always, always palpably starving despite my water- or fiber-filled gut—this did not feel like those ten years of active restriction. At first I believed this was another sign of having turned the corner, my hunger pulling back by another notch, my body not requiring as much fuel as repairs wound down. I was not at all obsessing over food, so I didn't suspect that the eating disorder was slithering through a crack in my vigilance. Still, as much as I maintained that I would take that bloated body over the dungeon of restriction, I quietly held hope that this reduction in intake was my body's way of shedding what I knew with every sluggish movement of excess flesh was an overshoot of my natural set point, that my body would begin burning the extra mass and release the water, that I would finally reach equilibrium and truly feel like myself. But there was a menacing cadence in the voice that reassured me that eating such low amounts was fine, that it was okay as long as my stomach, rather than my mind, were cutting my meals off halfway—it all sounded too much like the eating disorder. I had to question that voice, and question myself. I uncovered that I was happy that I was eating less and could possibly lose weight. This was not good. This was the first step to relapse.

Such a turn didn't make sense to me. I had been so careful never to skimp on meals or snacks; I always responded to hunger; I rose as far as I could above the appearance of my body; I surrounded myself with support; I empowered myself with writing my book; I rested, rested, rested. How could this be happening nine months into a slip-free recovery?

There must have been something I was not tackling, and I could feel that it was about Alex. I had been brushing the alcohol issue aside for a few weeks because I didn't know how to grapple with it and I was fearful of his reaction. I was convinced that no matter how much he worked on himself with the therapist, no matter how many joint sessions we had with her and date nights we set up, he and I would never enter into a true intimacy if he did not stop drinking. I agonized that he might laugh off the problem and refuse, and our marriage would be over, or he might retaliate with even more drinking and possibly actually hurl that fist next time, and our marriage would be over. My new self required a partner who tackled problems directly, who knew and embraced himself. But lately I hadn't been that for myself as I stuffed down the prospect of confrontation, postponing it until our next couples' session when we could be in a safe space and let the therapist drive the process. But this neglected pain and delayed response had ulcerated in my gut, burning a hole to be filled with something comforting and familiar, something like that felt like control. The eating disorder had found a new wormhole. I had to talk to Alex right away, else risk throwing away almost a year of recovery and potentially the rest of my life.

A few nights later, I asked him to sit on our bed. He pushed his back into the wooden headboard, a yard from me, as I hugged my knees into my chest, bracing and protecting myself for what seemed the most tricky and nerve-wracking conversation I'd ever commenced. I told him how that recent evening when he was drunkenly snapping at me and the kids was intolerable, and how that behavior reflected the unnerving side of him I saw years before, the one I was convinced was an insane aberration that I would never see again. As I began narrating that night with Eliza, I expected to choke my way through descriptions of his face and eyes and fist, enumerating the epithets I could recall, the ones I heard before my ears went deaf to everything but hysteria, and that he would sit dumbfounded, eyes widening and watering, regretful and penitent for treating me in such a way, even if he was reluctant to admit the alcohol's hefty role. I expected him to be shocked and sorry. Instead he interceded after my first sentence and told it all in startling detail, including that he had been watching a basketball game, listing names that I didn't remember him calling me.

Apparently he had even said that our relationship was over, which I hadn't heard through the pulsating panic.

He wanted the marriage over? How could I have not heard that? Where would we be if I had? Probably in the same place; the eating disorder would have eaten those words.

He explained that he was cognizant of his actions that night and he would have said all those things sober, that the surge of hatred and threatened violence was the release of frustrations building inside him for more than a year—since we moved upstate, since we had more children—because he sensed that I had been pulling away from him. He said that he attacked me in the only way he knew would hurt me, to roar the most hateful language he could muster. He admitted that, the next morning, when he acted like he couldn't recall what happened the previous night, he had in fact awoken still angry with me for taking Eliza from him. He said that in hungover daylight he still felt justified for acting and speaking the way he did.

As he spoke, those few feet of bed between us felt like they were protracting, and I dug my nails into my shins to make sure I wasn't just dreaming. He did not apologize for his outrageous and vicious behavior and he did not connect it with alcohol. I was plunged in a terror I didn't know to have: *my husband can be a monster with or without the drinking.* I could have fallen apart right then, but there was still work to do, to drive the point of that crucial and long-overdue conversation, so I removed that suffocating helmet of shock and betrayal and set it next to me, to be dealt with later.

"Alex, this is a really hard thing to ask, but for our relationship to have a chance to heal and grow, I think you need to stop drinking entirely. I understand that this is a major request and isn't easy, and I don't want a response right now. I just want you to think about it."

With a hushed "okay," our talk was done. Lying alone on the bed, I was astounded that he meant every verbal dagger he had hurled at me that one horrid night, that what I had witnessed was not in fact an anomaly but what had lain deep and true and festering. On one hand I was appalled and plain disgusted; on the other I couldn't deny the basis of his frustrations. Indeed after the girls were born I had burrowed more deeply in the eating disorder, become even more machine and less myself, not to mention less sexually desirous for anyone at all. He hadn't been getting anything from me, in every sense. Perhaps to an outsider his dramatic snapping wouldn't seem as outrageous as it had been to me, who had her head in her own quicksand. But I couldn't excuse his pushing down these matters until he lashed at me, which I suspected had been facilitated by drinking, in a way that could destroy our relationship. After years of occasional gentle requests and short-term agreements that he cut back on his alcohol consumption or stop for a little while, I was finally putting our marriage on the line.

The next morning, sitting down to add to the second chapter of my book, I found that I could easily eat my full cup of trail mix and then my entire breakfast. I was correct in my suspicion that Alex's drinking had been the source of my potential relapse, and I was learning to trust the gut even deeper than the one in my abdomen, to understand that recovery was not a permanent vacation from anorexia but a daily practice to remain in remission. Those worn pathways would always lie in wait for me, when I wasn't watching where I was going, when I was hoping that I could look the other way and still proceed forward. I would have to be vigilant not only about eating, but about allowing myself to feel my feelings and immediately fighting the battles that came my way for the rest of my life. I had been tripped up, but I felt empowered for stopping the sly eating disorder from dragging me back to the dungeon.

But after Alex awoke, my confidence waned. He communicated with me minimally about the kids, stomping through the morning with his bottom lip protruding, the pout indicating that he had slipped into little-boy mode. I struggled to respect him in moments of such behavior, but I figured he had decided to concede to my request that he stop drinking and simply had to sulk for a bit at the prospect of no longer having wine with dinner, beer with a book on a warm summer afternoon, three single-malt Scotches after everyone else had gone to bed. Some hours later, when the girls were napping and Charlie was conceiving his next LEGO construction, I approached Alex as he was finishing his lunch. I asked what his current feelings were about our conversation.

His eyes were desperate. "What about when we go on vacation? If we go back to Key West, and I want to take off with you and stop at a bar, I can't have just one drink?"

I recognized what he was doing, pointing out instances in which his drinking was innocuous. "Well, that's really far ahead in the future." Since my body probably couldn't handle all the walking and sweltering sun, we had already decided not to book that vacation for the approaching winter. "I think we can deal with that when we get to that point, which is more than a year from now."

"But I can't go into this thinking that I'm never going to have another glass of wine with dinner ever again. I need to know that you and I can go out on a date and have a good time."

I sighed. "Here's the thing. If you don't stop drinking, and the fact is that the majority happens at night, when you're alone . . . if you don't move this roadblock to truly healing yourself and the years of all this stuff, our marriage has very little chance of getting back on track and to a better place, where we really can go out and enjoy each other on a date. I can't guarantee that this will work, but I know that our marriage definitely will not work if you don't do this, because we can't continue like this. I want to try to fix us, but we can't do much if you don't stop drinking entirely, at least for a long time." I leaned on the stove, awaiting the verdict. His lip pudged out further, then his head began to nod side to side, scornfully.

"I just know it's not going to end here. If I do this, you're still going to come up with something else I have to do, some other reason why you think our relationship isn't working and you won't have sex with me."

I wasn't doing all this just to toy with him, but I couldn't say that he was entirely off base. "Well, you're right. I can't guarantee that more hurdles won't come up. This is a lot like my recovery process—it could be a longer journey than we expect. But I think we can make it if we stay on track."

6

As my world was coming into focus, I was also due to get my eyes checked. As a six-month-old baby, and later at two and eleven years old, I had surgeries aimed to correct the movement of the muscles controlling my eyes, since one of them had a propensity for wandering, which ophthalmologists cruelly labeled "lazy." As I spoke, kids occasionally turned to look over their right shoulder to spot whatever my roaming left eye seemed to be tracking, their confusion embarrassing me and flushing my cheeks as I willed that eye to cooperate. I came to understand that, unlike most people, I simply could not focus through both eyes at once. I learned to hold gazes only briefly and to shift my focus from my right eye to my lazy left for just a second, just enough to return it to center, like a toddler who had to be corralled back to the group again.

In this way I'd adapted. By adulthood, the over-the-shoulder glances became rare, and I considered my plight a cosmetic inconvenience rather than a practical disadvantage. I didn't feel like I was missing out on anything besides the freedom to lock eyes unselfconsciously. But in the early weeks of recovery, as my size was increasing dramatically, I began thinking about perception—how I see myself, how I see others, and how others see me, all in terms of fatness—and that curiosity, as well as the lingering concern about my size and attractiveness, led me to wonder about the popular notion that cameras make people appear ten pounds heavier. I assumed it a fault of self-perception, that we wishfully envision ourselves a certain way and view ourselves in mirrors at flattering angles but the lens catches the truth of our flesh. However, I couldn't recall ever noticing that I looked larger in photographs than I imagined myself; rather, when I had been restricting, I was often surprised at how thin I appeared and I chalked that discrepancy up to the dysmorphia of anorexia. But, I pondered, as I continued to recover and the layers of body-based fears flaked off, would eventually I, too, be disappointed or incredulous at my size in a photo or video? I had to learn more about how all this worked, to prepare myself for this potential threat to my self-image and recovery journey. And through a mere Internet search, I found more than I could have ever anticipated.

I found a diagram contrasting how a lens sees—one "eye," taking in what is straight ahead—and how two human eyes function, with each sightline approaching the center from a complementary angle and converging at the point of focus. The brain then fuses the two images perceived through the eyes into a single three-dimensional one—something with depth, versus the flat, two-dimensional image of the lens. When the two eyes and brain cooperate in such a way, the person experiences stereovision, which creates the three-dimensional result. In addition, since the left eye perceives a bit of the area behind the center of object, and the right eye perceives that area from the other side, the fusion of those two slivers of background forces the object between them, the point of focus, to appear narrower than it is. Since my brain did not do this, I had always been seeing myself as larger than others see me, like I had been walking around my whole life with "fat" goggles. By the same token, when others view a photo of themselves, they see how I perceive them. Further, to me, a scene on a television screen was like those photographs; a movie or TV show was no less detailed or dynamic than how I would experience it in the real world. I recalled my car accident, how the other car seemed to emerge out of nowhere, how I hadn't perceived that movement toward me. And that was because, I now realized, I had never seen the world in three dimensions.

I couldn't begin to conceive how that might appear. At first it felt superfluous, like the fleeting magic trick of the 3D movies I'd never been able to appreciate. I believed I had been absorbing the world just fine for my entire life, so I let it go until I came across Susan R. Barry's book *Fixing My Gaze: A Scientist's Journey into Seeing in Three Dimensions.* This neuroscientist had, like me, been unable to fuse images from two eyes since infancy, but with extensive vision therapy as an adult she had achieved stereovision—and she found that this was no minor enhancement in perception. She was astounded by the difference, the experience of witnessing the distance between herself and an object rather than guessing it, of walking through woods or standing among falling snowflakes and feeling truly in the scene rather than watching it unfold in front of her like a projection screen wrapped tightly over her eyes. A new life in three dimensions was so striking that she could spend hours walking around a single room in her house, marveling at simple objects, in a sense seeing them for the first time. For her and others she interviewed, this shift was a life-changing revelation. I had to have it, too.

After all my work through recovery to heave my entire self out of the black-and-white, two-dimensional world of anorexia and into the rich complexities of my soul, heart, and mind, now there was something more: I could fuse not only within myself but with the world around me, another step toward wholeness. Once I discovered this unexpected level of healing and contentedness, I believed all I had to do was go out and get it, that my re-fed eyes and brain would of course concede to my efforts and this stereovision would be the cherry on top of recovery. I imagined that once I began seeing the world in a truly new way, I could finally leave all these struggles behind.

But I wondered if I might lose something vital to my identity. With the world always at a remove, I watched merely a video of reality, and my sense of self lay primarily inside. During our next session, Sil suggested that my heart and mind had compensated for this disconnect from the external world, developing themselves into the three dimensions that my universe had been missing. That theory felt true, that my impaired outer compass seemed to have freed the energy for a finely calibrated inner one. So I worried that one of my greatest strengths would atrophy if I became a "normal" in my visual perceptions, similar to how I had once dreaded recovery because I would lose my identity as a thin person. But once again the rousing potential of the unknown prevailed, and I made an appointment with a local optometrist also listed as a vision therapist. I prepared myself with exercises using a Brock string—a series of colored beads on a rope—to cajole my eyes to begin to work in unison. After I forced both eyes to focus on a single object in front of me and perceive an object behind as doubled, I was flooded with pride and hope. I was sure this venture would be the most incredible turn in my recovery journey and perhaps my most profound reward.

The assistant who conducted the basic eye exam was warm and sympathetic to my plight, and I quickly grew comfortable discussing this long-embarrassing issue. But when Dr. Rose walked in the room, the temperature seemed to drop a degree. In a tan pantsuit she marched to her desk while reading my chart rather than greeting my face. Then she regarded only her computer as I explained the main reason for my appointment. Still fixed on the screen she asked, "But did you ever have stereovision at all, maybe as a baby?" I recalled photos of myself as a very young infant, my eye way off to the side. "Because if not, then you'll probably never have it. The cells in your brain that fuse the images have probably been dead for a long time."

My hope absorbed a blow. I imagined the decade of starvation hammering shut the coffin holding those precious cells. But I pushed that thought away, reminding myself of my body's amazing ability to rebuild. And Susan Barry didn't have stereovision as a baby, either. I was sure that once I pointed out that it was possible, Dr. Rose would change her tune.

"But in that book, which you've probably heard about, *Fixing My Gaze*, the author didn't have it at all until she underwent a lot of therapy, and I'd like to try that."

"Well, it's probably not going to work, you know. You really should have gotten vision therapy along with those eye surgeries as a child. I really only see success with very young patients." The second blow, and a deep one: perhaps my parents didn't fight hard enough for me. "Anyway, it's just some fine tuning. Over your life you've developed adaptive techniques to judge distance and depth, while others can only rely on their vision."

What does that even mean? And really? If a deaf person is desperate to hear music, do you brush it off and console with his or her acute sense of smell? Just the previous day I had been sitting across from Sil, who always spoke to me with compassion; I was flabbergasted by the contrast. Although I was lacking the three-dimensional vision, Dr. Rose seemed to be the one severely deficient in deep perception, unable to detect how important all this was to me. Even as my eyes welled and reddened and my nose flushed with the heartbreak of hearing that I couldn't have this one amazing thing that others could so easily and naturally, she observed me with a glacial stare. I sat silently, willing myself not to completely fall apart until I was in my car. I still had to endure the standard examination, with all the lights and lenses and straining to read letters across the room.

I boxed up my nascent dreams of stereovision and placed them on a mental shelf, allowing the familiar protocol of an eye exam to lull me into pretending that I was there for just that. I was surprised that she bothered to experiment with my eyes, using ever-elaborate configurations of thick prisms to force the focus from each eye to converge at the same spot. I was amazed that without great concentration I could manage simultaneous perception, in which I could use both eyes at the same time, but the dot I perceived with my left eye simply wouldn't overlap with the one I saw through my right; one dot was always a little higher and over to the side. As much as Dr. Rose tried, she concluded that likely all I could ever achieve would be double vision, which was obviously functionally worse than what my body had naturally worked out. She then examined inside my eye with a special light tool that confirmed that the internal structures of my left eye were not properly centered, which seemed the reason why I couldn't get those dots on the screen to fuse no matter how I tilted my head. She didn't offer any surgical solution, and I was so emotionally drained that I didn't ask—I couldn't weather any more disappointments that morning. I ordered my new lens prescription and rushed out into the sunny chill of that bright November morning.

Charlie was in school and our babysitter was with the girls for a few hours, so I drove the smooth, familiar roads through neighboring towns, grieving the loss of that dream, struck down in its adorable, chubby infancy.

Driving aimlessly, my chest ached with disappointment, but I also reflected on how fortunate I really was: all those healthy, loving children, a body and mind that could heal itself, a life that was ultimately rather comfortable. Brooding over the eye issue felt like weeping over a denied cookie, as my daughters did. I felt a little ridiculous as I mourned the unlikelihood that I would ever see the world, in a physiological sense, in a way different than I had been managing for my entire life. But still, although I was deeply grateful for all that recovery had already given me, merging so much inside me, I always strove for more—and I was hungry for that fusion to be comprehensive, to extend to the synthesis of my left and right eyes, to dissolve the boundary between myself and the world. I wanted wholeness, both internally and externally, and I was furious that my stubborn will couldn't get me there. I had always been able to accomplish whatever I set my mind to: with my intelligence, courage, and determination I had scored incredible grades in school; jobs and professional recognition; a body scraped down to skin, muscle, and bone; and in the past year, my greatest endeavor, pulling myself not only out of the trenches of a decade-long eating disorder but up to a soulful plane that some never reach. I had been on a rapturous trajectory, but a glass ceiling smacked me to the ground. Even if surgery were a possibility, carving the time required to recover and for extensive vision therapy felt like a pipe dream.

I also felt stalled elsewhere. Alex and I weren't discussing the alcohol issue or really talking much at all; I feared that he was might choose drinking over salvaging his relationship with me. I couldn't deny that he was correct that my request for this change in him—like couples' therapy and individual therapy—was another hoop for him. However, I was coaxing him along not as torment but to offer him tools to grow into the kind of person I needed now. Through the awakening of recovery, my heart had been mingling with men from my past, like Matteo and Danny, with each rekindling parts of myself or bringing new ones into consciousness. I experienced the thrill of my once-buried qualities reaching the sunshine, under many suns. However, I ultimately wanted Alex—the man I chose to marry, the father of my children, my best friend—to illuminate and nurture the entire field of flowers within me. I wanted my heart to renew our vows, to choose him again as a life partner for my renewed life.

But so much was out of my control and thwarting my efforts. I was facedown in the dirt, attempting to coordinate my arms and legs to crawl forward, but ropes restricted each limb. My recovery was curtailed by the physical demands of my children; my writing was slowed by my physical and emotional exhaustion; my desire and responsibility to play with my children was hindered by my body's need for rest and my mind's for calmness; and my marriage revealed further fractures as both recovery and our therapy sessions continued to uncover truths of our dynamic—how we married too young, how we unconsciously enabled each other not to grow. My life was threatening to draw and quarter me. If I cut one of my ambitions loose, perhaps the rest could get somewhere, but I couldn't amputate parts of myself anymore. I had to drag myself forth slower than a snail every day by the determination of my chin. On some days I collapsed, pebbles boring into my cheek, and cried for how I didn't sign up for this agony, how I wanted to be anywhere else. But, once realized, there's no retreat from the self.

Still, on some days I was blessed with signs of progress. At our next couples' therapy session, which I expected would revolve around alcohol but produce no resolution, Alex surprised me: he declared that he would stop drinking, at least for a long stretch, so that he could work on himself and so that our marriage had a chance. The room oxygenated and I inhaled relief and hope, smiling for what seemed like the first time in weeks. He also admitted that, when he insisted he meant every horrible name he had called me that night we were fighting over Eliza, he had lied. "That night I didn't really mean those names I called you and other things I said. I told you later that I had meant them because I didn't want to admit to myself or you that drinking was such a problem." Alex, Paula, and I were silent, perhaps all acknowledging that it was indeed a problem. "I'm so sorry."

I then breathed another kind of air—truth and promise for our marriage. Alex stopped drinking immediately and seemingly effortlessly. The rest seemed to have a chance to fall into place.

All over the Internet I read about all those children brutally shot dead in Newtown, twenty minutes from where I grew up, in a cute town where Danny and I had driven on dappled summer evenings to watch second-run movies in an old balconied theater on its main avenue. All those children and teachers, who breezed an hour earlier into that one-story brick school—one that looked just like the one I attended, just like the one Charlie was in at that moment—mowed down in an instant. All those children, my son's very age.

Like 9/11, I didn't know anyone lost that day, but the sympathetic pain was agonizing. Alex and I sat on the coffee table and held each other during President Obama's televised speech that afternoon, and we counted the minutes until Charlie leaped off the bus, grateful for his ignorance of the senseless tragedy in the world, for our happy son safe and sound in our home. I cried for three days, waking in the night to imagine the scene from the perspective of the teachers, of the last child standing. I imagined being a parent of one of the students, rushing to the school—the panic and the inconceivable disbelief and devastation upon learning that mine lay bloody on the classroom floor. I was disoriented, rattled, and overtired, and I feared it was more than enough to drive me to restrict, to awaken that primal part of myself that could order the chaos through food control, to access the stonewalled corner of my brain where nothing could get in and I might not ever get out again.

But I heeded Sil's advice: I was good to myself and allowed myself to cry whenever I needed to, keeping the television off and walking away from Internet coverage whenever it became too much, and, as I had been for many months, simply eating to hunger. Although my emotional upset was knotting my stomach and I sensed that I wasn't eating as much as normal, I didn't confirm it with a calculator, whose numerals were the entrance ramp to restrictive compulsions. Fortunately I didn't have to, because as the initial shock of the school shooting wore off and many of us forced ourselves back to our weekday routines, my hunger quickly swelled. I sidestepped potential relapse by listening to my body.

But then our household came down with the flu. The lingering horror of Newtown was absorbed by this full-body viral assault. My world reduced to breathing, coughing, and lying still enough to keep the worst chills at bay, when I wasn't spending hours in the middle of the night changing my children's bedding slick with vomit. Naturally there wasn't much eating, and for a week I was too ill to even worry about it. As the worst symptoms subsided, I noticed that the quantities on my plate continued to be small because I could not stomach any more, as well as how the remaining wisps of pain in my calves and hands had taken flight. A seductive inner voice whispered, *Look at how much better your joints feel, and you don't even need to eat that much anymore! Your body is finally normalizing and your size will start to taper down.* But when I heard, *It's okay not to push the food! You're not hungry, so it's all fine!* I knew I was listening to a rose of wishful thinking barbed with the eating disorder—always there, always waiting to snag me.

After I fully recovered from the virus, my appetite indeed roared back and I was flooded for a few days with extra swelling and pain as my body strove to catch up with the calorie deficits. I was sick of my body yanking me around like that and demanding that I rest, eat, rest, when my soul felt ready to fly and simply live again without the albatross of the eating disorder. Like with the relentless cold and snow of that winter, I wanted to be done with recovery already. But it was only the end of December.

I dreaded the turn into the new year—another milestone, another date by which I had once imagined being completely finished with the process. Yes, I was spending fewer hours each day lying motionless and enduring the surges of pain in my hands, calves, and feet until they abated and I allowed myself to move again, my daily penance. The worst was clearly behind me. I could only continue to feel better, and the new year held the promise of my old body. But I still felt frozen in a holding pattern, waiting for it to emerge, and waiting for my marriage to announce itself renewed or irreparably botched, like my sixteen-year-old philodendron plant, which I was nursing each morning in front of a full-spectrum lamp, hoping something could revive its sparse brown leaves. I couldn't comprehend how things that flourished so effortlessly for so long could suddenly turn toward death.

With frigid glass separating me from the snow, the bedroom door guarding me from the careening chaos of three children in a tornado of new Christmas toys, the boisterous cabin fever at the end of the holiday break, I spent many hours on the bed, fanning out my arms and legs, feeling my inner expansion as I considered the emotional trials of my past that my writing time was raising to high relief, the present pain of my repairing body and struggling marriage, and the future hope of a gratifying romantic partnership with someone with self-awareness and aspirations for growth, someone with the qualities that recovery had allowed me to reclaim in myself. With each breath I accepted them all, growing wider, calmer. Just as my body seemed to require as many hours in repose as it had once been overworked in order to reverse the damage, my soul needed to inhale in solitude the all of me that had been kept at bay for ten years. In one of our couples' therapy sessions, Alex had conceded to allow me this space on the weekends, to respect the closed bedroom door, but that didn't last. One dazzlingly bright winter Saturday he appeared in the doorway, forearm leveraging his torso on the frame, head down but bobbing with deep breaths. Rather than flushing with annoyance that he was breaking our agreement, my heart jolted; I thought someone had died. Wide eyed, I waited, until he raised his drawn face.

"I was clearing old stuff off the computer, and I found—I found a story. That I assume you wrote." *Oh, God.* His eyes, red and watery, skated around mine. "Is it? Is it true?"

I immediately knew what he found. I recalled saving it under some generic-enough file name on our shared computer one Friday afternoon three or four years earlier, when Charlie was napping, in the quiet hours before retrieving Alex at the train station for another weekend at what had at the time been merely our getaway house upstate. I was always terrible at fiction, yet I had been so moved by an arousing dream about Matteo that I was compelled to explore on the page the possibilities and ramifications of pursuing an affair. Characters were lightly veiled, so I couldn't fault Alex for presuming that the tale was about us and others he knew about.

But was it "true"? That simple notion was complicated. Had I not only imagined but craved the events described? Yes, with a desire that had disturbed me and seemed the first sign, well before recovery, that my marriage was not fulfilling me. Did anything beyond the dream occur? No.

I stumbled into a "no, not really." Alex staggered down the hall to the bathroom, to sob. "Is it true?" I gently returned to the question as he slumped on the kids' sink stool. His face was wet; his eyes huge. "Did I write it? Yes, of course. But did any of it actually happen? No. It's a story. I've never touched anyone else since we've been together." He continued to cry, his tears falling on his folded hands, and without a blink of relief. He looked to me like a little boy, or at most a man who couldn't handle the truth of human desire. It probably wasn't reasonable to expect him to be okay with my fantasies about other men, but at that moment, deep in those months of self-exploration and self-embrace, I thought he was pathetic.

I didn't want to schedule any more couples' therapy appointments for a while. During those two-hour sessions in our separate chairs angled slightly toward each other, I felt more like Alex's mother than his partner, observing as he nervously tugged on his pants and ran his hands through his ill-kempt hair as I described to Paula yet another thing I felt he was or was not doing, for himself or for the relationship. The conversation often began with a seemingly innocuous point—his unwillingness to drag himself to a dental checkup since Charlie was born or, despite my invitations and then eventual pestering, his minimal involvement in choosing birthday or Christmas gifts for the kids time and again—but they were manifestations of what felt to me to be Alex's reliance on me as a safety net or simply his relinquishment of husbandly or fatherly duty. The more we delved into issues of responsibility and ambition, the more I sensed that I was sitting near a man without the self-awareness and confidence and motivation that I needed more than ever from a partner—I needed a peer on those levels. Since beginning recovery almost a year prior, I felt that I had been accelerating exhilaratingly and Alex was running alongside but falling further behind no matter the progress he did make, namely giving up drinking. I wanted to be patient—I knew I should be patient—for the sake of preserving our relationship, which I still valued profoundly, as well as the harmonious lives of our children, but I couldn't stop my course and I couldn't deny what seemed his. Continuing those couples' therapy sessions felt like stepping on a scale during recovery, subjecting myself to the numbers, the black-and-white quantification of how bad it's getting, the needle that can tempt me to walk away from the whole thing. And I had grown so tired of fighting for our marriage to slide over to the new track I had begun carving out for us. Working on myself—thinking and feeling and resting my body, along with caring for my children, working, and writing—was more than enough for me; I didn't want the responsibility of shepherding another adult.

In a teary collapse I told Alex that I was so tired of all my fighting for everything and that, for a while, he should book only individual sessions with Paula, to which he acquiesced. I had lost any remaining confidence that we could talk our marriage into saving itself. To me, we were now pieces from different jigsaw puzzles; I wanted us to work on ourselves individually, with the hope that we would fit together in the end, authentically.

Exactly one year ago, I had awakened to the unwavering resolution that I would recover from my eating disorder, that I was turning my life around. I recounted that February morning when I had met Jen for breakfast, and after a hard swallow of eggs and fear—that choked moment of dropping a love letter into the thin mouth of a blue mailbox, knowing that once you let go it will be done and known—I had told her my history and my plans. And now I was marking one full year in recovery.

Occasionally during the darkest, most despairing moments of that first year I recalled how I used to be so small in tiny jeans, parading in the weekend sunshine rather than constantly resting and pained. I had considered that perhaps, in a certain way, I had been happier back then. Despite my deep understanding that an eating disorder is at best stagnation, I lamented that I felt even worse in recovery. But with each month of that first year, another stitch pulled the wound tighter together, leaving less room for me to worry it with my finger, to curiously and nostalgically reach for the familiar throb. And now, with the first anniversary of the day I chose to recover—when my whole self had somehow leaped over the yawning chasm of fear of food and fatness—the final stitch was sewn, separating me from what was. From that point, whenever I pondered where I was one year ago, I would remember myself worse than I was at that moment. My body was clearly closer to the end of recovery than the beginning. There was only the promise of flying forth. Still, turning in various directions, my soul saw the same dusty field, horizon, overcast sky. I'd have to wait for the sun to show me the way west.

I was washing my cereal bowl in the sink when Alex approached the kitchen, all boxers and wet hair.

"When I was in the shower I was thinking about what certain people have been saying, how you seem so different now than before. I've felt terrible, like such a monster, for not being able to see it. And now I know why. It's because I've always focused on only the good parts of you, putting the negative parts in a box I didn't have to look at. I couldn't see when those parts got better." My eyes fell on Sierra's dog bowls: one water, one food, never mixing. I agreed with him that both of us had been separating me, trimming the unsavory gristle, and now we both recognized the error, how it was costing our relationship after it almost cost my life. Seeping in one ear and up into my head was the hope that, after we both achieved awareness of all the facets of ourselves and each other, we could land on the same page and move forward, but seeping through the other and washing my heart was the dread that this was all as bad I feared, that our dozen-year relationship was based on denial and too sick to heal.

Alex continued, "I want to see those parts of you. I want to know all of you, and love all of you. Please let me in so we can really connect in the ways you need."

It was everything I ever wanted to hear—from a partner and originally and ultimately from my parents. But deep down and reverberating undeniably was the full, even, calm voice that I last heard on our anniversary when I felt nothing when he kissed me. The one that told me this isn't working. This time it somehow both boomed and whispered, *It will never be enough. It will never be enough.* It stunned me, this seeming truth from my soul.

I squirmed away from the conversation, mumbling something about being willing to try. I spent the morning hours—brushing mouths, buckling car seats, folding laundry—delving into why all the effort and good intentions driven by the love he and I did have for each other couldn't save us, or why I wouldn't allow it to. Alex had just given me an extravagant diamond necklace to celebrate my recovery anniversary. He was sweet and thoughtful and wanted to make it work. I didn't hold grudges, I gave people the benefit of the doubt, and I was always forward-thinking. Why was this so different, and why couldn't I do these things for one of the most important people in my life, for this critical relationship?

The answer emerged as a hideous feeling, the one I had begun unearthing in therapy that spring: the resentment. Alex hadn't seen me, how I was falling apart. When I had begged him to find me a psychiatrist, he stopped after one dead-end phone call. He did nothing after I told him I had an eating disorder, and still nothing as I was relapsing and disappearing through the years. And the whole time he grazed his hands over my withered body, telling me I was sexy and beautiful, those skin and bones, halfway to the grave. I didn't want those blind hands on me anymore. I couldn't just turn my focus to how wonderful a man, friend, and father he is and was otherwise, to how he had begun to grow and was willing to try, because those years were like a metastasized cancer in my body, in the lips that wanted nothing to do with his.

My friends had sensibly been urging me to forgive and forget, but deep down I didn't see why I should. I felt too betrayed, like someone with a debilitating disease whose spouse was having a romantic affair rather than properly taking care of her. And Alex's affair had been with avoidance. The betrayal had been one of neglect. My body and mind had been dying, and, as passively and unintentionally as it may have been, he still let it happen. Alex was entwined with the eating disorder that I was heaving over the edge, eager to toss it in the wake of my revived self. I wasn't sure if I could, or even wanted to try to, untangle them.

I arranged a long weekend for myself in Manhattan. I knew that even if I spent much of those three days just resting and reading and writing the next chapter of my book in the tiny apartment Alex used for his overnight stays, I would still reap a physical and mental break from the pandemonium of the winter-trapped children and the reminders of my marriage going south. I should have stuck with that vision, but I made too many plans—meals with friends, my brother, his girlfriend—and walking to subway stations and restaurants left me short of breath and aching to lie down. The fiery throbs in my calves and feet and hands ensnared me for hours on the bed before I could manage to move to do anything else. And in those hours of simply being, with nothing in my ears but the intermittent hiss of the radiator, I was not at all content. The relentless heat was suffocating and seeming to swell my body further, and I tore off my sweaty leggings and sweater and socks. I sat in front of the air conditioner, which I desperately dialed to its highest setting, cooling my half-naked body as if the city were oppressed by a July heat wave rather than adorned by mounds of blackening snow along the sidewalks.

This was not like my late-summer getaway to the Mohonk Mountain House, where on the hotel bed the breeze had soothed my limbs and soul and I could write for two hours in the early morning. Here in wintry New York I woke in a tropical rainforest of a one-room apartment, prying open the window to the soothing frost well before a good breakfast could be procured in the neighborhood, engaging in a stand-off with my laptop. I sat at the desk my parents gave to me in the third grade—the place where I completed thousands of homework assignments, pined over dozens of boys, stared into a mirror on Saturday nights and wondered if there was something about my face or body that wasn't good enough to be invited to those middle-school parties where spin the bottle awarded so many others with their first kiss, and where a decade later I sought the answers on the Internet, in recipes and calorie information. Now, at age thirty-four, at that desk, I was frozen. In prior weeks I had been progressing with my writing every day, but here my mind was short circuited by furniture and furnishings, the trappings of my years in anorexia.

When I was pregnant with the girls and we moved upstate, Alex ferried most of the remaining items from our Brooklyn apartment to this little Manhattan studio, and there it all was, prominently displayed on cheap particle-board bookcases, wedged in corners, piled high in the sole closet. On the wall above the air conditioner were my silly paint-by-numbers of birds, one of many attempts to relieve my overdriven brain with a task both mechanical and creative; in the kitchen area was the shiny metal cart that once held cookies that taunted me with their dense calories my body needed so desperately; on the fridge was the strip of faded photo booth pictures of the day I broke down and asked Alex to get help for me but we ended up at Coney Island; and then the dishtowels, the framed photos from our wedding, the sticky and dusty candles, the refrigerator magnets that were the backdrop for my nightmare—all the objects on which I would fix my dead gaze as I recalculated what I had eaten that day, what I could eat, what I should weigh. That apartment felt like a packed elevator in which former selves kept bumping my shoulders.

The last time I had stayed there, just a few months before I began recovering, I considered quaint that Alex had kept so many things from our Brooklyn life. I thought him sweet and nostalgic and even a little cute for not knowing how to make something of a new space. But now I was disgusted that he had left it in such a state for four full years, apparently not having touched a thing since the day he moved in. I opened the closet to hang a shirt that had wrinkled in my suitcase, and I was stunned that the space was crammed with table lamps and garbage bags filled with who knows what. Instead of rolling my eyes or laughing at the laziness, I was infuriated by this emblem of an inability and unwillingness to sort through old stuff and acquire new, more adult things. Rather than investing in moving forward, he chucked it all up in the closet, perhaps hoping no one goes there and the shelf doesn't collapse. Each of us had also done that with the unsettling parts of the other. With recovery and individuation I was going there, finally allowing myself to see and sort through it all, but I felt that he was clearing his side of the mess too slowly, and I was losing patience. I was suffocating in that metaphorical apartment. I wanted a new one, with someone who already knew how to be an adult. I already had three children; I didn't want to be anyone else's mother or teacher.

I lay in the dark on that bed, and then days later on the one in our house upstate, in the dark of my soul, waiting for signs, an answer. I really did love Alex, and I plain liked him, too. He made me laugh harder than anyone, and I had spent essentially all of my adult life with him. I couldn't imagine my world without him. And we had three young children together, the sweetest little beings whom I couldn't imagine thrusting down the path of a broken home, confusing and likely breaking their hearts. But Alex and I weren't connecting on the deep, intimate levels that I needed, and he didn't seem even to understand what those were. I worried he might not ultimately be capable of reaching them, no matter the time and effort spent.

I was holding the tension of the opposites—a Jungian concept that Sil was often underscoring and celebrating—but all I felt was just that: tense. A week after I returned from New York City, a surge of freelance work reminded me that, despite depending heavily on Alex's income for so long, I retained the ability to be self-sufficient if I needed to be. Perhaps I could do it without him. Maybe not. I was clawing around on a moonless night to ascertain on which side the grass was truly greener, trying to decide between the devil I knew and the one I didn't. If I stayed in my marriage, I'd maintain financial and other simplicity, the children would stay in a single home, and perhaps Alex and I could be free to discreetly seek gratification elsewhere if the spark between us was indeed completely extinguished. Still, if I left my marriage, I'd be following my truest self. But how to decide between myself and my three children? That was a stalemate. I had to remain in the howling black, accepting it, keeping my eyes open to it all, because only then could I ever spot the crack of light indicating the location of the door. I had to sit with uncertainty, as I'd done with my legs, hands, feet, arms, everything.

While eating a sandwich dripping grilled cheddar and tomatoes in front of my laptop, I entertained myself with an Internet article about a mother having a romantic affair, a story that was unremarkable except for the reader comments. Here were many dozens of women and men recounting the ongoing emotional destruction of their unhappy parents staying together for their children, and here also were commenters celebrating the relief they experienced after their parents split. Not one person claimed they were glad their parents stayed together for him or her. I was blown away; I'd been assuming that children were invariably shattered by divorce and thus I would be doing them a considerable favor by staying with Alex, regardless of the strain on me. But those reader comments shifted my thinking to another angle, enlightening me to the continuous damage of such an arrangement. Many of them described how much, even decades later, their adult romantic relationships continued to suffer because they had lacked the example of a genuine partnership.

That afternoon my brain finally fused the images of my eating disorder and my marriage: I had been negotiating and justifying the quality of that relationship—*it's not that bad; he's a really great person and friend; we have three children together; maybe it will get better if we keep going to therapy and "trying"*—as I had with anorexia, which I had once rationalized wasn't that bad, that I could always bring my weight up just a little, that maybe I could try using estimated numbers to tally my calories rather than maddeningly precise ones, that maybe I can make it all workable. Regardless of those attempts to validate the starvation, I was always hungry, and my soul knew it was not sustainable and I would never be happy, no matter how straight and smooth my body was, clothes barely catching on me. Similarly, I knew deep down that no matter how well Alex and I could skate on our rapport, a surface so shiny—like the perfect tiny size—that I had long believed it was all I ever needed, it wasn't going to be enough. I'd been feeling it in my bones for months. My limbs had been flaring with the knowledge that recovery wasn't going to be over until I dealt fully with my marriage, which I now understood would require extricating myself from it.

In time for Charlie's afternoon bus from school, I walked toward north end of our semicircular driveway and stared across the street at the water tower, a high, wide cylinder of muted green that blended into the trees, which I otherwise didn't notice as I hustled about a day. But to avoid a tract of ice I moved along the edge of the driveway rather than down the center, and my breath caught at what appeared to be the margin of another tower. I slunk a bit down the road to confirm that behind that water tower was in fact a second one, exactly the same as my familiar, silent neighbor. *There were two the entire time!* I had opened my ears to the universe, and she was speaking to me. In this journey, the eating disorder was the obvious first water tower; my marriage was the unforeseen second one to which my focus had been shifting, the monolithic issue that the eating disorder had enabled me to avoid.

Still, I avoided discussing with Alex anything other than the kids, and I retreated quickly from rooms where he and I were alone. I continued to believe that remaining in our separate corners was the best chance at growth as individuals and eventually as a couple, but I sensed that strategy was ceding to the shadow of impatience and forfeit, that our marriage was entering the endgame. My body seemed to be telling me so with a persistent series of stomach bugs and flus—by far the sickest winter I'd ever experienced. One morning Alex and I argued about the latest round of illness in our household, a barrage of vomiting and fevers among myself and the kids, which he didn't leave the city to help with.

"I couldn't just up and leave work that day. And I would have gotten home too late to really help, anyway."

"Yeah, well, maybe I wouldn't have had to spend all night holding myself up on the washing machine, waiting to put another load of sheets in the dryer before we ran out of them because our kids were puking all night. You could have helped. You should have. If one parent is too sick to take care of them, the other one steps in. I don't know why this was even a question."

This argument was typical fare for us—what each person could reasonably be expected to handle, who had it harder. I could recognize we both did in different ways, that we were both just doing our best in a situation that was more than we could chew: three very young and needy children; husband working more than two hours from home and often staying there overnight; wife recovering from an eating disorder. But I was indignant that I had been so ill and still had to take care of three sick kids.

"Seriously, what's happening here?" Alex asked. "We barely talk. We're not going to therapy together. I feel like we're not making any progress." With arms now crossed over our chests, each of us glared at the other's frustrated face.

Then I felt the ugliness of truth emerging, like a painful pimple that has nowhere to go but out. But I had to release it kindly. I gripped the back of my desk chair and exhaled. "When we got together, we were pretty young and I wasn't really sure who I was yet, and to make our relationship really work I gave up on certain parts of myself, the angsty and passionate parts that at the time I figured were just immature things I should leave behind as I became an adult. And then the eating disorder became a way for me to stay on the surface and not be bothered by them. But since I began recovering, I've been reclaiming all those parts and realizing how important they are to me being whole. But they can't yet find corresponding parts on you to plug into. And so the disconnect is very deep and was always there, but I want to try to make it work now. I love you, and we have this marriage and these three children, and I don't want to leave that all behind. I want you to understand that I haven't given up on this. But I think that the best chance is through your continuing to see Paula and working on yourself, and me continuing to push along in recovery, so that we can eventually connect in the way I need to be happy." I searched his frowning face. "Please tell me that makes some sense."

"No, I don't think there was anything missing from our relationship in the beginning. And I don't see how that makes sense. I don't see how we're ever going to connect if we're not going to therapy and working on it and talking about all these things there, and here in our house and out on dates sometimes. If you don't start opening up to me, I don't see how we're going to get anywhere."

I swallowed hard the disappointment. His viewpoint was not unreasonable, but I had hoped that we could agree to stay on our individual tracks for a while, rather than push into each other too fast, before I felt we were ready. Next, per the law of emotions, what went down then came up. My chest, throat, and forehead flushed with the hot panic of pressing that red button, of saying, "I think it's all over now," because if my explanation didn't ring a bell, I wasn't sure what ever would. My tongue tingled with the words that could end it all, and I waited for them to tumble out before I could stop them, but it wasn't time yet. Maybe we just needed more time. Or I needed more time to be certain.

"Sierra! Sierra pooped on the floor! Mommy, Daddy, she pooped a big poop on the floor!" Charlie hollered as he scampered up the stairs to our bedroom. I never thought that hearing about poop would be a relief.

"Are you sure it's Sierra's?" Alex asked him. "Maybe Mommy did it earlier!"

"Oh, MOMMY!" Charlie squealed.

Alex turned to me. "You know, maybe you should just admit you had a little accident earlier. This would be a great opportunity for you to share with me and create a connection." I reached for one of the damp, holey socks he had left on the floor and I smacked him with it.

This was how we coped. When the conflict was too deep and on an uncomfortable plane, we sublimated the issue to where we could tackle it: on the slick, polished surface of humor, where the heat of our laughter might evaporate it.

It was a black, bitter winter. I couldn't trudge through a single day without another snowstorm, another school or babysitter cancellation, my stomach throwing up another virus, my throat coughing another cold. If the kids weren't sick and home unexpectedly, I was ambushed with proofreading. I couldn't get a grip on the day, the week, or myself, and I was drowning in snow. I was angry at recovery, exasperated with my ailing body, and raging against the cosmic forces that dole out the good and the bad for providing almost none of the sunshine to temper it all. I was feeling only profound pain—in my bones, my muscles, my heart continuing to discern signs that my marriage was over, and my brain flickering on and off, the congestion and coughing having robbed it of sleep. And still, deadlines had to be met, decisions to be made.

One Friday night, when Alex arrived home and I was thus relieved of most child duties for another weekend, I felt only more despair. I collapsed on the stained bathroom rug and cried for how I haven't made anything better, that it all just gets worse. *If I didn't have these three kids, I would like someone to take me out back and shoot me.* I felt that I was losing all the battles, and I was on my last drops of energy to fight them. I just wanted to be done, for someone to take it all away.

I was in excruciating psychic turmoil, but the only way out was through, so I had to continue down the black tunnel, the palms of my hands on the rocky walls, the naked soles of my feet on the pebbly ground. My head recognized all of Alex's positive traits and our compatibilities and strove to make our marriage work, but my body wanted nothing to do with those hands on me. And in my heart, the jury was out. I was torn, wondering if another four months in therapy could get us back on track, if I was just patient enough; if the stress and chaos of divorce would be enough to push me into relapse; if he would be so crushed by the declared dissolution of our marriage that he would return to drinking to cope. I feared that, upon asking for a divorce, I'd feel a rush of relief for ceding to what one part of me clearly wanted, but moments later I would topple and be eye to eye with something I cannot take back, a fire that consumes my house and all that I imagined my future to be. Pushing myself further down that lightless tunnel, I was terrified of something I'd almost never felt: regret. I waited for my heart to weigh in, but it was still pounding rhythmic jibberish.

Desperately I grasped for logic. I listed the five types of connection—mental, intellectual, emotional, spiritual, and physical—and evaluated which were strong between us and which were not. I listed all the qualities I needed Alex to display for me to be fulfilled in that marriage—self-awareness, responsibility for his self-growth, passion for work, and acceptance of other men occupying certain parts of me—and I gauged how much progress I'd witnessed in those areas since he started therapy, and how likely he seemed to achieve them, if at all. Meanwhile, well-paying, long-term work was coming my way, and I calculated how I could manage my own income, along with child support, if he and I divorced. I was seeking a crystal ball, a clear road that would ferry me to certain happiness, as I had with recovery, as I had with the eating disorder. But, once again, the answer was in the muck, or through the journey of the muck. No truth would appear if I didn't truly wade in with him.

One morning when Alex was working from home, I knew I was ready. As he threaded a belt through his jeans, I sat on the edge of the bed and grasped my own fingers for some steadiness, and my lungs expelled fear. "I just don't know if this is working—all the therapy and just waiting. I'm starting to believe that maybe this, our marriage, isn't really working." Rolling to my lips were tears for arriving there, for its truth, and for how he would respond.

His eyes, too, were wet, but with rage. He crossed his arms over his chest. "So you're just giving up? On me and our marriage? We have three kids! And I just started making progress. I know I've been changing and will continue to, but I guess it's not good enough, and now you just want to call it all off!" Alex shook his head and stalked down the stairs to make the children breakfast. I couldn't argue with his words, and that's exactly why we had to get to the bottom of them.

Around lunchtime we asked the kids to play downstairs for a little while so we could talk again. I sat at my desk chair, and he perched on the adjacent wooden chest, resting his hands inches from mine, kneading them on the desk that years prior he had sanded and stained three times without a grumble until I was happy with the color. And that's when I told him about the other men. "When I said in therapy that I wanted to tell you more about my other relationships, it wasn't really to talk about who they were and what we did together, but about how I always carry them with me.

These guys don't just go away when I move onto another relationship." I expected Alex to bring up the story he had found, to ask again if I had cheated on him.

"I know you're still friends with some of them, like Danny. I'm really okay with that. I know I didn't act that way in the beginning of our relationship, because I didn't know yet how to have a relationship and how to handle things like that. But I don't mind if you still communicate with them."

Maybe I should give him more credit. "Well, the thing is, they aren't purely friendships. They're not affairs, either, but these people, the important ones, connected with a certain part of me that no one else has, because no one person is going to do that for all of me. So, every once in a while I need to reach out to one of them, and I can't claim that the feelings are entirely platonic." His face didn't fall. "Are you really okay with that?"

Then Alex told me about Simone. When he and I were dating, I had heard his former college roommates bat around her name a few times with winks and snickers, but without any real story I had figured she was a passing crush. However, as he explained, he had fallen in love with this girl. And in a heated moment he divulged his feelings to her, which, tragically for him, were not quite requited, since she was still hung up on her ex-boyfriend. He spent almost a year nursing that heartache, and I was shocked that I never knew about it—about her, the second water tower hiding behind the first, myself. I felt no jealousy; there was more to him than I had known. And he understood how those romantic feelings do not entirely disappear. My body and heart sighed and softened with this newborn connection between us, and his hand enveloped mine. But trailing the grand hope was the crushing despair, the thing I had to say.

As the words arranged themselves in my head and marched down in order to my tongue, the tears poured down my face for having to reveal the underbelly of it all. I squeaked it out, heaving oxygen every few words. "I'm so sorry to have to say this, and I'm not doing it to hurt you, but you have to know because it's just the truth. And I hate it—I hate that it's true. But whenever you kiss me now, I don't feel anything."

As I sobbed into my hands, I heard him stand up and utter, "oh, my God." He walked out of the room and closed another door, down the hall, behind him. And then I heard the most distressing sound, the moaning and wailing of his heart wrenched out of place by those awful words I detested myself for having in me, for having the nerve to approach and share—but I knew that we'd never get anywhere, not even the end, that he'd never perceive the gravity of the situation if I didn't release them. I gripped my desk as I listened to what was no less than keening, to his receiving more news of one-sided romance, our relationship in demise. It was the worst thing I'd ever said to anyone, but I didn't regret it.

The kids didn't seem to hear any of it through their play downstairs, and in the stunned haze at becoming a monster, at what has become of my marriage, I processed requests for lunch sandwiches, with always an ear to where he was above us, seemingly shifting furniture. As I cleaned dishes he plodded downstairs, a limp, sodden curve of a man, and he read them a story before putting the girls down for their nap. I entered our bedroom, to weep for something, to think about something, to figure my next move, or to simply to check my e-mail and push away what happened, but my desk was carpeted with gigantic confetti that seemed frozen at odd angles as the pieces hit the wooden surface. As I approached, they revealed themselves as every birthday, Christmas, Valentine's Day, and anniversary card I had given him and inside were written the sweetest, most passionate declarations. I was supposed to be reminded of what I felt many years ago, and not so many years ago. I didn't want to look—I was afraid the words would ring as false, that I would understand that I never really felt those things, that they were all lies I had been telling myself so that I could tell him the same. But I owed him and myself that confrontation with the truth, just as I had hoisted another piece of it upon him an hour earlier. Reading the devotion and appreciation of him in those cards, I flushed with the love I felt when I wrote it, because I had indeed felt it; it had been a genuine expression at the time. But that was before all the cracks caught up with it, before the recovery and growth, before the resentment. The most brutal to read was the note I wrote to him the day of our wedding, my first thoughts upon waking in my childhood bedroom, that it was like Christmas morning and I was about to receive the most amazing gift Santa could ever bestow, a committed life with my soulmate and true love. I slumped into my chair, gagging on sobs. *Why did we have to move from there to here? It was so good, and now it's so bad.* The contrast was so stark. It couldn't be reconciled without the knowledge of what came before and what after, without the understanding that all the forces that brought us together would eventually take us down.

I shoved my swollen arms through the tight armholes of my trenchcoat and scuttled into the stark sunshine of late March, the thawing of branches and souls. It was the first time I'd strolled our neighborhood in almost a year, as I'd been denying myself that meditative pleasure so my body could use as many calories as possible to continue to repair. But everything that was happening in our bedroom was so intense and surreal that I needed the outside air, to check with the cosmos that this was all actually happening. As I walked and wept, a car raced past with music skidding out the window, a woman whooped into a cell phone as her dog yanked its leash to sniff another treasure in the earthiness of spring. The world proceeded as mine fell apart—creation and destruction. After a half hour, I returned to the house. I noticed that my calves, feet, and hands were not pulsing with that familiar fire of overexertion, nor did I want to lie down for a few hours. My body seemed to be able to handle it; I was ready for whatever came next.

Alex and I had both been wounded that morning, and in the afternoon we were able to talk with kindness. I folded and stacked the cards on his nightstand, in which he had been storing those former versions of our love. "What I wrote in there weren't lies. I meant all those words and I felt them at the time. But even during the eating disorder, those cards stopped, because something was starting to come out. And now that I'm in recovery it's right in front of us." I stared at some knots in the hardwood floor.

Alex spoke. "I'm starting to understand that you're not making a big decision based on a vague feeling. I know that you love me, but I see that a part of you hates me. And that's for letting you starve yourself for so long. And I realize that you may never be able to forgive me for it, but please know that I truly didn't know that was going on. Through most of our relationship I was always waiting for the thing in front of us to get out of the way so that you could finally be happy, and we could be happy together. First it was the job that depressed you into the eating disorder, and then the fertility treatments, and then dealing with a baby, and then fertility treatments again, and then a toddler and two babies when I was in the city most of the week, and then the house renovation . . . always something that just needed to be waited out, and then we'd get there."

I weakly smiled that we could agree. "I always thought the same. And I was convinced that recovery was the last hurdle—that once I was myself again, and wanted to have sex again, that I would finally be happy both in myself and with you. And that was the worst disappointment of the recovery process—that I wasn't, and all this came out."

He huffed with frustration. "But even though you don't know if you could ever forgive me for letting the eating disorder continue, and I might not ever be the kind of person you want to be with, you still won't hammer the last nail and ask for a divorce."

Because I wasn't confident that was what I wanted. I still loved him, but it was all so jumbled. "I'm not totally sure," I murmured.

He stepped forward and cupped his hands around my hunched shoulders. In a soft voice he asked, "Do you want me to sleep somewhere else?"

Before thought could emerge, the tears were rushing to my chin and I choked out, "don't go anywhere." My body might not have wanted him touching me intimately, but it didn't want to lose all of him, either.

Someone knocked on the front door, and the dog was still barking when Alex reappeared in the bedroom with a package. "Well, ironically enough, I ordered these earlier this week." He split open the shipping box and a held up a smaller one featuring a lingerie-clad lady blindfolded and handcuffed.

"I thought maybe you'd like having sex with me if you didn't have to look at me." It felt like the funniest and saddest thing I'd ever heard.

We spent much of that weekend, and the next one, in discussion. I presented the option of an open marriage on the premise that we could still enjoy the parts of our relationship that worked but each of us would be free to seek sexual and spiritual satisfaction elsewhere. Alex said he could never handle sharing me like that, and in researching open marriage I realized I was going about it all wrong—such an arrangement is based on the strength of the primary relationship, whereas I was seeking permissible cheating on something that was decaying. I was hoping to graft different trees onto us in order to hold us up. I was attempting to cobble together fulfillment.

The lines were becoming even murkier, so I retreated to what seemed clearer waters. Alex and I deliberated the damning issues—my resentment that he didn't intervene as the eating disorder roared back and nearly destroyed me, and what seemed to me his inability to exercise the kind of self-awareness and drive for growth that I now wanted for both of us—and I found myself vacillating between the two, pointing to the other whenever we seemed to agree that the one could be contended with. Perhaps he was more intuitive than I had been crediting him, because he asked me if I even wanted to make it work; apparently Paula had proposed to him that I might not even want to do this anymore. When weeks earlier Sil had asked me the same question, I felt my body and heart wrestling a little too much, as if a nasty truth resided there. Indeed something fierce inside wanted only to shed everything from those ten years—the exercise, the menu planning, the enabling and fragmentary relationship with my husband—and thrust forth into a new era, like a winter coat ripped off upon entering an overheated living room. As much as I wanted to believe that one of my hands was straining for an irrefutable excuse to end my marriage while the other was flailing for it to be revived, what I really, really wanted was out, and that was petrifying. Separation and divorce were so huge; they seemed to require an ironclad justification or at least a substantial list of bullet points. But my heart was speaking from the potent acknowledgment that I had become a different person and he and I simply didn't fit. I was different, and I was done. I had to accept that as enough.

We cried and fought, and cried some more. And then we returned to couples therapy with Paula. She knew what had been in the works, since Alex had seen her a week earlier. Paula considered the latest developments before she locked my eyes and explained that he and I had a chance of working through this, but we would need to return for perhaps a half dozen more sessions. I envisioned those additional twelve hours rehashing the same issues, riding that tired emotional merry-go-round, and still getting nowhere. I wanted nothing to do with those extra sessions. I wanted the issue to be resolved there and then. Whatever the final outcome, I knew it would reveal itself on that early April Saturday.

Paula wanted to know more about my resentment, whether I had really tackled it with my own therapist. I had, of course, and I knew it wasn't budging by virtue of some thinking, probing or magical. I sensed that perhaps with time, with a very long stretch of time, I could forget and thus forgive, or at least not actively hold it against him, but for now it was a boulder between me and Alex. And then she asked me, "During your marriage, during the eating disorder, how did you express anger toward Alex? Did you ever express it?" My eyes fixed on the empty wooden chair across the room, the point in her office where my gaze could rest as I allowed thoughts and feelings to rise into articulation. But nothing was emerging, because I couldn't remember times when I was angry. I could recall barely anything of emotional substance from those zombie years.

"I—I don't remember what I did. I don't remember much of anything from then." The tears were unstoppable, this agony of the broken little girl fusing with the woman I would continue to possess. "I've lost so much time. So much time. I can't spend much more time with something that just isn't working anymore."

I was suddenly elated and empty, like when I pushed out my son in the hospital bed. There it was, out in the world, from such a pure place that I didn't even realize it was crowning. I hadn't felt those words rumbling like when my soul had told me it would never be enough, that this isn't working. This time they sprung like a tiger out of a bush, and Alex and I looked at each other, both of us aghast. When Paula again mentioned returning for additional sessions, I nodded out of obligation, but I knew they would never happen.

On the drive home we hopefully and even cheerfully batted around the idea of open marriage, but it was a death throe: soon after we arrived at the house, he concluded he couldn't go ahead with it, and I knew that it wasn't right, either. "Where do you want to live?" he asked. And there it was, finally.

We both knew how it had to be. "Here, in the house."

"Okay. I'll find a place elsewhere. But I don't think we should divorce, at least right away. Let's just keep the financial stuff as is."

"I'd be fine if we never divorced." The words and tears poured out so fast. I wasn't ready for it yet, either.

That night he slept on the futon downstairs, and I woke up even earlier than usual. For hours of blackness I wept and whimpered into the sheets. It was Sunday, so he would stand at his two irons and make endless waffles for all of us, the somehow both chewy and crunchy treats that soon we would no longer eat together. I cried for the waffles. I cried for his laughably off-key singing accompaniment to the ukulele tunes he occasionally played for the kids, which started when Charlie was a baby on our bed in Brooklyn. I cried for sunny late afternoons playing baseball or shooting rockets into the air. I cried for his wit, his hilarity that often left me in belly-aching tears. I cried for Paris. I cried for the returns to Key West that wouldn't include me. I cried for all the beautiful, funny, loving, and lovely pieces of him I would no longer experience because my heart told me that it just wasn't right anymore, that it was time to move on. And I cried for all the memories that would strike me in the weeks and months to come, evermore things that I would remember that I would have to forget. I cried because I loved him, and I loved my children, and I hated that I—the real, recovering me—was tearing our family apart.

I moved through that day slowly, meandering through wreckage. *At least it's over.* After dinner I went up to our bedroom, noting that soon it would be simply my bedroom. I pulled out the same bleach-spattered sweatpants that I'd been wearing as pajamas since October because I couldn't bear to enter a dressing room and watch my body not fit in a size I could swallow. A little fist knocked low on the door. "Mommy, can I come in?" sang Eliza's distinctly melodious voice.

"Sweetie, I'm getting dressed. I'll come right out as soon as I'm finished."

"But Mommy, I want to see you! Let me in!" I could hear her tiny three-year-old body slump to the floor, the sobs. This time I couldn't tell her to go downstairs and see Daddy instead. They had to know how much they were loved, before their world would be thrown into confusion.

Eliza climbed onto the bed and watched. As I stripped off my leggings and a shirt losing its hem, I answered once again that the thing around my chest was a bra. I braced myself for one of those maddeningly sincere toddler comments like, "Mommy, your butt is big!" which I'd already heard at least once in the past month. *Please don't say anything. I can't take it today.* I turned away from her as I dressed, and not until I had the shirt completely over the belly I loathed—the extra fat that my body was still hoarding around my vital organs in case of another bout of starvation; the extra me that lipped over the C-section scar—did I spin to face her, expecting her to be focused on pulling at a loose thread in the duvet, she had been so quiet.

Her eyes, her cheeks, her wide smile framed by the rounded lips she inherited from me—all of her—were beaming at me as she remained seated at attention, hands in her lap. "Mommy, you look beautiful." And she smiled some more. I grasped her soft upper arms, and tears rolled down my face. She kept smiling.

At first I cried because someone could think I was pretty even in that swollen body topped by a sleepless face. Then my perception pushed into three dimensions, and I cried for my daughter's innate capacity to recognize beauty purely—not as a certain combination of straight and curved planes on a body, but as any shape illuminated from within, lighted by the soul fire that I had been stoking through my recovery. Cradling her head and smoothing her fine hair I wished for her a lifelong path toward such higher meaning, never to be shot down by the societal pressure to be anything that isn't authentically Eliza, and absolutely never to be shackled by an eating disorder. And the only way for her and her siblings to fly like that was for me to continue my own course, to accept destiny, to go wherever recovery was taking me, even if that entailed the end of my marriage, their family as they knew it. I had to lead, and to be the example.

Those four words from a three-year-old—*Mommy, you look beautiful*—reconciled the terrible doubt that I was choosing myself over them. I was, in fact, choosing all of us.

7

The next morning was delightfully warm for early April, as well as calm and vibrant, like when the world is draped in dewy sparkle for the sunny hour after a hurricane blows through. With Alex at work and the kids in school, I perched on the steps of the deck and admired the dappled expanse of our yard. My eyes settled on the sprawling oak tree framing much of the space; when I was pregnant with the girls and Alex and I were creating our wills, we chose that peaceful spot under the tree for our cremated ashes to mingle, that vantage for our spirits to watch the bluebirds flit out of the birdhouses and perhaps grandchildren tumble down the soft slope. I wondered if he would want his remains elsewhere—maybe not now, but after the real drifting happened. In the disintegration of a marriage, even death could die.

Now on the other side of the emotional hill, I could see that during the months leading to the decision to separate, our marriage had been like a loved one with a terminal illness, and I had been watching the slow failure with tears and rage. In my attempts to place blame for it I was moving through the reluctant understanding that the end is nigh, the contrary desires for it to expire already and for it never to end, and the hours of slight improvement that lend false hope that perhaps it can turn around. The inevitable perish held sad relief, the end of the struggle. However, the death was not of the past—in fact, the past is what remains—but the death of the future, together into the gray and wrinkle, that had been presumed.

Alex and I made arrangements. Our work schedules dictated that I have the kids at the house during the week and he have them at his new place, wherever in the area that would be, every late Friday through Sunday. Also, we agreed to eat Sunday dinners as a family, a lingering togetherness that we both wanted and probably needed just as much as the kids would. Ironically, the seemingly drastic shift of separating parents was yielding a rhythm not that different from what we had already been living, especially in the past year when Alex had been primarily caring for the kids on weekends while I rested my healing body. The more he and I considered and discussed it, in this place beyond the battle and angst, the more we agreed that this new phase seemed like a natural progression of things. It seemed to me that the growing apart had been happening all along, but now we were consciously moving with it.

The prospect of weekends in the house by myself, the promise of soothing silence for forty-eight consecutive hours every week, felt like a gift to my soul and perhaps the fast track to concluding my physical recovery. There would be all that time to simply rest, all that time when the kids were exclusively with Alex, simply not here. And there was the rub: I wouldn't be with them on the days when fun tended to happen. With him they would build beautiful memories in which I wouldn't figure. My heart tightened into a fist of loss and jealousy.

When Alex called from work to tell me he had found possible rentals in the area, with a cracked voice I asked, "Do you think that maybe sometimes I could meet up with you all? For some of the fun stuff you'll be doing on weekends?" I waited to be told to lie in the bed that I had made for myself, to accept that this was the price of my freedom.

"Of course. Of course we can do things together, whenever you want," he replied soothingly, and my eyes welled and my heart unclenched. *I'm not necessarily losing them, or even him.*

"Thank you. It means a lot and . . ." My throat closed around the bulge of a sob.

"I know. This is hard for all of us."

I felt reassured that Alex and I could still be on the same team and we would continue to talk and see each other, but we were no longer forcing all the pieces to fit. I was confident we would always be kind to one another and we could fashion a new kind of relationship with the indissoluble substance of friendship, kinship, history, and blood between us.

For the next few days I surged with an energy similar to the one I experienced in the first weeks of recovery: the relief of being finished with such a painful era, garnished with the novelty and thrill of finally flipping to a new chapter, a truer and fuller one of authenticity and the accompanying potential. The tears ceased and I was buzzing to explore this territory, the freedom of being even more genuine, of not lying next to a man in whom I was no longer interested romantically. But first Alex needed to sign a lease on a home, furnish it, and move his personal effects out of our house, which would be just mine. So I turned to sharing the news.

Since I had been regularly leaning on my closest friends, such as Jen and Amanda, for support, many in my circle were already aware of the latest happenings. However, for further-flung friends I had to awkwardly fold the announcement into conversations, an act of storytelling as I trimmed away the messiness to crystallize the reasons into a morsel that felt small enough to swallow but large enough to justify a forfeit of marriage. *There were a lot of deep-seated, ongoing issues. We grew apart. But it's almost absurdly amicable.* I received much sympathy and encouragement. Like when I had sent the mass e-mail announcing my eating disorder and recovery to dozens of friends, family, and acquaintances, I felt myself wrapped in a blanket of love, understanding, and acceptance.

Until now, neither my parents nor Alex's had known of any relationship trouble; like with our fertility struggles, dealing with our rocky marriage seemed difficult enough without inviting weekly interrogations about how the latest efforts were panning out.

"*What?*" my mother whispered into the phone. "But you two have always been like peas and carrots!" That broke my heart all over again—because the metaphor was true, but only on certain levels. The problem lay in the other, deeper planes on which he and I didn't mesh in such a way, which I explained to her had revealed themselves through my recovery process. Then she did some her own revealing. "You wouldn't know this, but when you were two, Dad and I almost didn't make it. And for reasons that were similar to yours. I felt like something was missing. I understand where you're coming from." My mind rushed to a memory of being two years old and flying with her across the country to San Diego to visit her mother for a week. I had always imagined that my father didn't accompany us because of work, or perhaps because he and my grandmother never liked each other much, but suddenly the narrative shifted and deepened: at that time their relationship hadn't been so stable, and my mother, whom I had been assuming wouldn't recognize a need for soulful growth if it were gnawing off her left foot, had that drive in her. I was stunned as my heart dashed toward hers in solidarity, and for a few silent moments we shared a compassion that we may never have before, even without her explaining the situation in detail. I already knew the end of the tale, that my parents chose to stay together and push on, have another child, my brother, and continue the life they had planned. Part of me hoped that would eventually happen for me and Alex, that we would find each other again in our own way. After my mother and I hung up, I wondered if I had always been underestimating her.

Three days later she called to poke further into the topic. "But is life really so bad with him?" And that was a snag in the whole operation, that he and I didn't fight much or even clash often over domestic matters. Life with him included financial security, a partnership in parenting, and simply having someone around. But the separation was about acknowledging a profound hunger.

"Okay, yes, we do get along generally quite well. We're very alike in certain ways and care for each other, even now. Maybe even more now than the past few years. But all of that doesn't make a complete marriage. Some pieces are missing, and I need them. And as hard as it may be on the kids, they're not going to benefit from two semi-miserable parents modeling a relationship that's mediocre."

"Well, you're not going to find some perfect person out there. He doesn't exist." *Be happy with what you've got. That's what I chose thirty-two years ago. Just settle. It's not worth making waves.* That's what I heard in her words, and I imagined that my news earlier in the week may have launched her down a recollection of her own process. I imagined that when she, too, had been overcome with feelings of discontent in her marriage, perhaps she didn't push forward and seize what she really wanted, despite my father's great qualities. Perhaps for her a higher relationship wasn't worth the risk of paddling into the unknown. "I'm just really worried about you, honey. I just don't want to see you . . . ALONE." That final word was spoken with almost comical gravity, as if the worst possible scenario were not having a man by my side, living in my house, killing my bugs. I stifled a giggle.

"Mom, don't you see how my life isn't really going to be all that much different? He never helped me much during the week, anyway, and now I'll have the weekends to rest and pull everything back together. And I still have all my friends and our babysitter. I'm never going to be 'alone.'"

"I do see that. I just want to see you happy, and raising these three kids by yourself is going to be a lot of work."

"By myself? What do you mean? Alex is taking them every weekend."

"*Every* weekend? Do you really think he's going to do that?"

"Um, yes. He wouldn't have it any other way. He's already heartbroken that he's going to have to go five days in a row each week without them. He's not about to skip weekends! He loves and adores these kids. They're his just as much as they're mine." I envisioned a nightmare from which she may have recoiled decades earlier, one in which she would raise me on her own, my dad floating away to start a new life elsewhere, and she, "alone," never yoking herself to another man. Maybe she remembered how miserable her own mother was after her father suddenly passed away. Maybe she believed none of the good ones would be attracted to a mother of so many children. And maybe she was right; maybe I was kidding myself that I could pull this off. Although I'd have weekends completely free for adventure and sexy overnights, would anyone amazing enough to check off all my boxes also be willing to eventually fold into such a demanding life, with so many kids never truly his own? And how would I ever find him, anyway?

The pinnacle of my childhood fears was my mom or dad dying, and a close second was their divorcing. The thought of my parents not being together—or with new partners—was, in my very young perspective, unequivocally bad. Although I witnessed little fighting or tension between my parents, any time they called me and my brother into the living room for a "family meeting," my heart quivered in anticipation of the D word, but the discussion always veered toward something fun or relatively innocuous, like an upcoming vacation. No matter how strained my parents' marriage must have been through my dad's various job losses, I believed I had won something by witnessing them stay together, by not watching my ancestral foundation crumble.

Now I no longer believed I had won anything if I hadn't witnessed my mother pushing for the kind of authenticity and growth that I craved for myself. Both Sil and Paula had suggested that subconsciously I had modeled my own marriage on my parents', and my body had paid dearly. I was determined to break the cycle, to snap and reset that inherited warped bone in my children's bodies so that they could grow properly. I told Alex that I could do most of the talking.

We lined them up on the couch, three luminous faces giggling and then scowling at the others as legs and arms jangled and poked. *Is this a mistake. How could I do this to them.* But there were no question marks. I had to go down that road. I sat on the chair facing them; Alex was next to me, balancing on the armrest. "Listen, guys. We need to tell you about a change that's happening. Daddy and I haven't been getting along so well lately, and it has nothing to do with any of you. Just like you might get into a fight with each other, grown-ups can get into fights, too. And it isn't because of anything that any of you did or didn't do. It's really important that you know that, and that we always love you so much. And that I love Daddy and he loves me." Six blank eyes blinked at me; they had no idea what was coming. I was trying to say enough for them to understand they were innocent, but my words felt like a compilation of after-school TV special scripts. "But kind of like how you get a time-out when you're not getting along with everyone, Daddy and I need a time-out from each other. And that means that he and I can't live in the same house, at least right now." The girls seemed to be purely absorbing, but Charlie's eyes were darting around, brow slightly furrowing as he processed confusion. "This won't be forever, but for now you all will stay here in this house, with me, during the week, and go to school and see your friends like you have been. But on the weekends you'll go to a new house, where Daddy lives, where you'll have new playgrounds and places to visit, and different toys, and all kinds of fun. So, it will be like a great new adventure!" I smiled and chirped at them, overcompensating with happiness and excitement in the hope of such in return, to reassure myself that I wasn't crushing their hearts or spinning their worlds into oblivion.

Alex chimed in. "I'm already thinking of all the fun, crazy things we're going to do every weekend. And you can help me pick out your new beds, and new toys! Does that sound like fun?"

"Yay!" the girls squealed and gave us hugs. Charlie remained on the couch, the corners of his mouth turning up for a small smile, but then he looked away, and it fell.

After a winter so cold and long and full of snow and sickness that I genuinely wondered if the Earth had finally collapsed and spring wouldn't in fact make an appearance that year, the sight of tender green dotting the landscape's hard gray and brown felt miraculous. It was May now. We were emerging.

I was opening windows. Walking through the house, I was making lists. I noted all the nooks in the house I wanted Alex to clean out before he left: the shed; the utility closet; the nightstand on his side of the bed, which contained those loving birthday cards and a seemingly ancient box of condoms we hadn't had enough sex to use; the extra bedroom that for a moment in Paris I had believed was destined to be for our "recovery baby"—the recovery of my body and our marriage, the chance of new life all around—which was used only for storing outgrown clothes and odds and ends. This time I wouldn't let him leave his messes, neglect, or mere disorganization behind for me; I refused to have to figure out what to do with his things, like I do for the children. I was determined that he move out like an adult.

I imagined the place free of his crumpled ATM receipts, the box of "special" paper he had to buy for the final printing of his college thesis which I always knew would just gather dust, along with piles of obsolete electronics and their serpentine cords. I felt lighter by grams of anxiety. I walked around the house again with my notebook and jotted down all the drawers and cabinets I would purge and the toys and useless items I would give away. I imagined how I would spend some time each weekend moving from one room to the next, making it mine, reclaiming it as my space. Alex joked that I would finally have the house I always wanted. I laughed it off, but in a way he was right. The adrenaline at the prospect of such a controlled environment led me to wonder if a facet of my decision to separate was to appease my introversion, which had been increasingly aggravated by so many people in the house. With a husband, and a child, and then three children and a babysitter, daily life had spiraled into a

Sisyphean exercise against entropy. This was my chance to keep the boulder at the top of the hill for a few restful moments each week, to sit in a calm, uncluttered, silent space, allowing my psyche to roam and evolve further.

But again I was slugged by the vision of Alex and the kids having their own fun, just the four of them. I imagined him taking them to new playgrounds and pools, the children making delightful memories during unfettered weekend hours. Although I might join them sporadically for blueberry picking or a movie, for the most part I wouldn't be included. I already had few photographs of me and the kids together, but now I would have only rare opportunities to ask Alex to take one, just to prove my existence later. And perhaps I would begin to appear less in the kids' mental photo albums, too. It didn't seem likely that they would recall with glowing appreciation how I shepherded them through frenetic school weeks, remembering to put Charlie's latest library book in his backpack every Friday or asking the girls to choose something for their sharing day at preschool, getting everyone fed and dressed and fed and undressed again, never one minute late for a commitment. I would be all business, and Daddy all play; there would be more than one separation. My hand had found its way to the underbelly of the arrangement, the wet, cold place where I grasped what I would lose. I couldn't have my cake and eat it, too.

A couple dozen families sprawled Jen's living room and lawn, and children filed into the inflated bounce house borrowed for the occasion, her husband's birthday. There were plenty of opposite corners to which Alex and I could have retreated, separate conversations to have with friends and acquaintances, our own children to wrangle and feed dinner from the catered spread. I expected avoidance, but he and I gravitated toward each other, perhaps by the secret of the separation that hardly anyone knew about yet but I sensed also by our unbreakable friendship. No one at the party would have guessed that our marriage was falling apart. After we laughed over Josie throwing one of her stomping fits that instantly evaporated into a wide smile once she was offered a cookie, Alex reached around my back and squeezed my upper arm, holding me for just a moment that felt so comforting and familiar but was released quickly, at the second that I recalled, and perhaps he did, too, that we weren't doing that anymore. But I knew that tenderness would continue to hover between us. We would always be friends. We would always be more than friends. We would never be everything I needed.

Later that May weekend, on our freshly mowed, bright green grass checkered by the shadows of oaks and ashes under the late afternoon sun, in that golden hour before the dinner proceedings began, we found our sweet spot. I canvassed the lawn, yanking weeds from beds and between walk stones, a pleasant maintenance task, then migrated toward the laughing and screeching of children as Alex played baseball with them. He was positioned behind Josie, holding and moving her arms through a swing as Charlie used the pitching machine to send a ball their way. I ran inside for my camera, begging the universe that the moment last long enough, and then I stood at the sideline, cheering the children and playfully heckling Alex as I snapped those minutes of classic childhood joy—classic parental joy. My heart was gripped by nostalgia for past moments of family togetherness, which would never to be enjoyed in such a way ever again. There was packing to do.

Although I had recently been exhilarated by the thought of uncluttered spaces and the breathing room in bookshelves that had long been jammed, my watching Alex as he extracted parts of himself from our home, parts of me that were him, was excruciating. When he was in the living room, I hid upstairs in our bedroom; when he came up to work on his clothes and personal things, I observed for a moment with the morbid curiosity of watching a surgeon run a scalpel through your own flesh, and then I fled downstairs in tears. His vacating our bedroom, our intimate shared space, was the most painful. Who would come to fill that slot, lie in bed with me, a swollen, still recovering thirty-four-year-old woman with three young children? *Who would ever want to be with me?*

He officially moved out at the start of the long Memorial Day weekend, damp and cold that year. I woke at my usual early time but did not carefully slide out of bed before he could grab me or initiate a conversation. I rolled to face his resting body, which had been inhabiting our bed again with mine for weeks, and I surveyed him: the coarse almost-black hair, once medium brown, with grays fringing the shorn curve around his ear; the mauve bags under his eyes, like muted bruises from his emotional burdens; the stench in his every exhale. But I still loved him and wanted to feel loved, just once more. My hand found the waistband of his pajama pants and wriggled in, stroking and tugging him lightly. Half a moment after his eyes regarded me he was on top of me, yanking off my bottoms, and we were in a rhythm before a condom could even be considered. "Just don't finish inside me," I breathed, imagining the raw irony of a child conceived on the day officially commencing our separation. As we moved together between the sheets I felt every sexual encounter we'd had, the deep friendship and care we'd developed, and the sadness that it would not progress on the prescribed path of marriage, like our life together flashing before my eyes. And it was a last goodbye to the comfort of being coupled, a final moment of feeling wanted and not alone. But I was not deeply turned on and I didn't want him "back." This was not a sign that I wanted to reverse the decision to separate, and he seemed to understand. When it was over, I curled around myself, the pillowcase blotting my tears that silently howled the unutterable loss. For once I had no words to give.

He sat up and spoke. "I know we have to do this. If we continue living together, you're never going to see any changes in me, and we're not going to have a chance at coming together again. I don't want to, but I know we have to do it. At least that is what I keep telling myself." He said the words I couldn't right then, and he was demonstrating more mature awareness. Maybe, in the end, if he held onto that thread and allowed it to pull him through growth, we could be saved.

That optimism propelled me through our family morning routine of cleaning up breakfast messes and herding the children out of pajamas and into toothbrushings. And once that familiar dust storm had settled, there was the matter of the final packing up, and then the leaving. For weeks I had been envisioning a melodramatic scene of the kids dashing unaware to the minivan, and Alex remaining in the kitchen doorway for a long moment, us holding a gaze of love and loss, a hug or maybe a kiss goodbye, and then endless tears after I collapsed on the kitchen floor, sobbing for it all, even reaching for a vodka bottle at ten in the morning, spending the entire day like that. But as he and the kids toured the house for toys and books to bring over to the newly minted "Daddy house," the event somehow didn't feel so apocalyptic anymore and I didn't want such a scene. I also didn't want to have to watch the departure. We already had our goodbye between our sheets.

I announced, "I have to head out. I have errands." I kissed and hugged each of the kids and told them to have so much fun that weekend, shopping for new toys and sleeping in their new beds. Alex was stacking bags in the trunk of the minivan as I marched to our sedan, wrapped in a coat and scarf at the end of May. I was on a mission to just get out of there, not to watch it anymore. But he approached me and spoke.

"Well, I hope you find what you're looking for." My heart caught in my chest as it took a sharp breath. "At the grocery store." I panted a soft laugh, exhaling the tension of the moment, and I smiled I buckled myself into the car. Once again we met on the plane of the humor. And that was where we parted.

As I pulled the car out of the carport, Alex was already inside for another load to pack, and Eliza was behind the screen door, smiling and waving. My eyes welled as I waved back at my daughter, whom I may never again have in the house every day of the week, holding my hand on every outing, and then I tore out of there.

I drove through that drizzly morning to a garden store. After pacing their indoor plant area for something that needed very little light and would fit in a pot I'd had for more than a decade, I chose a small ivy, pretty and seemingly symbolic in its spreading—what my body had done and my soul was continuing to do. I drove home through more rain, and as I wound up our road I remembered all those days I wanted desperately to be able to arrive home after a shopping trip to a perfectly empty house, to drop my things, put away my coat and shoes, and fold the newly purchased items into the rooms where they belonged, all deliberately and in silence rather than have to navigate the accost of screeches and demands and beings underfoot as they created only more messes. I thought it would taste like sweet freedom, but as I walked in the kitchen, with the thin paper bag crackling like a fire in my hand, I encountered a vacuum of emotion and possibility. The only sound was the purr of the furnace. I felt nothing. I had to make my something.

I began on the surface. I scanned each room for fresh pockets—the corner of the counter where Alex's coffee machine had been; the shelves of bookcases now fragmented, like Charlie's gapped smile—and I shifted items over and around, pushing back, utilizing the new space, making it all mine, settled. I became electric with the task, sprinting down the hall with towels to clean the dust and gummy grime in and around the ghost of what had been taken away, to wipe clean the pain of its absence, to celebrate what was taking its place. This was my house now.

In the bedroom was the old philodendron plant, the one I had spent the winter months attempting to nurse with my full-spectrum lamp I used to minimize my seasonal depression symptoms, and on warmer spring days I had been setting on the deck for some nurturing sunlight. The plant had been a gift on my eighteenth birthday, surviving all odds of apartment moves and lack of care, but in its seventeenth year it decided it was time to perish. For weeks there had been only a stub of bright green in the middle of the brown and crackly death, which I willed to shoot into the sky as new life, but—as an almost cloying metaphor for my marriage—it just wasn't happening. It was time to call it quits. I cradled the pot as I carried it downstairs, through the kitchen door, and into the bleary day. "I'm so sorry," I consoled it as I pulled it out, block of soil still attached, an extensive tangle of roots grabbing hard through the holes in the bottom of the pot. *I'm so sorry this failed. I'm so sorry we're done.* Once freed, I didn't simply fling it into the woods, the usual fate for my dead deck plants come late autumn; instead I dug it a little grave along the back of the house, and I left the top poking out, like an intentional planting. I knew the situation was beyond dire, but in my heart was a beat of hope that, if left alone somewhere else like that, something could blossom.

❖

I had a brand-new garden space professionally built with tall wooden beams and wire to keep out the deer and other hungry creatures. It had a locking gate below an entryway of decorative cedar posts that I would encourage morning glories to creep around. I hauled home a carful of small but hardy-looking plants—zucchini, cucumber, basil, oregano, peppers, and a slew of tomatoes—and stared thoughtfully at the rows of neat raised beds, strategizing placement according to prospective height, hoping to fake it until I make it into a real gardener. After more than an hour of snuggling each green thing in the soil, constantly reminding myself to move it a couple of inches over so the plants didn't choke one another, my promise of a summer bounty, my visions of late-afternoon waterings and weedings as the kids squealed on the swings and slide a few feet away, were all laid in the ground. Carrying tools back to the shed with sun toasting the backs of my arms, I felt accomplishment and a bright sense that this would be a strange but good summer.

But I would be at the mercy of my body, because I was already exhausted. For longer than a year I had spent weekends resting as much as possible, but now, with the entire house to myself for those stretches, that self-imposed bed rest was no longer tempting. Chores and the summer sun called. One Saturday I took the commuter train into the city to reconnect with a couple of good friends and note the new and old shops near our last apartment in the Brooklyn neighborhood I hadn't visited since I drove off with a belly full of babies and our toddler son and dog in the back of the car. Although my body swelled to overfill my flip-flops flapping on the city sidewalk, I was revitalized once again by freedom and potentiality, much like the sudden expansion of my mental landscape once I was no longer obsessing over what I would be eating and not eating, plotting at least two meals ahead, and panicking about when I could snag thirty minutes to burn another hundred calories. The choice inherent in two free days a week—to cultivate myself, enjoy myself, perhaps meet someone new—was downright intoxicating, but the execution was hindering my recovery, because I was no longer harnessing those hours to lie still and undo further damage done by trudging up and down the stairs to corral the children all week and gather energy for another five-day stretch of proofreading and shuttling to school or camp and cooking and errands. So a few minutes after I would stop—lying on the couch with a novel as the summer air swished the oaks and maples before sweeping through the screens to caress the skin on my arms and legs—the pain in my overused bones and muscles reemerged. A tingle in my calves and hands dilated to a throbbing throughout my arms, down to the tips of my toes. My extremities ached for idleness, and to be soothed.

Amanda advised me to get a massage. She claimed that, in her dating days, a solid rubdown had proven an effective way to relieve the loss of that physical closeness of a relationship. At first her suggestion seemed irrelevant, since Alex and I had rarely touched each other, anyway, but as a new sensation of loneliness set into my heart and the burn of neglected healing into my bones, a massage became more appealing, even if I had to present parts of my naked body. I'd received more than a dozen massages for birthdays and Mother's Days and in-the-middle-of-a-horrid-winter days, but once recovery was in full swing I'd been avoiding my go-to spa just five minutes away from my house; I hadn't wanted to show my bloated self and explain my situation to another acquaintance. But I was ready to take care of myself now.

I couldn't deny that a male massage therapist's hands held a familiar sensuality, a welcomed appreciation for my body that was deeper than sexual, a feeling of ease that I just didn't feel when a woman was working my flesh. So when the spa receptionist explained that only a female therapist was available on that Saturday morning, I sensed that a lesson was awaiting me. As the therapist and I talked in the therapy room, she struck me as a very nurturing grandmother type as she hummed through her words while offering sympathy for my struggles around my separation, three children, anorexia recovery. Through those broad strokes I revealed so much of myself, and then I did so with my body. As she plied my muscles to release them from entanglement, the tips of her fingers barely gliding across my skin as she moved to the next area, never leaving my body, maintaining that connection, reminding me that she was always there, my closed eyes seeped tears with the delicious sensation of being consciously cared for by an older woman, initiated into my own womanness—a deliberate connection and guidance I couldn't recall experiencing with my own mother. Sil had initiated my soul, and this massage therapist was a conduit for integrating with my body again. Through that touching I felt a circle complete. Through that hour I opened myself to be mothered, and that opening was an act of self-care, even just the seeking of it.

I took that home with me. I became mother not only to others but to myself, taking care of household chores and writing and running errands when energized, and taking physical and emotional breaks when my body felt run down and my heart overwhelmed. I reminded myself that of course I felt that way, with so much going on. I became more self-compassionate. I started to embrace both the joys and pinches of this adjustment period, not arguing with changes in schedule or my fluctuating feelings, or putting deadlines on my emotional healing or my to-do lists. *Things would simply happen as they would.* I had already learned that my metabolism was not actually just a neat conditional of eating x to weigh y, nor did a certain amount of time and dedication to recovery yield a predictable amount of healing and the return to my body's set point. Those were lessons of surrender to my body, and this was the beginning of true surrender—that is, to my life and my growth within it. I began experiencing how openness and awareness and acting true to one's nature, not simply committing whatever stringent routine that logic suggested would guarantee results, created the possibility of a genuine path, with all the associated pain and happiness, even if that meant that my marriage would fall apart and in some senses I would be adrift. But I was awake and paddling.

By the ends of those summer weekends—watering plants, organizing cabinets, reading, cooking, meeting up with friends, breathing and resting, all without schedule—I was recharged for another week, ready to pick up the kids. I headed to Alex's apartment for dinner with everyone on late Sunday afternoons, arriving to the girls' squeals and leaps into my arms, new toys thrust in my face, and jabber about the weekend's excitement: a new playground, a new hiking trail, a new breakfast restaurant, the farmer's market, a movie, a puppet show. I was truly glad and grateful that someone was taking them out for such fun, since my body couldn't handle that many consecutive hours of activity, but I also wondered where this man had been when he similarly had weekend charge of them but wouldn't take them further than the grocery store. Back then I had pleaded with him to take them somewhere, anywhere, for an entire morning or afternoon if not a long day, perhaps visiting his parents just an hour away, so my mind could have a chance to settle. So I couldn't help my annoyance that he had this energy and motivation in him, and I wondered if subconsciously he was using it now to create a dichotomy of experience for the children, to coerce them into preferring him and thus to hurt me. At his new place, nothing got in the way of fun. Instead of milk at lunch they got to have lemonade, and the girls were foregoing naps. Over there, no wish seemed off-limits. By the time I was corralling them into their shoes to head to the car, one would guess they were crashing down from a two-day cake and ice cream festival; they were overtired, crying, and screaming that they didn't want to leave. "We don't want to go to the Mommy house!" I felt myself dissociate in order to bear those words.

Alex was as teary as they were, hugging them again and again as he buckled them in the car, assuring them that next weekend was coming soon and they would have even more fun. Even through his pain he must have noticed me despondently walking toward the car and loading bags in the trunk, because I heard him say, "Now, when Mommy gets in the car, I want you all to tell her that you love her." As I settled into the driver's seat, he prodded them, "Okay, guys, what do you want to tell Mommy?" But there were no words, neither singsong nor begrudging. Glancing in the rearview mirror, Charlie was staring, teary and puffy-faced, out the window. For the first time, my children didn't want to be with me, and that silence was the spiniest stake through my heart.

I navigated the minivan home through a sheet of my own tears. Still, I could recognize that they were likely behaving out of exhaustion—both girls fell asleep in their car seats at barely six o'clock—and once I got them bathed and ready for bed, they were hugging me and telling me they loved me, that they were looking forward to swimming and then ice cream before their much-needed nap the next afternoon. I had enrolled Charlie in a weekday summer camp, but I was keeping him home on Mondays, when I had replenished my energy stores enough for a day of fun altogether that could also show them that Daddy wasn't the only one who could give them a good time. But it just wasn't the same for Charlie, who like many little boys had grown to idolize his father, and he was struggling with not seeing Alex for five days, apart from a mid-week video chat. That evening he claimed that he forgot to say goodbye to him, crying until I offered to get Alex on the phone, into which Charlie choked and blubbered. After all three of their overstimulated heads succumbed to an extra-long Sunday night sleep, I sat at my computer to confirm the weather for our fun Monday ahead, and I wept for them and for me. I never meant to break their hearts.

"We're going to the beach!" the girls sang as they leaped out of bed the next morning.

As I gave Charlie a good-morning hug I asked him, "Has Daddy taken you to the beach this summer?"

He shook his head. "No . . . and I love swimming! Thank you, Mom!"

I already knew the answer, so it was just a cheap shot to establish that I was fun, too, dammit. After the exasperating parade of swimsuits and sunscreen application and packing the towels, toys, and snacks, we drove twenty-five minutes to the wide, sandy edge of the Hudson River—not a true ocean beach, but they were perfectly happy wading into their knees, covering each other with mud and sand, competing to find the largest rock, and making footprints under the late morning sun before the pressing July heat set in. I sat on a towel nearby, taking snapshots of these idyllic summer moments among three young siblings, feeling excluded in my long skirt and camisole, lamenting my swollen body and wondering if I would gain the confidence to put on a swimsuit before they were too old to want to frolic like that anymore. I didn't want to be the mom who never joined in. I didn't want them to remember me that way.

As the sun rose higher and stronger, I called them from the water. "Okay, guys, it's time to head out! We'll come back here soon, but right now we're going to get ice cream . . . as a morning snack!" Josie stomped and bawled; Eliza cast her gaze down and simply wouldn't move. *This is where it goes downhill.* After coaxing them to the car and back into their clothes, leaving sand sparkling on the floor mats, I was ready for a nap as much as they were.

As we pulled out of the lot, Eliza announced, "I love the Daddy house AND the Mommy house."

"I love Mommy AND I love Daddy," Josie added.

I was both delighted and shocked. *Where did they get that from? Who said they ever had to choose?* "I love all of you, too. And I love Daddy." I did, in my own way.

Even at three years old, their language revealed a sophisticated awareness and sentiment: that Alex and I lived in separate places, in separate clauses of the sentence, but their affection for each of us remained unchanged. Underneath all the turmoil, their love—and my love—was secure, which likely made this transition both simple and confusing. We were all adjusting and moving through our own flavors of pain. This movement was the price of the separation, but it also afforded what I so desperately wanted, and that was the freedom to explore not only within, but beyond.

I longed for fun and companionship and intimacy with a man, fantasizing an improved life with a weekend boyfriend who could introduce me to restaurants and lovely quiet spots in the region and spend nights in my bed, on Alex's old side, now available for another warm body. But my lifestyle was so insular, with local friends also busy parents with careers and not much time to hang out at all, never mind devote an entire evening to a bar crawl with me. I craved someone new but I didn't know how to make it happen, so I was leaving it to the cosmos until I figured I'd resort to online dating. I kept my eyes open to attractive men as I ran my errands, generating glances but no conversation; I scanned the newspaper for weekend events that could attract some prospects, but not much appealed to me; I put on a cute dress and lipstick and ate dinner at bustling enough restaurants, but in the end my book was my only date. Perhaps he'd be at the grocery store, like Amanda's husband, who first approached her to dissuade her from purchasing grapes that would rot too quickly. *Magic will happen*, I told myself. Then Alex told me very tentatively, as if he were asking for my blessing, that he was going to start dating. In fact, he had plans for later in the week.

I felt threatened. I had been the driver of the separation, the one conveying that our relationship was not good enough and I was heading to what I believed to be greener pastures, yet here I was spinning in place, unsure how to get there. And he was about to get on his first horse. *This is not how it's supposed to be.* I'd understood intellectually that one day he would date, and then have a girlfriend, and one day I would meet her and see our children sending smiles her way as he held her hand, but I imagined that I really wouldn't care that much. Even if I still hadn't yet hitched my wagon elsewhere, I didn't want his, anyway, so why would I care what he did? But I did care. I was smacked not only with the reality of our lives growing apart but also his capacity to look elsewhere, to feel such enjoyment through other women. Until then I hadn't been able to envision him involved with someone else because, besides his deep crush on Simone in college, I had ostensibly been the only one. It was a blow to my ego to experience that I did not in fact have a lifetime monopoly on his romantic energies and, potentially, love.

Competition prodded me to set up an online dating profile. I thought it would be easy enough for me, with my adequate self-awareness and facility with personal writing, but I struggled to distill myself into a few attractive paragraphs that balanced honesty with self-advertisement. So I brainstormed a list of qualities about myself—I'm a morning person; I'm organized and conscientious; I'm a hearty laugher; I prefer one-on-one conversations; I'm honest, ambitious, and affectionate; I need quiet and sunlight; I'm impatient—and I strung them into sentences sprinkled with a little self-deprecation. I was forthright about my weeks revolving around my three young children yet my weekends free for local adventures. The final prompt of the form asked for the most private thing I am willing to admit, and that rang as my opportunity to mention my eating disorder history, since I knew the topic would come up quickly in any discussion of my work, anyway. I preferred being up front about so many potential dealbreakers, reasoning that if someone didn't want all that, I simply wouldn't hear from that guy. And if he needed to see a ton of photos and especially a preview of my entire body, well, then I wouldn't hear from that guy, either. When the form asked for my body type, I froze; I'd have almost rather stepped on a scale and posted a number than choose whether I thought myself "slender," "curvy," or "with a few extra pounds," or what a man would think I was, and which of the options hit the sweet spot of being both true and attractive. When I looked at my body, I still saw a funhouse mirror of proportion: my thighs and butt too wide and the belly I had never had, but draped in flattering clothes I could concede that I appeared decent overall. I couldn't pin down what I saw, and I couldn't imagine how a man would react when I was naked on a bed, or how I would feel when I was, being not yet at home in my skin. Scrolling through the options for my body type, I chose "average," which seemed safest for everyone involved. Then I posted my profile.

The rush of possibility was tempered by the lurking fear that hardly anyone would be interested in me. I knew that my personality and heart had much to offer, but I imagined only a few would be willing to look past my red flag–ridden surface. For perhaps the first time in my life I wasn't confident that I looked good on paper. But man after man was visiting my profile, some rating it highly, some sending a message—often the short and empty "hey good morning" or "nice glasses" or "ur sexy" type to be dismissed, but sometimes I opened my inbox to a thoughtful comment about one of my favorite authors and an enticingly witty joke. Some lived close, some an hour or two away; some seemed cute, and others were surprisingly doughy and older looking than I expected for a man close to my age. I was instantly overwhelmed the first day, elated by new conversations and unsure when to give my phone number or suggest a meeting. I had no idea how it all worked, because I had never really dated. I had met Alex when I was twenty-two, and my previous relationships and flings had grown organically out of social interactions through school or friends. This was the first time I was meeting people with the explicit agenda of trying each other on for size, and I was dismayed at how ephemeral the experience was, how promising prospects could suddenly turn into creeps, sprightly conversations could fizzle out, and rapport in person could be nothing like the online exchanges. And then these guys were just gone from my life, like through a revolving door. I was disoriented and quickly disheartened.

But within a month I did meet someone who seemed to have some traction. He lived almost two hours away, which precluded any serious relationship potential, but his clever and lengthy profile was the best I'd read so far. Chris was sharp, considerate, candid, and hysterically funny, and we instantly accelerated from multiple messages a day to texting for hours in the afternoons, especially when the girls were napping and Charlie was at camp. I was giddy with the communication and delectable anticipation of it, and I became intoxicated by the forgotten bliss of the beginning of falling for someone. Dormant desires rose up, their energy propelling me through the cacophony of the kids' baths and the chore of dragging around the garden hose. Although during our first phone conversation Chris divulged that he'd never fallen in love during his long-term relationships, I was on no mission to change anyone's ingrained patterns, so I still wanted to meet this man who gave me butterflies and whose typed words could turn me on so much. He had been up front about his involvement in the BDSM world, specifically his role as a dominant male, which included elaborate rope ties and other scenarios of helplessness, his descriptions of which not only satiated my curiosity but stoked my desire to experience it. He inquired into my interest and sexual history, and in that space of openness and compassion I was able to admit to myself that my hottest fantasies and best moments in realized sex had often involved being held down or otherwise overpowered by a man, the precise opposite of what I felt I "should" want—that is, to engage in parity in the bedroom, to be on top at least as often as the bottom, if I was truly the strong feminist I believed I was. But the being in charge and micromanaging were what I did all day long, and for years I had wielded the flogger of starvation and exercise over myself.

What revved my engines now was handing it all over, surrendering, not having to figure out the next move because someone else was doing it. As the flip side of my daily life, submission was erotic, a different kind of control; after growing up with parents who didn't seem sure what to do with me, that surrender to sanctioned authority was my deepest desire. And after college years of lying on beds and letting sex happen, hoping it meant something, and ten years of a libido starved away, I was exhilarated to be finally cracking open and embracing—surrendering to—my sexuality. I was eager to wade into that new space where my emotional and physical hungers mingled.

When we finally met, Chris was not what I expected from his photos and his personality over messages: he was taller and wider and sweeter and more neurotic, like a teddy bear that spoke too fast. During dinner I found myself reassessing my attraction, which grew slowly and genuinely as the night progressed. Still, as we talked on my couch he kept his physical distance, out of gentlemanly respect, he explained. After he left, I wished he had kissed me more than on the cheek in the doorway. That withholding of desire only intensified my appetite, and when we he came over again two weekends later, like teenagers we began putting subtle advances on each other while watching a movie. As soon as he rotated in front of me to kiss me assertively, all pretense of tentativeness was off. He pushed me back into the pillows simply by his weight, and without breaking our gaze he pinned my wrists above my head, rendering me exquisitely helpless as he bit my lip and elsewhere. He yanked on my hair, he grasped my neck, he growled dirty things in my ear while deftly stroking me to the brink. The living room lamp was still blazing and clothes were coming off, and I was seeing his body, not as an abdomen not quite narrow or flat enough, but as simply the vessel that held the true target of my yearning, the passionate person who awakened and wished to pleasure the inner and outer, seeking the right way to do it for me, in the end always respectful of my wishes and call to stop. I was euphoric with the experience I'd never had with my husband, but I wasn't thinking of Alex at all; this was an entirely new game, this expression of my sexuality. And as I continued to surrender—even surrendering to surrender itself—I forgot to be embarrassed of my body, the shape of me that held the sexiness Chris desired. As his hands caressed my swollen thighs and my breasts deflated by years of nursing, I yielded to the enjoyment of his body interacting with mine. I was truly inhabiting my skin for the first time since recovery, and perhaps for the first time ever with a man.

Chris and I saw each other only once more. The arrangement had run its course, as by both emotional and geographic distance, he was just never going to be my boyfriend. I liked and respected him and we remained in friendly contact, but long term I was looking to love and be loved wholly with someone I could see at least once a week from the start. I returned to the dating site in search for men in my area, and my heart bounced when I spotted that familiar face: Alex. I instantly imagined other women with him, even simply flirting with him online; I had to know what they were reading. His profile was funny, sweet, and accurate, and I rated it five stars. His photos—a brief montage of recent years' memories—were some of the cutest I'd seen on the site, and I suspected he must receive a lot of attention, despite the three children mentioned. It was confusing, wanting to date that guy but not actually wanting him back. As I sat with that seeming paradox, I realized that I longed for the kind of first date he and I had a dozen years earlier: both of us nervously arriving ten minutes early to the restaurant; the immediate attraction; the effortless conversation and laughing over drinks at the bar down my block; extending the date by idiotically walking through the black, empty park past midnight; him asking to kiss me outside my front door at two-thirty in the morning; and just knowing, as I turned into the apartment that we would eventually share, that this was something lovely and real. Now someone else might feel that magic with him, begin down a path with him that could be more conscious and not inevitably implode. I wondered if he and I could do that, could push into a second marriage, as Sil had once described that potential for our relationship. Although I was actively pursuing other men, at times I deliberately opened my heart to Alex, inviting my affection to grow beyond congenial, like when he wrestled to free my jammed garden gate in one-hundred-degree heat and yet again mowed the lawn at the house where he no longer lived, as we bantered and joked and even bonded over absurd messages I regularly received through the dating site. I wondered if I could wait and see if things could organically turn around.

I was especially hoping that they would by the time of his Alex's sister's wedding—that he and I would be closer to "together," that my body would have settled to a point where I would be comfortable presenting myself to his extended family, who hadn't seen me since I was rail thin and may not know the circumstances of my physical transformation. But those cards hadn't been dealt as the wedding date approached. I was sending dress and shoe sizes to the bride for my daughters' flower girl ensembles; Alex was taking Charlie to be fitted for a tux. My feet were sweating and swelling in my flip-flops as I marched from store to store for my own dress, rejecting garments that happened not to be proportioned well for my shape and exaggerated the foreignness of my exterior. The dread of an overnight hotel stay with Alex, sleeping next to him after we attended a wedding of all things, eclipsed my desire to support my sister-in-law and witness my adorable children's part in the event. So less than two weeks before the wedding I told Alex that I just couldn't handle it. He responded with disappointment lightened with kindness, even offering to ask his mother to pass the news that I wished to attend the ceremony but couldn't bear to stay for the reception or overnight. I took responsibility and e-mailed the bride directly, explaining myself honestly and humbly and deeply apologizing for this very late change of plans that would affect the seating at the reception. After I received her gracious reply, a sick lump of regret in my stomach chastised me for not having faced the issue earlier. I had often prided myself for not shying away from the tough stuff, for always pushing and growing and accepting consequences, but this instance was supersaturated with tender elements—embarrassment in dressing and presenting my body; the piercing nostalgia of a marriage beginning while mine was ending; the worry that Alex would brush my body in bed and I would recoil—and here I saw how fallible I was. Still, I was grateful for ultimately having taken care of myself, for skirting what would have undoubtedly been a twenty-four-hour exercise in anxiety management.

A few days later my parents visited to help with the kids for the day, and during lunch my mother asked how everything was gearing up for the wedding. "Well, I made a decision that I really should have thought about earlier. I'm going to drive back home right after the ceremony." She shot me a dark look. "I felt bad about changing the plan at the last minute, but Alex is okay with it and his sister was understanding, too. I feel much better about that whole situation now." I smiled and awaited some validation that I had made a good move for myself.

"But weren't you going to take the kids back to the hotel room so Alex could enjoy the reception?"

"Uh, no? I never said that. I mean, because I tend to tire out early I'd probably want to head to bed earlier than he would, and I'd take the kids with me, but not because I want him to have fun . . ."

"Or why couldn't you just drive back upstate with all the kids after the ceremony and let Alex have a good time? You could even spend the night with them at our house, since we're closer than driving all the way. How do you expect him to handle all those kids like that?"

My eyes widened with indignation. "Because he has them every weekend, and that's when they're his responsibility. He has his whole family there, and he will figure it out. He's not helpless. And it's not my job right now to go out of my way to make his life easier."

My father remained silent and unreadable as he finished his plate, likely to avoid entering the conflict. I didn't want to discuss it further, either, so for once I was grateful for Josie spilling her milk across the table and onto the floor, the flurry of cleanup ending that conversation.

For the remaining few days before the wedding, I grew incensed that my parents were not seemingly supportive of the huge upheavals in my life and the marvelous growth accompanying them. They didn't seem to understand the grounds of my marriage separation; they did not respect putting my own needs above Alex's; my mother had been calling Alex to ask how he'd been faring the separation but never asked how I was holding up; they were expressing no excitement about the book I was writing and only weak and belated congratulations after I published a well-received piece on Gwyneth Olwyn's recovery site.[44] I was crushed by the lack of encouragement and I had to retreat. Over the next two weeks my mother left several voicemails expressing concern that I hadn't responded to her casual check-ins, so I left on their phone a message in which I calmly explained that I loved them but because they were not being supportive in various ways through such a difficult time in my life, I needed some space from that negativity and would call them at a later point. She countered with a heated message that this was my fault and that I had to let them in first. I resolved that I would contact them when I felt ready to wage those battles again. Plus, first I had a wedding to face.

Wearing the black-and-white flouncy dress I had purchased for our fanciest meal in Paris a year earlier, I sat where Alex had instructed me to receive him and the children after they walked down the aisle. With the rows of pews in front of me remaining empty and reserved for the wedding party, only the shuffles and low voices indicated the church filling behind me. I clicked around on my phone to drown my fretful thoughts, the ones imagining the thoughts of all the others: *There she is. Did you hear they separated? Yeah, he doesn't live in the house anymore. He works all week and takes care of those kids all weekend. What a saint. Looks like she gained a lot of weight, too.*

When the music finally rose and we all turned, I was thankful for the organized proceedings. I aimed my camera down the aisle as Alex's other sister held the tiny hand of Josie—all confused smiles—and Alex coaxed Charlie and his ring pillow forward while leading his grandmother and as well as lugging a very grumpy-looking Eliza on his hip. They were a beautiful wreck. I was struck by how handsome Alex was in his tux, noting how he always looked good in a well-fitting suit, remembering what he looked like at our own wedding. Remembering that we were hardly married anymore.

All three children tumbled into the pew, grousing for seat positions, and Alex's parents greeted me with lukewarm smiles. Alex locked on my eyes and said, "Come here. I love you," and kissed me full on the mouth, the first time since he moved out, perhaps to show everyone watching that he and I were not yet a defeat, perhaps to strike my heart while the iron was hot with the emotion of a wedding. I was desperate to feel something, to turn myself over to it, but again I felt no passion. Between shushing the

---

[44] "Sweet Surrender: The Empowering Gift of Recovery," *The Eating Disorder Institute*, accessed October 11, 2017, https://www.edinstitute.org/blog/2013/7/21/guest-post-sweet-surrender.

overtired children through the Mass, I glanced at him—a good father, kind and funny even through such a stressful episode—and I wished I were feeling something that could allow us to skip into the sunset altogether, not to force our children to grow up in two homes. After the ceremony, as everyone gathered at the entrance of the church to witness the newly wedded couple ecstatically skipping down the steps into their supposedly blissful future, the one that we, too, had truly believed was ours, our children grabbed at our legs, asking for snacks, and Alex asked me to change my plan and stay for the reception. But deep down nothing had changed yet.

On my thirty-fifth birthday, I awoke to the sterile hum of a dim hotel room in Montréal, where I chose to spend the final week in August when Alex's parents were taking the kids. Without those little ones to cheer on the next year of my life, and with my local friends out of town to get ahead of the long Labor Day weekend, I would have had to spend the occasion alone in my house, so I opted to be alone in a vibrant city instead. *Thirty-five.* I was undeniably an adult now. With no pressing agenda for the day, I was still in bed, sheets twisted around my legs stiffened by the previous days' exertion, when my cell phone rang.

"Happy birthday . . . I wanted to wish you first thing." It was Alex.

"Thank you. It's strange to be waking up alone in a different country, even if it's only, you know, Canada, and know that I'll be spending the day by myself. But Montréal has been great so far. Like Paris lite. I think you'd love it."

"I'm actually in a hotel, too. In Albany. That's why I can't sleep. I was supposed to have a date, but she canceled."

"A hotel room? Well, that's presumptuous!" Although it was just a casual tease, I could feel a light tug in my chest.

"No . . . I got it just so I wouldn't have to drive all the way back home so late." I wondered how much therapy had been helping him with the panic attacks. I wondered if he drank at all on these dates. I wondered if I was being silly, if two people who obviously cared about each other and built a life together should really be separate and alone like this, especially on her birthday, when she has a reservation at a reportedly fantastic restaurant, and he has time off work, and the kids are taken care of for days. So far I had been content with freely eating every delectable meal alone, choosing every route and shop and museum, and not speaking to anyone for hours and hours, but now I was craving loving company on that day of all days.

"Well, you're almost halfway here. What if you just came up, maybe just for the day and overnight?" We dissected the option, deterred by his passport lying back at his apartment, inconvenient flight times, and then a clash over how long he would stay—he was pushing for longer than I was. I wanted just a brief visit to our old, comfortable relationship, to amble down the Parisian cobbled streets of Old Montréal outside my hotel and laugh at his attempts at French pronunciation, to sit across from someone at dinner. I didn't want him to kiss me or push himself against me in bed that night. I wasn't welcoming him as much as I was resisting the supreme aloneness that my mother had foretold. And I couldn't brush that under the rug. To grow, I had to wade into what I was and how I felt when I had nothing but myself to lean on. We decided it was best if he stayed in New York.

My birthday was peppered with calls and texts from well-wishing friends and family, including a short, cordial e-mail from my parents, who didn't know that I was out of the country. Not speaking on my birthday to the ones who created me was surreal but not painful—just simply where I was. As I chatted on the phone with the kids, who were having a blast cheering the racehorses in Saratoga with my in-laws, I tried to be as chipper as their chirpy voices. I tried to revel in all the luxurious meals; I tried to savor the secret of my birthday in a city that didn't know that someone was flipping to another stage of her life; I tried to transcend the whole thing. But I was driven back to my hotel bed, legs and feet pulsing with a severity of pain I thought was far behind me, now a year and a half into recovery.

A year and a half! And you once thought that you'd be fancy free in your "old" body by a year ago! But here you are, still swollen and needing to lie still on this bed for hours so that you can head out again for your birthday dinner. Alone. Not even with your children. And the only man who regarded you here was that borderline creepy waiter in the hotel restaurant, the one who comped your wine. So how does it feel, now that you've gotten your freedom? How does it feel?

It felt like failure.

The next morning I wanted to cut the trip short, just go home already and soothe myself with familiarity, but my faithful stubbornness propelled me to the street with my guidebook, staying the course to visit the reportedly stunning Jardin botanique de Montréal. The day was different— cooler, less humid—and my body failed to sweat and swell as I navigated the subway to an outlying neighborhood. Once off the sidewalks and into nature, I followed throngs of elderly tourists down the main path of the botanic garden, mirroring their pensive speed as we frequently stopped to appreciate the manicured scenery, a summer exhibition of colorful topiaries conceived and designed by dozens of international artists. They were majestic and meticulous: horses mid-stride, mythical creatures, ladybugs I photographed to show my daughters, who would gasp at such spirited life made of shrubbery. I was in a world of magic and delight, for an hour walking and pausing, respecting my body's pace. Too often I had been focusing on the ways in which my own little world hadn't been meeting my expectations and wishes, but now my body and mind were receptive to the joys that were always on offer.

As I entered a narrow path bordered by tall hedges, I remembered that it was the very end of summer, right before that turn into September that inevitably gifts renewal. *It's that time of year. It will happen. Something is right around the corner, if I both wait and keep moving.* I turned the corner in the path, and there it was, the tallest and most stunning of the topiaries, and I recognized her before my sight could settle to the title plate: Mother Earth. Her head and neck rose from the soil, her eyes cast downward, and she bestowed a smile that was serene, wise, and nurturing. Past her colorful, flowing hair, her arm reached up from the earth and water spilled over her palm, this giver and celebrator of life. Like so many observers around me, I was startled into place, eyes watering, for this was the mother I never had, the one I wanted to be for my children, the one I wanted to be for myself, the one stirring in my soul to care for my battered body and the one in my body aching to care for my fiery soul. I knew right then that I had no need to blame anyone else anymore—not my mother, not Alex—for not mothering me. I suddenly understood that she was in every movement of the earth, that she was the thoughtful cosmic design that has been caring for me even when all seems like chaos. She was in front of me; she was in me; she was everywhere. There was no need to look for her anymore.

I pushed forward, feeling centered, filled, and expansive, through the elegant Japanese garden, wild and rocky Alpine garden, and vibrant rose garden, experiencing them as various parts of myself, walking through them and appreciating their distinct beauty. At an empty bench along a wide pond I rested my weary limbs, slipping my feet out of my sweaty flats and into the grass the temperature of bathwater, feeling her, Mother Earth, always supporting me. Dragonflies darted over the surface of the water, and I recalled that they are considered symbols of transformation. Recovery had indeed given me a second set of wings, allowing me to fly higher than I ever imagined.

Then one dragonfly stopped and suspended a foot in front of me, seemingly making eye contact, and my torso bounced with surprise. The tiny thing dashed off, but in its faintly buzzy wake I heard it, the earth, my soul, and myself resonate in harmony: *Transformation is happening. It's right in front of you. Do not be scared, my love.*

That night I slept soundly for the first time in months. I dreamed that I stabbed myself through the heart with a long, thin rod like a metal knitting needle for no reason other than it needed to be done. As I pulled it out I was fascinated by the painlessness as well as the scantness of blood that remained on the shaft and leaked from the hole in my chest. It was like a superficial wound that I needed only to clutch in my hand for a few moments to allow it to clot. I knew there was no need to rush to a hospital, that I would be fine, that I could take care of myself, that nothing could bleed me out.

EPILOGUE

"Mommy, hurry up! We want to go in!"

One year later, on my thirty-sixth birthday, I drop the tote bags of towels and shovels and snacks on the sand as the kids rush to the edge, squealing and leaping as the water licks their feet and they heed my demand to wait for me before walking further into the ocean. I glance at other families setting up for the day on that quiet stretch of the Jersey shore, other mothers with bodies that my brain registers as thinner, plumper, taller, rounder than mine. But the comparisons have lost significance, as the shapes themselves do not suggest worth or beauty.

I note with neither terror nor fanfare that this is the first time I'm exposing my post-recovery body fully to the sun and world, and then I unceremoniously pull off my shirt and skirt. I trudge through the sand in the first swimsuit I've worn in three years, back when I was twenty or thirty pounds lighter and miserable. And now I'm twenty or thirty times more confident. I think I look good, because I look like me. After two and a half years of recovery, I'm no longer sidelined by the associated bone and muscle pain and exhaustion. The swelling and overshoot of my natural fat mass have slowly fallen away without any food restriction. I can recognize my body as a reflection of the one I abandoned at twenty-three years old; and it is a homecoming, to be forgiven, to be trusted not to starve it. I've finally recouped what I desperately desired through the ten years of anorexia: the ability to move through my life with both physical and mental freedom and to eat not by numbers. To my refurbished mind it's the most simple, natural thing to do—but it's also a miracle.

Charlie whoops as another wave crashes him and he flails on the sand. The water is rough, so I position myself between the girls and grab their

177

five-year-old hands in mine, anchoring them as they jump and inevitably lose their balance in the undertow. My jangled arms grow sore after a while, so I insist that we all take a break back at our towels. There the kids build sand castles as I lie back in the sun, for a moment wishing for another adult to share the load of taking three young children on vacation, but I feel empowered for pulling this off: the beach, the pool, an amusement park, a mini golf course, a water park, three restaurants a day.

"Thank you!" I chirp into my cell phone when my parents call to sing happy birthday. "I thought I'd be miserable at least half the time doing all this by myself with the kids, but it's actually been one of the best times I've had with them. It's strange that this is turning out to be one of my best birthdays." I tell my mother that the kids have been so well behaved and are regularly showering me with "Mommy, you're the best"s and "this is the best vacation ever"s. I tell her how I haven't been too tired, how I've been swimming—I've been sharing more and more with her. During the past year she seems slowly to have grown to accept and embrace both me and the divorce, and I've grown not to seek that buttressing from her, because I harnessed the mothering in myself. As a result we've met somewhere in the middle, and from there we grow: four months later I'd cry on the phone to her about the boyfriend who crushed my heart, and for weeks afterward she would console and check on me. But through many dating debacles I would always be okay, because I never lost myself again; and because I loved myself, I could freely give and receive love. And soon enough I met my match in Tim, a wonderful man who was up for that, for all of me.

"Mom, do you want some of mine?" Charlie offers his strawberry licorice, which he chose at the deli for his beach snack and he knows is my favorite movie candy. He drops a sandy fistful of red ropes into my hand.

"Thank you, sweetie. That is very generous. I'm pretty hungry." As we eat, the kids observe the swooping seagulls and shake sand off their snacks, exaggerating tales about the biggest waves. Eliza smiles and hands me one of her cashews, and I'm glad to be the mother who eats intuitively and without restraint, that I do not set the example that women should turn down food.

Before I can gather the husks of wrappers, the kids are all at the lip of the water again, hollering at me to come down. We assume the same positions: a little girl holding each of my hands, and Charlie on his own just a few yards beyond. All three shriek in delight as the vigorous waves pitch them over, and I stand as the hinge, a coil of strength allowing movement and change.

ABOUT THE AUTHOR

Kerrie Baldwin is an editor and writer with twenty years' experience in children's and adult trade book publishing. Her interest in the science behind eating disorders is fueled by her additional work as a medical editor in the pharmaceutical industry. Kerrie has authored several children's educational titles. *I, Dragonfly* is her first book for an adult readership.

The aim of this memoir is to raise awareness around eating disorders, the journey of recovery, and the opportunity for remission, which Kerrie has maintained since 2014. To preserve that focus, this book does not specify her height and fluctuating weights, as an eating disorder can be active at any BMI. For further information about this neurobiological condition, she encourages readers to visit The Eating Disorder Institute at www.edinstitute.org, founded by Gwyneth Olwyn.

Kerrie lives with her family in the Catskill Mountains of upstate New York, and she can be followed on Twitter at @kerrie_baldwin.

ACKNOWLEDGMENTS

My reclaimed body and mind, and this resulting book, would not exist without the tireless work of Gwyneth Olwyn. I cannot adequately express my boundless appreciation for her contributing the foreword, supplying citations throughout, and showing great enthusiasm for my project, and all after unequivocally saving my life by guiding me—as she has so many others—through an evidence-based path to remission from an eating disorder. Further, I deeply thank the online community of recovery comrades for their support around my journey as well as their urging that I publish an account of what it all really looks like. This book was produced for the millions out there who aren't sure if the dragon of restriction can be truly slayed. My story is proof that it can.

The physical and psychological changes of my recovery process would not have been manageable without counseling by Risë Finkle, Lysa Ingalsbe, Patti Knoblauch, and Parinda Parikh. I owe my soul's journey of individuation to my beloved therapist, Sil Reynolds.

I thank all my friends and family who cheered my recovery and writing processes—you know who you are because you are all of you. For the extra encouragement, tips, and draft reads that I needed to bring this memoir to light, I thank Máté Adámkovics, Meghan Lynch Baldwin, Eliza Berkowitz, Hanna Otero Bird, Cheryl Chandler, Denise Hoffman, Josh Jacoby, Pat Latshaw, Dustin Malstrom, David Smith, Christina Stanley, and my late father, Geoffrey Baldwin. I am deeply grateful for my dear friends who happen also to be professional writers and editors. This book owes its development to my cosmic sisters Suzanna Cramer, Aileen Weintraub, and Suzanne Wentley, who offered their time to read my work at various stages and provided forthright feedback over long phone calls or meals together. I thank Yassmeen Angarola for catching the rest of my mistakes and giving the text a final polish.

For alleviating my imposter syndrome and making me look like the real deal, I thank Leyla Cadabal and Michael Hunt.

For believing that I'm confident enough not to need his emotional backing for this project but giving it to me in spades regardless, I thank my husband, my love, Tim Baroni.

And for being my unrelenting motivation to persist through recovery, I thank my three children. May they never experience my anguish, but on their own paths may they, too, grow into their authentic selves.